Date Due

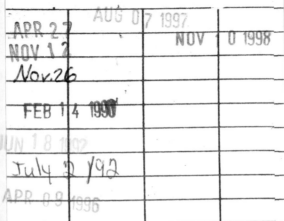

	AUG 0 7 1997		
APR 27		NOV 1 0 1998	
NOV 1 2			
Nov.26			
FEB 1 4 1990			
JUN 1 8 1992			
July 2 /92			
APR 0 8 1996			

They Shared to Survive

The Native Peoples of Canada

Selwyn Dewdney

Illustrated by Franklin Arbuckle

Macmillan of Canada/Toronto

Acknowledgements

They Shared to Survive was conceived some twelve years ago as a series of drawings, supplemented with explanatory text, that I hoped would bring to the native people of Canada a fresh view of how their ancestors lived in early historical times. Circumstances made it possible for me to involve the interest of Franklin Arbuckle. No Canadian artist has drawn and painted so broad a span of the Canadian landscape, nor did I know of any artist who could bring the Canadian past alive as vividly and authentically as he. I am grateful to the Canada Council for the grant that made his participation possible.

With Arbuckle as artist I was free to revise and expand the original manuscript to its present proportions. Along the way I had help from many individuals. Dr. R. G. Forbis gave me new insights into early bison-hunting techniques. Dr. E. S. Rogers, with his enthusiasm for the drawings and his criticisms of my text, gave us a lift when we most needed it. Most of my Micmac reading came by courtesy of John S. Erskine. And I must extend my thanks to Terry Leeder, of Macmillan's, whose editorial sensitivity helped immensely in clarifying what I wanted to say.

Wilfred Pelletier was kind enough to read an earlier manuscript. Others of native ancestry were helpful, especially James Red Sky Senior and Norval Morrisseau, whose friendship and insight into the oral traditions of their people gave me new perspectives into the Ojibway life style.

Nor can I forget the constant support and encouragement of Drs. A. D. Tushingham and Walter Kenyon of the Royal Ontario Museum. It was their consistent support of my field work over the years that brought me into contact with so many of the native people whose histories Arbuckle and I have attempted to record.

Contents

On What Authority?

The reader of a book as ambitious as this has the right to know about its author's background and bias.

Both go back to a boyhood in Prince Albert, Saskatchewan. On any warm day fifty years ago, you could pass a dozen Cree families loitering along River Street between Revillon Frères and the Firehall. Here were moccasined men with long black braids that hung over the shoulders of shabby dark suitcoats, and bright-shawled wives toting skilfully embroidered cradle-boards, from the laced-in security of which the bright eyes of fat little babies looked out on an indifferent world. Sometimes we would play at *Métis* and Mounties, and re-fight the Riel uprising. And if we got up early enough on a summer morning, we could watch a pair of Royal North West Mounted Police, in the brown service coats they wore on prairie patrol, riding past our house on 20th Street.

The winters were sub-Arctic in intensity. I recall going to school one morning in a breathless fifty below, and many another day when my eyelashes stuck together with the cold. Our family summers were spent under canvas on the shore of a little sandy lake. I remember one wonderful summer when we were the sole campers, and I tasted a naked kind of freedom I have known all too rarely since. I was the only one of five brothers who had a strong interest in the canoe, and I spent hours of every day in it, too absorbed in the wind and the waves and the life along the shore to have any sense of being alone.

I had just turned twelve when we moved to Kenora, Ontario, into a land where, for the Ojibway, the canoe was a way of life. And it became a way of life for me too, with Lake of the Woods at my doorstep and an endless maze of islands to paddle through. Sometimes I would

1

pass whole families travelling by canoe, gliding silently and almost invisibly along the shore; and I diligently acquired the quick, smooth, mile-eating Ojibway paddle stroke. Twice I saw birchbark canoes.

On Saturday nights there were "pow-wows" near the Tourist Hotel, but one June my father took me sixty miles down the lake to Neangoshing for the Treaty gathering, where the drums beat a more authentic note. As I wandered through the big encampment, watching and listening, I understood only that I was on the edge of another world — surrounded by strangers whose life fitted this wild, beautiful land in a way that was closed to me.

Yet I yearned "to be an Indian". All winter during high school, I wore beaded Ojibway moccasins, sewn by hand with sinew thread. I was the proud possessor, too, of slim-pointed snowshoes, beautifully crafted, on which I learned to lope over wind-hardened drifts out on a frozen lake, or to break a trail in the soft snow of my "bush trap line". Often my winter hiking companion was a schoolmate of Saulteaux-Ojibway extraction. It puzzled me to discover how few words he knew of his ancestral tongue, but I was shocked one day when he referred to his own people as "they" instead of "we". For I envied him his strong dark face. I had no inkling of how great the pressure was on him, as a member of a family that had crossed an invisible line, to dissociate himself from a racial minority that was then regarded by most of those in the mainstream with condescension or even contempt.

In love with the wilderness milieu, and growing up in a home that was saturated with nineteenth-century Anglican evangelism, it was only natural that I decided to become a missionary. My eldest brother was already serving a Cree community on the Churchill River, and would complete his missionary life ministering to the Loucheux of the Mackenzie delta. My father was an Anglican bishop, and his diocese of Keewatin (pronounced Kewaytin) extended up the west side of Hudson Bay. In 1928, after my first year of college, I grabbed the chance to go with him on a tour of the northern part of his diocese. At Norway House he hired two Cree canoemen, who broke me in as bowman on the 500-mile trip due east to Big Trout Lake. One of them, I was to learn forty years later, was both a staunch Anglican and a widely feared shaman, practising his ancient religious profession on the side. That the Church had no knowledge of this testifies eloquently to a communication gap that has persisted into the present.

From Island Lake east we met human inhabitants only once, pausing just long enough for our canoemen to barter some of their bean and sow-belly for bags of mushy "yellow-berries". Fifty-five portages later we arrived at Big Trout, then a thriving fur trade centre so isolated that every board in the place was whip-sawed by hand. Ammunition for ancient muzzle-loaders could be bought at the Bay store, and discharges from a few of those guns were no doubt included in the traditional welcome we got as our canoe neared the shore. Some of my delusions about the taciturnity of the "Red Man" were dissolved by the broad grins of the men and the shy smiles of the women and children as we shook hands with every inhabitant in the village on our way up the bank. On Sunday the whole population was jammed into the church till, for me, the air reeked of the fish that formed their staple diet, mingled with the odours of sweat and stale woodsmoke. But the smells were soon forgotten as the whole congregation joined in a hearty rendering of familiar Anglican tunes sung in Cree-Ojibway in a strange droning style that I learned later was typical of their ancient chants. As I stared blankly at the syllabic printing in my hymn book it suddenly came home to me that I was the least literate of all assembled there.

On Hudson Bay I had glimpses of the Cree of York Factory, the Chipewyan of Fort Churchill, and a band of the "People of the Deer" at Eskimo Point. In the Eskimo settlement I threw away my worn-out moccasins and donned a pair of waterproof sealskin boots. We came south with an Eskimo party, stopping for a day at a river mouth, where I paddled bow for two seal-hunters in an old freight canoe. As we chased a big seal in the shallow river mouth, I heard a .303 bang inches above my head and simultaneously saw a red splash in the back of the seal's head. The body sank to the bottom like a stone. That's how I learned what a harpoon was for. When we had recovered the body and towed it ashore, it was so bulky that it had to be cut into sections before we could load it into the canoe.

As a student-missionary I spent two idyllic summers at Lac Seul, then the declining centre of a fur trade that was once even more flourishing than the post at Big Trout. Very young, and equally earnest, I paddled to every fish and berry camp in the area. I was once greeted, as I rose stiffly from the canoe to disembark, with the Ojibway equivalent of "We thought you were an Indian". But this was mere flattery. There were nights when I lay awake in the old mission house listening to the drums from across the lake, aware that I had only to paddle over to witness the rites of the "White Dog Feast". But I never did. And if I plead, as an excuse, youth and an uncertainty about my role, I can think of none for my failure to record a single "Whiskey Jack" tale of the dozens that I heard on evenings in a neighbour's cabin. In recent years, seeking clues from local elders about the origin and meaning of the rock art sites I have been recording between the Rockies and the Atlantic, I tried to compensate. I took notes with such obsessive zeal on one occasion that a venerable old man made pointed comments on how weak the memories of the white men were!

3

My recollections of Hudson, the jumping-off point on the CNR for the Red Lake gold rush, need no notes. I happened to be there on the day of the arrival of the last fur brigade from Osnaburgh House — a flotilla of a dozen freight canoes, to be replaced by a single diesel-towed barge. Prohibition had made the place a bootleggers' bonanza. I saw the men being paid off in the Hudson's Bay store on arrival, and I saw some of them again in the morning, lying dead drunk along the railway right of way, or puking behind the CNR station. That afternoon, in the middle of an open-air service that I was conducting at a camp over at Frenchman's Head, the women suddenly melted into the bush with their children. I turned (attired in Anglican surplice and cassock) to face a man, ugly drunk, emerging from a nearby tent. With all the aplomb of an empire-builder facing the threat of "lesser breeds without the law", I stared him down. But it sickens me now to recall how readily I could assume the moral arrogance of my race; and I like to think that it was then that I began to question my missionary motives. It was near the end of that summer, reading the burial service in the graveyard back of the little mission church at Lac Seul, that I glanced across at a father who wept unashamedly while he held in his arms a little black coffin within which lay the fifth small child he had lost from tuberculosis. It was then that my missionary zeal died.

Perhaps with this book it has re-emerged in a less sentimental, more valid context. Behind this book are strong feelings, accumulated through a half-century, about the debt that all Canadians owe to the *original* Canadians. For there have been enduring, if subtle, contributions made by the first natives of this land to the emergence of Canada as a geographical entity, and of Canadians as a deeply different, if somewhat inarticulate, people. For I have come to believe that the impact of aboriginal values and attitudes has shaped us more than we know. On the surface we appear to be a minor sub-culture of a super-power; yet against all economic and political sense Canada as a nation survives. As I will try to show, the roots of this identity reach back through the history of the Anglo-American and French fur trade to the aboriginal traders who roamed the forests, mountains, prairies, and waterways of the northern half of this continent. This is my bias.

This does not pretend to be a "scholarly" work, but it is a serious one. In the last analysis the only authority I can claim is the strength of my desire that the people this book is about will find in it some reinforcement of their own identity. And I hope that these efforts, by one who does not share their ancestry, will increase for other readers the interest and respect all Canadians owe them.

4

1 Man in the Americas

What Manner of Man?

Little is known about the remote ancestors of the native people of Canada. We do know that, thirty thousand years ago, the whole of what was to be called Canada lay buried and barren under an incalculable burden of ice. At the peak of the Wisconsin ice age, so much of the earth's water was locked in ice that the level of the sea was lowered by over 100 feet. And, what is more, the land adjacent to the ice masses was forced upward to balance the land areas that were depressed by their growing burden of ice. So it was that the broad plain of the Yukon River in Alaska reached far out into the Bering Sea.

As the sea level dropped and the former sea bed rose, a broad plain — 800 to 1,000 miles wide — stretched from Alaska to the foothills of the Koryak Mountains in Siberia. No mere "land bridge", this huge region — never glaciated — united Eurasia and North America into one immense continent.

To the south of this newly formed "sub-continent", herds of bison, horses, and elephants grazed the fertile grassland. Northward the tundra vegetation offered ample forage for the musk-ox, woolly mammoth, and countless caribou. And men were there too, bands of big-game hunters, roaming over the very threshold of the Americas.

If we ask what manner of men first stood on the soil of what we now call Canada, prehistory has no answer. What we do know is that they were likely mammoth-hunters, for the earliest tools that have been discovered are clearly lance heads suitable for such hunting.

These sharp stone artifacts are known as Sandia points, and are possibly 20,000 years old. They were so

shaped, apparently, that the cutting edge on each side would be no wider than the thickness of the long shafts to which they were lashed. Such a weapon would be required for attacking an animal so large that if the first jab of the lance failed to reach a vital organ, it could easily be withdrawn for a more successful thrust. Obviously the attack would need to be made at close quarters. This would be possible on firm ground only if the animal were surrounded by a group of very agile hunters, but would be more likely to take place when the prey was mired in a bog. As such points are most frequently discovered with the remains of extinct mammoths and mastodons, few now doubt that they were used for hunting these animals. A later type of lance head—a Folsom point—was found near the ribs of a species of giant bison that became extinct some nine or ten thousand years ago.

We can work on the basis of such remains, and on our knowledge of other hunting societies, to make an imaginative reconstruction of what the first man who stood on the soil of Canada might have been like. As long as we keep clearly in mind that this is an invented scene, it may serve to bring us a little closer to these mammoth-hunters of the distant past.

A young skin-clad hunter, broad of cheek and stocky of stature, has disregarded the older hunters' decision not to pursue the wounded mammoth they had manoeuvred into a bog, where the black muck was too shallow to hold the great beast for more than a few hasty lance thrusts. Stubbornly the youth has followed the blood-stained trail, while noting with misgiving that the splashes from the wounds are getting fewer and farther between.

He pauses now to sniff for his quarry's scent in the glancier-chilled wind from the northeast, and to scan the lowering sky for signs that the wind will change. Fog banks hang persistently over the ice ramparts that block the upper reaches of this Yukon valley. Will they move in to end his hope of sighting the beast? Looking west, his eye locates the faint blue wisps of smoke that rise from the small cluster of skin huts sheltering the womenfolk. Beyond lie glimpses of the broad, spruce-edged river that snakes its way out into the wide Alaskan grasslands. The sun reveals itself momentarily through a break in the scudding clouds. Although it has begun to set in the northwest, its light will linger along the northern horizon until the midsummer twilight merges into dawn.

The youth stands irresolutely. Sixteen years old, he has already killed a bear to prove his manhood. He knows now that he will not find his quarry dying in its tracks. But he might still—if the fog holds off—locate the female and its calf, so winning the respect of his

7

elders. Only too well he knows the kind of witticisms that will greet him if he arrives empty-handed, words of ridicule that will ensure his future submission to the superior hunting wisdom of his elders. But there is something else that fills him with a deep unease, impelling him to retrace his steps slowly while he tries to recall . . . . Then it comes to him — blanked out until now by the excitement of the day's events. Two sunsets ago the Old Woman had told him that his woman's time was close. A panic seizes him. If he is not at hand to play his role in the birth rites there will be grim days ahead for the whole band. Swiftly he strides down the valley side, then breaks into a steady lope.

That night, we may imagine, his first son was born. If he survived and became a parent in his turn, his linear descendant may, even as these words are being read, be wailing his birth cry in an Argentinian shepherd's shack, or in a Cree trapper's cabin on the shore of a northern Saskatchewan lake. But so great a span of time has elapsed since that distant day that it is difficult to conceive of it in any meaningful way. In Europe Palaeolithic hunters were only beginning to develop obscure rites deep in the Cantabrian caves. Reckoning a human generation as thirty years, a thousand generations separate that hunter from his twentieth-century descendants.

The Wanderers

For the youthful mammoth-hunter, the great Cordilleran ice fields were an impenetrable barrier to the unknown lands beyond. Seemingly the great ice ramparts had stood — and would remain — through all eternity.

He could not have known that, even then, slow climatic changes were under way. Each summer, century after century, the glacial barriers retreated a little farther up the headwater valleys of the Yukon River. But many more centuries passed before an ice-free corridor lay open into the heart of the continent. And it is likely that, during this same period, as the oceans crept back to their pre-Wisconsin levels, the wide shores of the Arctic Ocean offered an alternative route into the continental interior.

Regardless of the paths they took, migrating herds of the large game animals by-passed the melting glaciers and emerged on the Mackenzie and Alberta plains, with bands of Alaskan hunters close behind. And the hunters' descendants, bold and resourceful, fanned out in scattered groups over the southern plains, or filtered into the eastern forests. Other wanderers and their succeeding generations penetrated ever farther southward, until a few bands had reached the bleak extremities of South America. As we shall see, these

A band of Alaskan hunters surround an old musk
ox that has been driven out of a herd by a
younger male.

wanderers were to prove, with the high civilizations they built in Yucatan, Peru, and Mexico, that their native intelligence and capacity for creation were equal to those of any other race on the planet.

Compared to the thousands of years these migrations covered, it is barely yesterday that scientists began to investigate the prehistory of early men in the Americas. Across North America over the past fifty years, archaeologists have been digging up the stones, bones, and earth layers that offer direct evidence of the men who lived in the interior of this continent long ago. Ethnologists, by studying recent and surviving societies of hunting people, can offer insights into the life styles of these prehistoric hunters. Many other scientists, both within and outside of the broad discipline of anthropology, are helping to fill in the blanks in our knowledge of man's past. Radioactive carbon dating has now become a familiar tool, and is the nuclear scientist's contribution. Less generally known is the skill of the palaeobotanist who, by examining microscopic pollen grains in an excavated soil sample, can describe the climate that prevailed when the site he is investigating was occupied.

Today there is general agreement among such scientists regarding the broad outline of North American prehistory.

A burial circa 1200 B.C.

10

Excavating the site, A.D. 1971

By 10,000 years before the present, most of Canada was free of its icy burden. Judging by the projectile points that have been discovered — the Sandia, Folsom, and Clovis — big-game hunting persisted until about 9,000 years ago. Indeed, some believe that the mammoth and mastodon were actually hunted out of existence. At any rate, smaller projectile points became more frequent, especially in the east, and the large fluted points began to dwindle in favour of those more suitable for heavy darts. Such projectiles were thrown by the leverage of a throwing stick, or *atlatl*, a device that gave greater thrust to a weapon than the unaided human arm. By 6000 B.C. modern bison, moose, elk, caribou, and bear had become the chief game animals.

During the next four millennia the western plains gradually dried up, and to the east, in the moister, forested regions, a *Boreal Archaic* culture developed that was to last until the sixth century B.C.. It placed a heavy emphasis on the use of wood, so that stone tools shaped for woodworking predominated. In the same period an *Early Woodland* culture appeared farther eastward yet, with the first burial mounds and pottery. Agriculture moved into the lower lakes region with the *Hopewell* people from the south. And, when a *Late Woodland* culture developed, a variety of subcultures 11 appeared, broadly divided between the ancestors of the wandering Algonkian hunters, and the prehistoric Iroquoians.

Authorities disagree as to when the bow and arrow came into use in North America. On the western plains the weapon was not known before A.D. 800, although arrow points began to appear in the Atlantic coastlands at least two millennia earlier. Probably the hunting methods on the plains, where bison were driven over the edge of a coulee and into pounds where they could be speared at close range, account for the late introduction of the bow and arrow in the prairies. But, interestingly enough, once the plains people learned of the bow, they created tiny flaked points popularly known as "bird points" that could penetrate the bison's hide and reach its vitals more efficiently than a coarser arrowhead.

Some Unanswered Questions

The most persistent problem that has confronted anthropologists from the beginning is the extent to which important cultural traits have been independently invented as compared with those which were transferred to the New World from the Old. Well into this century, most scholars attributed every significant feature of New World cultures to an Old World origin. As, literally, they dug deeper it became clear that many features were independent inventions — the Mayan pyramids, to mention only one example. But, recently, evidence has emerged that raises the possibility that cultural influences passed both to and from the Americas. It might be reasonable to suppose, for example, that the West Coast Nootka people had developed a method of manufacturing bark cloth on their own, even though Captain Cook declared he had seen identical techniques in use on the opposite side of the Pacific. But it is quite another thing to account for the discovery of cotton seeds, found in a 4,000-year-old deposit on the Peruvian coast, that some botanists are convinced are a hybrid of a wild American plant and a cultivated Asian one!

A majority of scientists believe that most, if not all, of the migrations into the Americas occurred after 30,000 B.C. But a number of excavations have raised speculations to the contrary.

One such site was discovered by an archaeological team from the National Museum of Man at Sheguiandah Hill, on the east end of Manitoulin Island, 150 miles east of Sault Ste. Marie. Here, in an outcrop of the white quartzite that also forms a ridge along the north shore of Lake Huron, an ancient quarry was found. Five levels of human occupation were excavated. The third level contained javelin and atlatl points of a type that had been found elsewhere in

10,000-year-old deposits. And a test pit, dug in a small swamp on the hill, disclosed artifacts lying *underneath* peat layers that themselves could be carbon-dated back to 9,000 years before the present. A controversy continues over the interpretation of this deepest layer. It was covered with a sterile deposit which some geologists identified as glacial in origin, although others were doubtful. If the former are right, then men were quarrying on Manitoulin Island *before* the first tongue of Wisconsin ice crept over Sheguiandah Hill some 40,000 years ago.

On the other hand, a problem faced by linguists is so simple that it may not, at first, seem to be a problem at all. This is the subtle effect that the word "Indian" has in perpetuating a mistaken concept of Canada's native peoples. Columbus had good reasons—and therefore scientific ones—for believing that he had reached the outlying islands of the true Indies, and to conclude, therefore, that the islanders he met were "Indians". Today, five centuries later, the name is a source of confusion, especially in Canada, where thousands of individuals—many of them professional people—have emigrated from India since 1945. But even more significantly, stubborn stereotypes persist, built up around the image of "the Indian". These are the result of romantic associations with the opening of the American West. Some anthropologists now use the composite term "Amerindian" to distinguish the aborigines of the Americas (including the Eskimo and Aleut) from the natives of India. Yet the image of the Plains Indian is so firmly fixed in our minds by the *word* that it is extraordinarily difficult to think of a Kwakiutl, Ojibway, or Micmac in terms of anything but tipis, scalps, war bonnets, and horses. Only if we change the word is it possible to change the image.

A related problem is that associated with the term "primitive", when it is applied to any human group. In Eurasia and Africa, ample evidence has accumulated that Palaeolithic Man had a brain capacity equal to that of men in the twentieth century. One has only to visit the caves these people occupied, in limestone and sandstone formations from northern Spain to the Ural Mountains, to have his image of crude "cave men" utterly shattered. Here, in a period when men — apparently — had not learned to build their own shelters, and made their stone tools coarsely, though skilfully, some of their number were able to create drawings, paintings, and sculpture that demand sensitivity and intelligence of the highest order. Subsequent examples of rock art found in all parts of the globe, including Canada, range from a naturalism that rivals the Palaeolithic art of 20,000 years ago, to a capacity for abstraction that is equally impressive. And a close examination of such "primitive" art reveals a sophistica- 13 tion of religious beliefs that continues to escape the complete understanding of the most "civilized" investigator.

Here science is confronted with the most enigmatic of all mysteries: the origin and significance of the human spirit. It may be that, although we learn to unravel the complex mysteries of the human brain, the enigma of human consciousness will still lie beyond the reach of scientific investigation. For thousands of years man had to be satisfied with the explanations offered in myths, and they could be the closest we will ever get to the meaning of our existence.

Spectacular as the advances in our knowledge of the past have been, we are still limited by the bias of our own time and place in our interpretation of each fact that comes to light. The reader who shares the spirit of science will approach the statements this book contains with a measure of scepticism, alert to separate what he can accept as fact from what he suspects to be based on the writer's bias. But he will also be aware that the true scientist, patiently picking away at the wall of our common ignorance about the past, is far too aware of the immensity of that ignorance to be anything but humble in its presence.

2 Civilized Man in the Americas

Mastering the Environment

In 1938 anthropologist Junius Bird made a significant discovery in Palli Aike cave, not far north of the Straits of Magellan: a series of deposits which proved that men had lived at the tip of South America 8,600 years before the present, hunting a subsequently extinct species of horse. There were four aboriginal groups in the region when they were first encountered by Europeans. One of these, the Yahgan, was studied at first hand by the nineteenth-century Anglican missionary, Bridges. Seemingly they were one of the earth's most backward people, with the crudest of dwellings, no footwear, and no other clothing than a fur robe for protection from the damp, freezing winters of southernmost Patagonia. Yet when Bridges completed a dictionary of their language, he found he had compiled a vocabulary exceed-ing 30,000 words, quite comparable with the working vocabulary of an educated English-speaking person in the twentieth century.

Thanks to the diet and diseases of the European intruders, all four tribes have now vanished. But the fact that their ancestors had penetrated so early to this bleak extremity of the New World points eloquently to the capacity of the Amerindian to adapt himself to the most varied environments of the western hemisphere.

Three of these environments gave the Amerindian unique opportunities to develop the intelligence and creative capacity that were his human heritage. In all three regions — the high, dry Peruvian plateaus, the low, moist plains of Yucatan, and the lake country of the central Mexican highlands — men began to form settled communities five or six thousand years ago, having found, and learned to cultivate, two basic foods, corn and beans.

So ancient is corn that the domesticated plant cannot re-seed itself without human help, and only recently have botanists been able to identify its wild ancestor. In the southwest United States, cobs a mere two inches long have been found and carbon-dated: they show that corn cultivation had penetrated this far north as early as 3000 B.C. Many more centuries were to pass before the seeds on so small a cob were developed into fat, starchy kernels that could be cooked as a vegetable for immediate use, or dried and stored for future needs.

Frijoles, a small black bean of the genus *Phaseolus*, was as widely cultivated as corn, and may have been domesticated a thousand years earlier. This was a food rich in the muscle-building protein that was formerly available to Amerindians only in meat and fish. The bean was undoubtedly a factor in the strenuous agricultural development of the high plateaus of Peru and Bolivia.

Once these foods were developed, early farmers were released from the need for constant food-getting. Their time and energies began to find more varied and special skills for clever fingers, more complex and stimulating ideas for active brains. From cord-twisting and basket-weaving they moved on to the spinning and weaving of fine fabrics. Simple drawings on rock, and picture writing on bark and hide, developed into sophisticated pictography, preparing the way for mathematics and astronomy. The informal leadership of small wandering bands grew into an ability to guide and govern the complex affairs of a whole state.

The Incredible Incas

The earliest farmers in Peru and Bolivia appear to have lived on the coastal lowlands, cultivating beans, squash, chili pepper, and cotton. As they moved inland, into the lower valleys of the Andes, they added some thirty food plants to their diet, including corn and the small red and purple tubers that were the ancestor of the potato.

But when settlement moved higher into the Andes, some remarkable things began to happen. It is far from certain where the high Andean people came from, or how early they began to occupy a land that was so far above sea level that, like the Sherpas of the Himalayas, their descendants developed lung capacities far beyond the human average. Whatever their origin, the obstacles overcome by these highlanders were beyond belief. With dogged toil in this high, harsh land they moved rocks and earth from miles around in order to build narrow terraces of soil up steep mountain slopes. And they dug ditches — sometimes hewn out of the living rock — to bring water to these terraces from distant mountain streams. They became the only pastoralists of the New World when they domesticated the *llama* as a beast of burden, and the *alpaca* as a source of meat. Two other cameloid species were exploited, 17 though not tamed: the *vicuna* was caught, sheared of its wool, and released, while the *guanaco* was hunted as game. The dog was kept as a pet and scavenger and eaten by some tribes. But the main source of meat for the common people was the domesticated guinea pig.

With ample sources of nutritious food and an amazing ingenuity, the Andean population multiplied. Trade and the arts flourished. Cotton fabrics were woven of a fineness and lightness that has never been excelled. Great temples were built for sun-worshipping ceremonies, their walls constructed with stone and copper tools out of huge, irregular blocks, blocks so perfectly shaped and fitted that even today a knife blade will rarely go between the mortarless joints. The *quipu*, a unique method of keeping records, was invented. Using a complex system of coloured and knotted cords, priests were able to memorize and recite long sequences of religious and historical data.

Ever since the first scientific excavations made by Max Uhle at Pachacmac in 1896, the story of Andean archaeology has been the discovery of one remarkable and individual culture after another. It was not until the fourteenth century A.D. that a small tribe from northwest of Lake Titicaca moved into the Cuzco valley and developed a powerful class of Inca rulers. These people—by sheer force of character it would appear—forged dozens of scattered communities, many of them highly developed and powerful, into the New World's first military empire. Between 1438 and 1493 the Inca rulers, Pachauti and his son Topa, expanded their sway to include at least two million people and the greater part of Andean America. No mountains were too rugged for their military roads and few chasms stopped their bridges. Using only human power and tools of stone and copper, they built triumphs of engineering that rival the roads and viaducts of ancient Rome.

The Peruvians under the Incas built a highly centralized, materialistic civilization based not only on a craving for wealth and power but also on a concern with permanence and political stability. To increase production, great works of agricultural engineering were undertaken. Whole populations of conquered states were transplanted, to be replaced by more subservient ones that were watched by picked troops and ruled by Incan administrators. The resulting empire was unlike any other the earth has known, and terms that have been invented to describe it, such as "autocratic socialism" or "theocratic monarchical communism", confuse rather than enlighten.

The Maya

Meanwhile, in the other half of the New World, other high cultures were emerging. The Olmec built a civilization along the southwest shore of the Gulf of Mexico as early as 1000 B.C. And later, in the dense forests of

Olmec sculptors

the interior, another extraordinary flowering of culture, influenced by the Olmec, took place.

Only in Cambodia has a great civilization been built in a setting that was more humid and tropical than the homeland of the Maya, in the Yucatan Peninsula. In this unpromising land, the Mayan farmer burned and hacked out a clearing, and planted, tilled, and harvested his staple crops of corn and beans, equipped with no more than a digging stick and a stone hoe. And, within ten years, the fertility of his clearing would begin to fail, forcing him to hack out a new clearing.

And even while his plot was still fertile, the rains of midsummer would activate the encroaching jungle, so that it was the farmer's constant concern to hold back the lush flow of tropical vegetation. Even today, archaeologists examining Mayan ruins must devote the first weeks of the digging season to rooting out the growth that has overrun their excavations during seven months of intermittent rain. And during the driest months their work may still be interrupted by unpredictable cloudbursts and flash floods. To the north, however, where less rain falls and forests thin out into savannah and scrubland, drought, not rain, was the major menace. Here, the Mayan communities grew up around the *cenote*, a natural, spring-fed rock well.

For the Mayan peasant, threatened by wilful and capricious weather gods, the only hope of survival was offered by dedicated priests. Willingly the peasant gave his surplus time and energy to support a centre where all the people could assemble for great religious festivals, and where the priests could spend all their time studying the signs and portents that enabled them to predict — and to believe they could control — the changing moods of the gods. At a time when Rome was young, such centres for ritual and priestly research were already growing. By the seventh century A.D., the great temple-cities of Yucatan had achieved a peak that has earned for the Mayan civilization the title "Athens of the New World".

As the priests learned about the cycles of the sun and moon, and the seemingly erratic motions of the planets against the majestic daily rotation of the stars, their observations became increasingly accurate. And thus the Mayan priest-astronomers developed a calendar by which even eclipses of the sun and moon could be predicted with great precision. At the same time, they created a system of numerology and mathematics, and recorded it in a form of picture-writing that was the closest approach to true writing ever developed in the western hemisphere. This mathematical system reached a level of sophistication beyond any achieved up to that point in Europe or Asia. Indeed, centuries before the Hindus, the Maya invented the *zero*, as revolutionary an advance in those days as Einstein's theory of relativity in our own. Unknown to the Old World, the Maya were then the world's foremost mathematicians.

The Mayan city never became an urban centre based on trade and industry. It remained a centre for collective ritual, with permanent quarters for the priestly scholars, clerks, and officials necessary for temple activities, for the staff and labourers working on current building projects, and, possibly, for soldiers. But during the weeks of the major festivals, the wide foot-highways that fanned out into the farmlands were choked with peasants and their families carrying provisions on their backs that they would need during the festivals. At these times, the population of the city was swelled by tens of thousands, who would stare with awe at the massive, elaborately carved *stelae* erected at specific intervals to record the passage of time, or gaze across the broad plaza towards a pyramid, 70 feet high, and capped by a temple.

Great care was lavished on such temples. Even the relatively small city of Bonampak could offer the spectacle — denied perhaps to common folk — of vividly painted murals decorating the walls within its temple. Here, in the words of anthropologist Jacques Soustelle, was "a sort of pictorial encyclopedia of a Maya city of the eighth century; the city comes to life . . . with its ceremonies and its processions, its stiff and solemn-looking dignitaries weighed down by their heavy plumed adornments, its warriors clothed in jaguar skins."

Elsewhere, the building on the pyramid had other uses. On a great stone platform in Chichen Itza, for example, stand the ruins of an astronomical observatory. And at Palenque, Piedras Negras, and Copan, the surviving structures are still eloquent of the greatness of a people who not only produced masterworks of sculpture and architecture, but excelled as painters, potters, and weavers, comparable with the world's best.

By A.D. 800, however, the Mayan states were beginning to decline and some had already collapsed. The reasons are obscure, but at least one factor is clear: a gulf had opened between priest and peasant. The former, advancing in both power and enlightenment, had made increasing demands upon the labour of the latter, whose farming techniques remained at the crude level of hand toil. Inevitably tensions between the two classes would have mounted, and there is some archaeological evidence — as at Altun Ha on the Honduras coast — which suggests that these tensions might have reached an explosion point. Rioting peasants — or soldiers, or both — smashed the sacred symbols and levelled temples to the ground.

But violent revolution was not necessary for the

disappearance of the Mayan temple-cities. Once the peasants started the practice of passive resistance to the priests' demands, a single season could begin a process that became more difficult to reverse with each passing year. For the jungle, ever encroaching, needed only two or three years of neglect to engulf the temple core beyond recovery. The whole process, accelerated by growing rumours that the gods had withdrawn their favour, would dishearten the people at the very time when all their energies were needed to cut back the encroaching jungle.

New Civilizations Emerge

Even as the Mayan civilization declined, a *Teotihuacan* culture had emerged in the Mexican highlands, and with it grew the first true city in the Americas, just northeast of where Mexico City now stands. But pressures had been building up farther north yet, as semi-civilized tribes moved into the Mexican region from as far away as Arizona and New Mexico. Teotihuacan was destroyed, and the Itza, one of the invading tribes, created a new and harsher *Toltec* culture. As the Mayan society continued its decline, and the power of its temple-cities weakened, the Itza took over the northern centres and came to dominate the whole of Middle America. At Chichen Itza, their activities in-

fused a new vigour into an aging Mayan city, and the old glory was briefly renewed. But the Mayan dominance had been ended decisively.

Although the Toltec absorbed and revived many of the old Mayan cultural characteristics, they brought with them a form of religion that was obsessed with the conviction that constant sacrifices were needed to satisfy the gods that moved the sun and fertilized the earth. Catastrophe was imminent, they believed, if they failed to sacrifice massive numbers of adult males to these gods. In the Mexican city-states that emerged under Toltec dominance, the mania for such slaughter grew until it became the practice to wage ritualistic wars for the sole purpose of acquiring captives whose hearts might be offered from the altars of the victor.

However, a bare two centuries before Columbus arrived in America, an obscure hunting tribe moved into the Mexican lake country from the northeast and took up a farming life. Soon, crowded out by stronger neighbours, they were forced to take refuge on some islands, where they lived by fishing and raising produce on large, earth-covered reed rafts. And then, with remarkable speed, this small *Aztec* tribe became formidable. Beginning on a single island, but expanding over a reclaimed lake bottom on top of wooden piles, *Tenochtitlan*, the greatest city of pre-Columbian America, emerged. By a combination of threats and alliances, the city gained power over its neighbours until, by the fifteenth century A.D., the whole of southern Mexico was dominated by the religious and military authority of the Aztec priest-emperor, Montezuma II.

From neighbouring states, the best minds and most skilled craftsmen were lured into the capital, infusing new energy into the arts of weaving, pottery, sculpture, and architecture. By A.D. 1500 Tenochtitlan, the "Venice of America", was a city of paved streets and busy canals. Here richly garbed nobles looked down from their litters on simple country folk paddling their boats to market. The boats were laden with all sorts of produce: turkeys, fish, game, tomatoes, sunflowers, beans, chocolate, cotton, pottery. Beside Montezuma's palace was a great zoo to amuse the populace, with an aviary where thousands of tropical birds were kept for their brilliantly coloured feathers.

To celebrate the festivals of the kindlier gods, laughing people filled the streets, honouring their deities with flowers, music, and dancing. But there were grim occasions, when the population assembled in the great square to witness the sacrifices that all believed were necessary for the welfare of the state. At the summit of a great pyramid stood the priests, armed with razor-sharp obsidian knives. One by one the captives were laid on the sacrificial stone where, with consummate skill, a priest slashed open the chest cavity to reach in and wrench out the victim's living heart, while the still twitching body rolled down the bloodied temple steps.

To ensure a steady flow of victims, almost constant war was necessary—although threats could sometimes prevail on a weaker state to provide a tribute of captives. When two armies met, there were no surprise tactics. Rather, the attackers gave the enemy ample time to gather all his forces before the decisive battle. For it was the war gods who decided the victor, and the greater the opposing force, the richer would be the human harvest for the winner. Even when the victors were absorbed in the sacrificial celebrations that followed the battle, there were no counterattacks, for the defeated army accepted its losses as a verdict of the gods that it would be impious to challenge.

Few economic ties bound this strange theocratic empire together; Aztec supremacy depended mainly on religious prestige. This, and the fatalistic attitude of the people toward the outcome of a single battle, would prove to be mortal weaknesses when they were faced with European invaders, whose aggressive fighting tactics and greed for booty would utterly demoralize Aztec resistance.

After Columbus's first landing, more than a quarter-century passed before the first Europeans stepped on Aztec soil. Throughout those years, the 23 rumours multiplied of strange visitors from the east—foreshadowings, perhaps, of the Aztec's deified folk-hero, *Quetzalcoatl*. This feathered Serpent-God was reputed to have sailed east in exile, after giving his people corn, the arts, and the calendar. He had vowed to return, so the old records said, and now a prophecy was circulating that he would soon arrive, in the form of a bearded, white-skinned man.

Soon, indeed, a whole company of extraordinary red-faced, hairy strangers arrived, whose skin, when uncovered, was white as the snow on Popocatapetl. They bestrode huge, hornless, long-tailed deer, were clothed in plates of a metal bright as silver but hard as obsidian, and carried weapons that belched forth thunder, fire, and death.

And all too soon others of their kind would follow, to change forever the ancient ways of man in the Americas.

3 Men out of Europe

Hairy-Faced Strangers

A wandering Eskimo hunter in a Greenland fiord a thousand years ago stared incredulously at what he saw emerging from behind a rocky headland. What kind of monstrous *umiak* could this be? Was that a great white wing over it? No, it was some kind of hide held up with poles and ropes and bellied by the wind. Never had he seen so many men in one boat. Clearly they were not *the people*, not *Inuit*. It was just one more of those strange things his dying father had told him about, of the changes coming over the land: strange plants that no man had known; channels opening up where ice had always been. Swiftly he paddled his kayak ashore and hid behind a rock to watch the Vikings land.

Today we know that a warm spell had begun that was to last into the fourteenth century. Erik the Red, view-ing the fiords and headlands of the southwest Green-land coast in that summer of 982, might well have seen a green land. The two Viking settlements he founded maintained themselves for four centuries, dying out only when the warm cycle ended and the grain and wild grasses on which the cattle economy depended would no longer grow.

A stone with Norse runes that was found in Min-nesota, and Norse relics that turned up north of Lake Superior, have raised fierce arguments as to whether or not the Vikings penetrated the interior of North America. Charges that this evidence was forged or deliberately planted have been neither proved nor convincingly refuted. The meaning of "Vinland", a word used in Icelandic sagas to refer to an unidentified part of the Atlantic coast of North America, remains ambiguous. "Vin-" translates into English as "grape", if 25 it is used with the long "i" — but with a short vowel it means "grass". Did some early scribe, unconsciously yielding to a "fondness of the marvelous", write the long vowel, instead of the short one, when he copied the saga?

Certainly the sagas tell us of landings on the mainland of North America: by Leif, Erik's son, in the year 1000, and by Thorfinn Karlsefni a few years later. The latter attempted to found a settlement and, in 1961, at L'Anse aux Meadows on the northern tip of Newfoundland, a party of Scandinavian scientists found a site that yielded evidence of Viking occupation.

Here eight houses had stood, the largest sixty feet long by forty-five feet wide. On the smithy floor, beside a large stone anvil, were numerous scraps of iron and slag. Nearby a charcoal-burning pit was found. Seven carbon samples yielded dates around the year A.D. 1000.

It is through the Icelandic sagas that we catch the first European glimpses of the inhabitants of the Americas. These people, whom the Vikings called *Skraeling*, were "swarthy men and ill-looking, and the hair of their heads was ugly: they had large eyes and broad cheeks."

But what did the Skraeling think of their visitors?

Perhaps they doubted whether these narrow-faced, hairy creatures with their spearlike noses were really human. What strange skin! On the faces and arms it was red as fire, but when it was uncovered, it was white as snow! Some had black hair; but on the heads of others, the hair was yellow or red, growing in waves. And the eyes of some were the colour of seawater! What clacks of disapproval must have passed among the women as they crowded around the new-born Snorri, first European child to be born in the New World. Imagine a baby being born completely *bald*!

Equally mystifying was a substance, like none the Skraeling had ever seen, out of which these strangers hammered their tools and weapons. Karlsefni and his men were too canny to trade the sharp axes that might be used against them if fighting broke out. But when it did, the weapons of the slain lay on the ground for the taking. Thus, after one battle, a saga tells us, "the Skraelings had found a dead man whose axe lay beside him. One of them picked up the axe and cut a tree with it, and so they did one after another, and thought it a treasure, and one which cut well. Afterwards one of them set to and cut at a stone, so that the axe broke, and then they thought it useless because it could not stand up to a stone, so threw it down."

Another saga relates that "one of the skraelings picked up an axe, and having looked at it for a time, he brandished it about one of his companions, and hewed at him, and on the instant the man fell dead. Thereupon the big man [already referred to as their leader] seized the axe, and after examining it for a moment, he hurled it as far as he could, out into the sea."

However we may interpret the peculiar action of the latter Skraeling, both accounts record the mixed reactions with which the iron weapon was viewed. Whether these natives of the Atlantic coast were Eskimo, Naskapi, or Beothuk, warfare would have been a rare experience for them: life was too hazardous and neighbours too few. Introduced to the axe as a weapon, they nevertheless saw its possibilities as a tool, and were delighted until they found it shattered on rock. Obviously a hammerstone was a much more effective rock-splitter. But as a weapon, it had supernatural power which could be turned against one's companions. The thing was not to be trusted. So even though they must have watched the Viking smith convert bog iron ore into iron castings, they probably regarded both process and product with great suspicion. And so, when the Vikings abandoned the settlement, they left the aborigines to continue in the Stone Age.

Axes for Beaver Robes

Five centuries elapsed before the next recorded visits of Europeans to America. Such a time span would have sufficed, in view of the briefness of Viking contact, to wipe out any tribal memory of the event. So the coastal natives would again have been totally unprepared for encounters with aliens from across the ocean. Nor are we of the twentieth century—familiar as we have been from childhood with pictures of strange people in far-away places—likely to comprehend the impact of those first meetings.

Columbus gives us a hint when he describes how his gifts "of little value . . . gave them great pleasure, and made them so much our friends that it was a marvel to see." Verrazano describes the natives of the Carolina coast as "seeming to rejoice very much at the sight of us". But Cartier, still farther north, gives us a more intimate glimpse of the reaction. "We sent two men unto them with hatchets, knives, beads, and other such like ware, whereat they were very glad, and by and by in clusters they came to the shore where they were, with their boates, bringing with them skinnes and other such things as they had, to have of our wares." Since these people whom he met in the Baie de Chaleur in 1534 had invited his men ashore by waving skins on the ends of poles, they must have met earlier Europeans who had exchanged axes and knives for fur pelts.

No doubt the Amerindian eagerly accepted beads and trinkets for their glitter and novelty. But Cartier heads his list with *hatchets*. We have only to compare the slow chipping of even a small tree by dozens of 27 blows from a stone hatchet with the effect of two or three swift blows from a steel axe to understand how amazed and delighted the aborigines must have been with the first demonstration of an axe. No matter how keen the edge of a stone axe might be ground, its brittleness demanded a thick, bluntly bevelled blade, incapable of biting deeply into the wood, so that its action would be one of chipping rather than cutting.

Even after the Amerindians had learned of the marvelous gifts the strangers brought, the early accounts make it clear that there was a period of suspense that prefaced each new encounter. We can only guess how much greater this must have been on the *first* unexpected meeting. Surely it would have had the impact of a supernatural visitation. On the edge of panic, already aware for hours of the approach of a strange object—a sort of gigantic water bird—the natives would study every detail as the vessel anchored, the ship's boat was lowered, and its crew paddled *backwards* towards them. What did this extraordinary event foreshadow? Was it good, or evil? They would glance at their shaman, only to sense in him the mounting tension that gripped them all.

For the master of that boat, there would also have been tension. Would these savages be friendly? Or would they flee, so that nothing could be learned from them? He would note the weapons held tensely at the natives' sides. . . .

Let us imagine now the master of the Portuguese vessel, shrewd and experienced in dealing with the native people of many lands. As he disembarks at a Micmac shore camp, followed by a single man carrying a sharp axe, his crew stands alertly by the boat. The men of the camp have moved closer, cautiously fingering their weapons, silent and watchful. The captain pauses to survey the shore. His axeman points to a tree on the ridge, a young aspen six inches through. The captain nods and they walk with calculated nonchalance toward it, ignoring the people who follow slowly, their headmen in advance. The axeman takes his position beside the tree, sizing it up and taking a firmer grip on his axe. The little crowd circles to watch. The captain, doffing his cap and bowing in the European manner of his time, gestures toward axeman and tree. "Now!"

The axeman lifts his steel hatchet. It glints in the sun, holding every eye. And each eye falls with the descending blade. Swiftly it bites, deep and true — *completely through* the trunk. The tree quivers as it slides, still standing, butt to earth, then leans and gently falls.

An audible sigh of astonishment sweeps through the audience, but no one yet moves. For no one yet knows what this ritual means. Until the captain takes the axe from his man, and holds it out — as a gift — to the boldest headman, who takes it in his hands, stares at it gravely a moment, then with gleaming eyes holds it up for all his people to see.

And pandemonium breaks loose.

Years later, reminiscing at an inn in his native seaport, the aging captain once more concludes the tale for his cronies.

"That joy — those people — how shall I describe them? A deluge of young and old reaching to touch you — caressing your arms and shoulders, falling at your feet — young men cavorting on the sand — and everywhere a din and hulabaloo of joyous shouts and cries. I can hear them yet. They ring in my ears, like the ecstasies of shriven souls newly admitted into paradise. It was as if — may the Blessed Virgin forgive the thought" — and the ancient mariner crosses himself — "as if I had been Her Sweet Son Himself at His Second Coming!"

As the decades passed into the third quarter of the 1500s European trade goods became familiar along the Atlantic shore. Canvas and woollen broadcloth were no longer strange, and curious women, pulling the strands apart, could understand that they had been woven together. But the material of which European headgear was often made must have puzzled them far longer. When it was shredded, they could see it was made of animal hair. So, in fact, it was, but the Amerindian could scarcely have guessed that the felted hair was manufactured from the short inner wool of the European beaver.

Since early medieval times, European feltmakers had known that the wool of the beaver, after the longer coarser "guard" hairs had been removed, was unsurpassed for making hat felt. Thus any style of head covering that was made of felt was known as a *beaver* in English, or a *castor* in French. By Columbus's time, however, European beaver was becoming extinct, and by 1550 the only known sources of supply were Scandinavia and Russia.

In the New World, however, it happened that the most widely worn garment among northern tribes was a rectangular robe made from six or more prime beaver pelts, worn with the fur turned in. It not only furnished extra warmth in the winter, but was also useful as a sleeping robe and a rain cape — perhaps, too, as a protection against mosquitoes. After about a year's wear, it underwent two significant changes. By frequent handling, as well as deliberate greasing, the outer side acquired an oily flexibility that made it waterproof and kept the hair in good condition. Meanwhile, the longer, coarser guard hairs, having been loosened by scraping while the hide was prepared, were shed during a winter's wear. And the gentle friction of the fur on the wearer's body had produced a peculiar downy quality in the wool itself. Such well-

29

worn clothing came to be known as *castor gras*, "greasy beaver".

History does not record which Paris hatmaker discovered the unique felting properties of *castor gras*. But it is recorded that in 1581 a cargo of furs from the Gulf of St. Lawrence was sold in Paris for a small fortune. And by 1600 the trade was already so extensive that supplies of beaver were being exhausted all along the Atlantic coast, and even in the Gulf of St. Lawrence.

The impact of the fur trade on the native people was massive and far-reaching. The Amerindian's craving for trade goods was matched only by the European demand for *castor gras*. Soon axes, knives, and pots from overseas were making their way inland far ahead of European penetration, carried by native middlemen. This trading activity was not unusual. Long before the arrival of Europeans, extensive inter-tribal trading had been going on throughout the continent. Obsidian from the Yellowstone area, which could be flaked for use as razor-sharp knives and "microblades", had been traded to the most distant points. Native copper from Lake Superior was bartered far afield. And agricultural people had regularly exchanged surplus corn and tobacco for the tanned hides and birchbark of northern hunters. These trading habits were quickly adapted to the fur economy. Tribes that had exhausted their own beaver supplies became middlemen, carrying trade goods inland to exchange them for beaver pelts. Back at the coast they exchanged the furs for more trade goods, at a handsome profit.

When the Europeans learned to by-pass such middlemen, the latter turned to poaching on the territory of neighbouring tribes, and warfare flared as raids and reprisals increased. With their more efficient trade weapons, the aggressors could take over new beaver lands, and with firearms, they proved irresistible. And they also carried previously unknown diseases, likewise imported from overseas. Thus, far in advance of actual European settlement, shock waves of warfare and epidemic rippled across the continent.

Guns, Horses, and Epidemics

The first impact of firearms had little to do with their efficiency as weapons, and a lot to do with their noise. When Cartier demonstrated the fire power of his twelve ship's cannon, although these were discharged in a harmless direction, the Stadacona villagers "took to howling so terribly that it seemed hell was empty". Even the sixteenth-century musket—actually a slower and clumsier weapon than the bow and arrow — was sufficiently frightening on first encounter to rout large enemy forces. Throughout the seventeenth century, the gun was used mainly for its dramatic effect. In 1673, writing of Illinois bands in the upper Mississippi country, Père Marquette noted: "They are active and very skilful with their bows and arrows. They also use guns, which they buy from our savage allies who trade with our French. They use them especially to inspire *through their noise and smoke* [italics added], terror in their enemies; the latter do not use guns and have never seen any, since they lived too far towards the West, . . . nor do they know anything of Iron, or of Copper, and they have only stone knives."

In the early nineteenth century, David Thompson smuggled guns across the Rockies to provide the Salish with protection against Blackfoot raids so they could get on with beaver hunting. He gives us a glimpse of how, even when the efficiency of the gun had improved to the point that it was superior to the bow and arrow, its supernatural associations continued. In his youth, a Salish elder informed Thompson, "he made a heavy war club, with which he felt himself confident of victory, [and] they formed a very large party against the Peeagans, and hoped for success, when for the first time their enemy had two Guns, and every shot killed a Man. We could not stand this, and thought they brought bad spirits," the old man related, so that "We all fled and hid ourselves . . . we had no defence until you crossed the mountains and brought us fire arms."

So, all across the continent, as each tribe acquired superior weapons, it moved in on those that lacked them. And thus the tribal territories that were discovered by the first traders were often well west of the hunting lands that had existed when Europeans arrived in America.

On the plains this westward shift was complicated by another event. Horses were appearing from the south. It is a strange fact that the horse had originated in the Americas some millions of years previously, and spread into Eurasia by way of the Bering route, lingering in the Americas well after the first men came. Then, for no known reason, about 8,000 years ago, the American herds became extinct. When Cortez brought horses from Spain in A.D. 1519 he completed the cycle that carried the horse completely around the globe, back to its homeland. Soon wild horses were again native to the New World. And with their appearance, knowledge of horse-handling spread rapidly northward, reaching the Canadian prairies in the mid-eighteenth century. Evidence of how strange these animals were to aboriginal eyes is carved into soft sandstone cliffs along the Milk River in southern Alberta. In the earliest renderings they look like long-tailed, hornless deer with human figures suspended in the air above them.

With the coming of the horse, the lives of the Plains people were transformed. Bands that had toiled slowly on foot after bison herds now pursued them swiftly on horseback. Even corn-growing tribes along the upper tributaries of the Mississippi were tempted to forsake their earth lodges for the adventurous free life of the mounted hunter. The simultaneous appearance of iron weapons and firearms set the whole population in a turmoil. Within a century a new culture had emerged, characterized by daring and skilful riders whose main obsession — outside of bison-hunting — was raiding neighbouring tribes for the horses that established tribal status, and for the scalps and *coups* on which personal reputations for bravery depended.

So strong an impression was made on the mind of the young American nation by this picturesque culture that it dominates our image of "the Indian" to this day. And thus history has suffered serious distortions. It has been forgotten, for example, that scalp-taking had an eastern origin, and may even have been introduced by the European. It is true that Cartier noted the skins of five human heads stretched out to dry in the village of Stadacona. But it is more significant that, at an early date, New England Puritans offered bounties to friendly natives for the heads of hostile ones. Later only the ears and hair were required, and the price rose to a fantastic 100 pounds sterling. This bounty, offered by a Massachusetts court, was fifty times the going price of a beaver pelt. Before long, the bloody practice became a feature of the wars between the French and the English in North America. The price dropped rapidly, but

it still paid the frontiersman and native alike to bring in the scalps of the enemy, including those of women and children. By the time the practice reached the plains, it had been formalized to the point where a small circle of skin with hair attached was sufficient as a trophy. Frequently the victim survived.

Of all the disturbances introduced by the men out of Europe, by far the most devastating were the deadly micro-organisms they unknowingly carried with them, against which Amerindians had no defence. Especially disastrous were typhus, smallpox, and a virulent form of measles. Tuberculosis appeared much later. As trade and warfare increased inter-tribal contacts, epidemics broke out with terrifying speed. Panic and starvation compounded the effects, and whole villages and bands were wiped out. David Thompson, travelling up the Hayes River from York Factory in the early 1800s, describes what he saw when he landed at a Cree camp to get supplies. "When we came to them, to our surprise they had marks of the small pox, were weak and just recovering.... None of us had the least idea of the desolation this dreadful disease had done, until we went up the bank to the camp and looked into the tents, in many of which they were all dead, and the stench was horrid; those that remained ... were in such a state of despair and despondence that they could hardly converse with us.... From what we could learn, three fifths had died under this disease. . . ."

And so, from the banks of the St. Lawrence to the delta of the Mackenzie, disease ravaged tribe after tribe. And the people came to realize that the evil the strangers brought with them could not be drummed away, sucked out, frightened by hideous masks, appeased, or controlled in any way, even by their most powerful shamans.

What To Do With the Strangers?

How would they deal with these men from across the salt-water seas? Clearly they were the bearers of powerful magic, with their firearms and their immunity from the diseases they sent ahead. Perhaps, in view of this power and the wonderful things they were willing to exchange for beaver pelts, it would be wisest to appease them and tolerate their presence. But, apart from their trade goods, they were not too admirable as human beings. "They often told me," writes a seventeenth-century Jesuit priest, "that at first we seemed ugly with hair upon our mouths and heads." Why, the Amerindians must often have asked themselves, did Europeans not have the decency to pluck out the offending hair, as every self-respecting man would? These strangers were unmannerly, too, interrupting rudely before one finished what one had to say, speaking with loud voices even to a single person, and laughing at beliefs and practices they made no attempt to understand. The majority seemed to be liars, making promises they quickly forgot—even when they put their promises in the writing that they needed to help out their weak memories. And what were their black-robed shamans up to, scurrying through epidemic-stricken villages, performing sinister rites with crossed sticks over dying babies? A Jesuit missionary to the Petun complained that "this whole country is filled with evil reports which are current about us. The children, seeing us arrive at any place, exclaim that famine and disease are coming; some women flee; others hide their children from us; almost all refuse us the hospitality which they grant even to the most unknown tribes."

Europeans, the natives noticed, were like children in their eagerness for beaver skins, which they took away but never seemed to use. They were like children, too, in their greed for bits of shiny gold and silver metal. But worst of all they were mean. Their traders, even when their lodges were filled with goods, required the poorest widow among their own people to make gifts of the few skins she had before they would give her the smallest articles she needed. Why were they not punished? For everyone knows that such meanness angers the supernatural powers.

Only with their fiery medicine drink were these newcomers generous. This was a wonderful but fearsome thing. With a few swallows a man could enter the shaman's world, seeing visions and rising out of his body, without the long fasting and abstaining from women that one used to need. But sometimes it changed a man into a murderous monster, from whom women and children — even his own — fled in terror. And it could make a man exchange his whole winter collection of furs for a single bottle.

And yet, for all their power, these pale people were strangely weak and ignorant. In the winter they starved and had to be fed. They had little knowledge of medicine, and could not cure the diseases they brought with them. Yet they could not be left to die. For where then could one get the sharp knives and axes and strong cooking pots? And there were some good men among them, who gave freely, who did not lie, who spoke the language of the land and grew skilful in its ways.

The fact is that the early settlements would never have survived without a mutual need — the natives' craving for the newcomers' trade goods, and the Europeans' greed for *castor gras*. Long ago the tough Norsemen had failed, and all through the 1500s attempts to settle along the north Atlantic seaboard ended in defeat or disaster. Undoubtedly the Spanish settlements in the south would eventually have crept up the coast, and the small fishing colonies of Newfoundland would have established footholds much as they actually did. But the Europeans showed little talent for adapting themselves to conditions in the New World. When their grain was planted too early or too late, it was ruined by unpredictable spring or fall frosts. When this happened, or a supply ship was wrecked on uncharted shores, the settlement faced starvation. In winter, European clothing was pitifully inadequate and scurvy killed the settlers off like flies, until they learned native remedies. They had no techniques for winter hunting, fishing, or travel. And in summer their boats were too heavy and clumsy for the rough inland rivers, while their wagons and even their horses were useless in the trackless wilderness. But yet, surrounded by an overwhelming majority of aliens, they persisted in an arrogance that frequently put their lives in danger.

Farmers, Traders, and Missionaries

Yet tolerated, taught, and frequently fed by the native people who wanted their trade goods, the men out of Europe endured hardships unknown in their native lands, and established settlements along the northern Atlantic seaboard: the French at Port Royal in 1605 and Quebec in 1608; the English at Jamestown in 1607; and the Dutch at New Amsterdam in 1615.

From the first, the French committed themselves to 35

the fur trade. Their young men quickly acquired the dialects of their Algonkian-speaking neighbours, a skill that would open up trading friendships with Algonkian speakers deep in the continent. Along with the language, they acquired native bush skills and an understanding of the gift system on which Amerindian trading was based. This rapport with the native tribes yielded rich rewards, opening to the French the intimate knowledge that each tribe had of its own territory, and of the ancient trading routes and meeting-places. So Father Marquette could write in 1673: "We obtained all the information that we could from the savages who frequented these regions [Algonkian-speaking tribes of the upper Mississippi], and we even traced out from their reports a Map of the whole of that New country; on it we indicated the rivers that we were to navigate, the names of the people and of the places through which we were to pass, the course of the Great River, and the direction we were to follow when we reached it. . . ."

A quite different relationship with the native people developed in the English colonies. The attitude of many settlers is illustrated by the comments of an early writer on "the great sickness at Patuxet" that raged among the natives from 1617 to 1619. This had been so severe that, "when the English arrived in the country their bones [i.e., those of the natives] were thick upon the ground in many places. This [the English] looked upon as a great providence, inasmuch as it had destroyed multitudes of the barbarous heathen to make way for the chosen people of God."

The English had not come to trade, or to fish, or to look for gold, or to find a route to the Indies, but to settle. For a few years, while they depended on the "barbarous heathen" to learn corn-raising and hunting skills, they cultivated friendship with the natives. Thereafter — except as allies during the French-English wars—the natives were a source of irritation to the English settlers. Time after time territorial boundaries that were established by earlier treaties became intolerable obstacles to expansion.

While the contrasting attitudes of French fur trader and English farmer were laying the foundations of future nations, a third element complicated the relationships of the newcomers to the aborigines. Seventeenth-century Europeans retained many beliefs that, in some cases, predated Christianity. For example, they brought with them from their native lands talk of wandering ghosts and wailing banshees, of the dread werewolf and the blood-sucking vampire. Witchcraft was still employed — albeit secretly — to injure an enemy, to win a bride, or to cure a malignancy. And dreams or portents were accepted as evidence of occult powers. Most Christian missionaries believed as firmly as anyone else in witches and werewolves. But they regarded every supernatural being or power that was not accounted for by Christian teaching as an agent of the Devil. Automatically, therefore, they took Amerindian beliefs in sorcery and supernatural powers seriously. But they failed to consider whether or not native religions, or any details of them, could be beneficial. Never dreaming that some of them could express a morality akin to that of Christianity itself, they lumped them all together as spawnings of the Devil or his infernal agents. So Père Perron wrote in the *Jesuit Relations*: "All their actions are dictated to them directly by the devil, who speaks to them now in the form of a crow or some similar bird, now in the form of a flame or ghost, and all this in their dreams, to which they show a great deference."

Superficial though Perron's accounts of the native religions were, they showed far less bias than the extreme example of Cotton Mather, the third of a line of Puritan pastors of that name, who wrote as late as 1702: "The natives of the country now possessed by the Newenglanders, had been forlorn and wretched *heathen* ever since their first herding here and though we know not how these Indians first became inhabitants of this mighty continent yet we may guess that probably the *Devil* decoyed these miserable savages hither, in hope that the gospel of the Lord Jesus Christ would never come here to destroy or disturb his absolute empire over them."

The story is not a happy one. Again and again, over the years that followed, the missionaries' zeal and moral arrogance confused and undermined the native cultures. For, by and large, these pioneers of Christianity in the Americas were humanely dedicated men and women, totally unaware that their desperately earnest efforts to "uplift" the heathen might end in dragging them down.

In the pages that follow, the reader will encounter each broad group of Canada's natives as they lived during the period of their first contact with Europeans, and in the order in which they were contacted. Undoubtedly the picture will be distorted by the limitations of the information that has come down to us, the bulk of it from sailors, traders, and missionaries who inevitably misunderstood some aspects of what they saw and heard. It was impossible for these observers to recognize the richness of the cultures they encountered. Today scientists are filling in some of the gaps, and the lingering oral traditions of the natives are being studied with new understanding. The best we will ever be able to do, however, is to stand at the edge of our knowledge and discern, through the fog of our continuing ignorance, the broad contours of a richly varied human shore.

4 Fishermen and Hunters of the Atlantic Coastlands

The Land Not Understood

Five years after Columbus's landfall in the Caribbean, a fellow Italian named Cabot, commanding an English vessel out of Bristol, stared through the lifting fog. Moments later came the magical "Land-ho!" from the crow's-nest, signalling the first recorded sighting of the Newfoundland coast since the Norse adventures. We may guess his impatience as he peered at the misty outlines of the nearing shore, possibly Cape Bonavista. And perhaps, as he changed into courtly clothes with which to impress the inhabitants, the fingers that tightened his hose might have trembled a little. Emerging again on the poop deck, he would have ordered the helmsman to change course so that they might anchor in the little estuary that promised a safe harbour for the night. Then, he probably planned to enter his ship's boat to row upstream, perhaps to turn a bend and meet a potentate of the Indies with all his courtly retinue to greet the stranger from the west. Even if such a meeting didn't occur, he could at least take on fresh water to sweeten and replenish the stinking barrels in the hold.

Attired in his finest furs and broadcloth, wearing his golden chain of authority, he steps into the ship's boat and silently appraises the shore. The rowers sense the doubt that seizes him, though he attempts to mask his troubled thoughts.

Where were the gleaming pinnacles he had dreamed of, the palaces roofed with gold, the busy coastal commerce that Marco Polo had described? Were these rugged barren rocks and forested slopes the Isles of the East? It was hardly likely, in so northern a latitude — but surely Cipangu could not be far away. Surely he would find at least a fishing village where they might ask their way. For already his ship had passed through great shoals where the water so boiled with codfish that they could be hoisted aboard in barrels.

An hour later he stands on the summit of a headland, vainly scanning the horizon for some sign of human habitation, while his men are busy trimming and peeling the pole on which they will raise the flag of the English king. But he sees nothing — nothing but the cursed lichen-crusted rock and the spruce trees that serrate the skyline.

One of his crew runs breathlessly up the rise to thrust a small stone and some strands of weathered hide into his captain's hand. There are men on the island! He had found a place where trees had been felled and rawhide snares had been set.

But his captain stares down gloomily at the flaked flint in his hand, drops it and grinds it into the moss with a contemptuous heel. His worst fears are confirmed. This new found land is a desert inhabited by savages. He must sail west again, around this uncharted barrier to his dreams.

Early Man in the Maritimes

No land could have offered a greater contrast to the islands of the Indies than the triangle of rugged coasts that border the Gulf of St. Lawrence. Here the great glaciers lingered long after they had retreated from the lower Great Lakes and the Canadian prairies, perhaps until mammoth and mastodon had passed into extinction. But in the more southerly valleys and gentler slopes the warmer summers gradually bared more ground. Reindeer moss took hold and the caribou came — as early, perhaps, as 10,000 years ago. And men, as ever, were not far behind.

Ancient hearths, found at the Debert site just west of Truro, reveal that these men were people of the barrens, for they had only shrubs and dwarf trees to burn in their fires. They knew nothing of the bow and arrow, hunted the caribou with the atlatl or lance, moved over the land in family bands, and packed their few possessions on their backs. Perhaps they improvised crude skin water-craft to cross the streams, but there is no evidence that they had boats. It is probable that — like the Eskimo who were only then entering the continent in the remote northwest — they made rude weirs and rock traps in the shallower streams. Perhaps they sampled the shellfish or edible seaweeds along the beaches and flats at low tide — foods unknown to their inland forebears.

Millennium after millennium Atlantic waves thundered on the bare headlands of the eastern seaboard, and salt-water surged with the changing tides through treacherous coastal channels, or up the narrowing estuaries. Gales lashed land and sea alike; coast fogs blanketed the shores; and the sun shone fitfully through the seasons. Out on the continental shelf, where arctic and tropical currents met, the sea teemed with plankton and the swarms of fish that fed on them.

But these first men of the Atlantic coastlands left no record of having reaped the harvests of the sea. Nor is there any evidence yet of where they came from or where they went.

Two thousand years were to pass before others came. There were forests now and the summer winds were warm. The newcomers were the Boreal Archaic people: fishermen, hunters, and foragers for seafoods along the shore. An inland tribe, adapting to these coasts, they learned new summer skills. But during the winter, back among the snow-burdened spruce, they lived again a life their people had known from times too remote to reckon. It was a white world, where the creak of snow underfoot or the chirp of a wintering bird might be the loudest sounds. A white world, where the widening red stains on the snow from the stone-slashed throat of a woodland caribou meant that there would be fresh hope for the hunter, and colour in his children's cheeks.

Their taste for shellfish was new, but their woodworking skills were already old. The ground-slate tools they used have been found far inland and could have served no other purpose but woodworking. With adzes and gouges they could—and probably did—chip and char large tree trunks into dugout canoes. They knew how to use a bow, but 500 years were to pass before the arrowhead gained preference over the atlatl point. Pottery appeared about A.D. 600, and snowshoes, along with the first dogs and toboggans, came into use while the Vikings were settling in Greenland.

We are not certain when the Micmac arrived in the area. Their own oral traditions state that they found Nova Scotia already inhabited and drove its occupants —the luckless Beothuk—across Cabot Strait to Newfoundland. In early times, the Micmac probably lived the year round on the seashore, subsisting mainly on sea foods; apparently it was about A.D. 1500 before they began to spend their winters inland, hunting moose or woodland caribou. In the same period they increased the size of their summer villages, perhaps to defend themselves from the Armouchiquais of Maine who were now making forays north in search of copper and jasper, and from Iroquoian seal-hunters who were intruding into the Gaspé. Archaeological work in the Gulf area, however, has been far too limited to establish any reliable prehistory for the Atlantic coastlands.

We do know, however, that by the time Europeans were coming to the Americas there were five aboriginal groups occupying the Atlantic coastlands. Eskimo, or *Inuit*, were hunting sea mammals along the Labrador coast and the adjacent shores of Newfoundland. In the spring the *Montagnais-Naskapi* emerged from the interior for sealing and eel-fishing on the north shore of the Gulf of St. Lawrence. Newfoundland was the home of the *Beothuk*, while all of what we now call the Maritime Provinces was occupied by bands of *Micmac*, and — south of the Saint John River — the closely related *Malecite* (mal-i-seet).

The Red Men

The Beothuk may have been the last survivors of Boreal Archaic bands who had occupied Newfoundland ever since the glacial retreat. Or they may have taken refuge there under pressure from aggressive people out of the south and west. Linguistically they seem to be distantly related to the mainland people: Micmac, Malecite, and Naskapi, who spoke dialects of the widespread Algonkian language-family. But too few Beothuk words have been recorded to solve this mystery. And there are reasons for believing they might have come from different stock. They had neither dogs nor pottery and, though their boats were made of birchbark, the design was unique on the continent. So was their routine practice of smearing themselves from head to foot with red ochre. This was the basis of the Micmac nickname for them that meant "Red Man". This in turn gave rise to the European

41

myth of a "Red Race" in the Americas, and the designation has recently been revived in the phrase "red power".

In the early 1600s, a Captain Whitbourne met a group of Beothuk, and left us a description. They wore on their heads "a great locke of heare platted with feathers, like a hawk's lure, with a feather standing upright by the crown of the head and a small locke platted before". They had "stores of dried deer meat" and deerskin coverings for their *mamateeks* (tents), although even as early as this a few had coverings of European sailcloth. Sheets of birchbark, however, were more common than either. Whitbourne noted that the Beothuk kept great stores of red ochre "with which they cover bodies, bows, arrows and canoes and every other utensil". He described large cooking vessels made of birch bark "sewn and fashioned like leather buckets". Some, he wrote, were big enough to boil twelve fowl at once. Smaller ones were used for storing dried meat and fish, or the egg powder made from the dried-out yolks of boiled seabird eggs.

It is possible that the earliest description of a Beothuk comes from the journal of Jacques Cartier. Landing on Blanc Sablon Island in the Gulf of St. Lawrence, he encountered a band of seal-hunters who could have been either Montagnais or Beothuk. "They wear their hair tied on top of their heads like a bunch of hay," writes Cartier, "passing through it a small piece of wood . . . and they also attach there some bird feathers. They wear skins, men and women, the latter being completely covered and girded at the waist (which the men are not). They paint themselves with certain red colour. They make their boats of the bark of the boul tree, and take large quantities of seals."

Early commentators were particularly struck by the unusual water-craft of the first Newfoundlanders. "The middle of the canoe," says John Guy, "is higher a great deal than bow and quarter." The canoes were somewhat longer than the typical Algonkian canoe and the V-shaped bottoms were filled with stone ballast, then padded with moss and covered sometimes with weather-separated sheets of balsam wood. The present writer was convinced, after a close examination of an exquisitely crafted model in Edinburgh, that this craft was designed so that the thwarts could be removed and the whole canoe folded flat. It could be buried in damp sand during the cold weather, which would prevent the bark from drying out and cracking along the fold of the keel. There is no record of this craft being encountered inland, and indeed it was eminently unsuited for portaging in freshwater travel. Clearly it was a sea-going canoe. So far there has been no explanation for the high peak midships.

That the Beothuk were expert seamen and offshore navigators is shown by the fact that at least twice a year they visited the Funk Islands to harvest eggs from the

millions of seabird nests on the rocks. Though Guy maintains that they "never put to sea but in calm fair weather," this forty-mile trip — far out of sight of the mainland — must often have been hazardous.

On these islands, the Beothuk could also slaughter the great auk. Cartier gives us the first European record of this bird, now extinct. It was almost flightless — "always on the water, being unable to fly high as the wings are small . . . they fly on the surface of the water as other birds do in the air. They are very fat." On land they were so clumsy that they could be clubbed to death at will and like the Beothuk, they were destined for extinction.

Living near the sea in the summer, the Beothuk moved inland for the fall hunting of the caribou. During the summer months, the great caribou herds fed on the deer lichen that still grows luxuriantly on the bleak hills of the Long Range. Here, unmolested by man, cows dropped their calves and the herds fattened through the warm months, mating in the early fall. But when the first skin of ice formed over the mountain pools and the wise old leaders smelled snow in the air, the caribou responded to an ancient urge and moved southward, seeking the forests of the Exploits River watershed. For the snow in the Long Range, glazed by the action of sun and frost, or ice-coated by freezing rains, or hammered dense and hard by free-sweeping gales, became impenetrable to pawing hooves. Only in the softer, deeper snows of the sheltered valleys to the south could an arctic deer always find winter forage.

As the herds began their fall migration, the bands of Beothuk were casting calculating glances at the changing sky. Storms were coating the rocky coves and open beaches with ice. And so family after family removed the ballast from their V-bottomed canoes, and buried them in the damp sand. Then, loaded with the dried flesh, fish, and egg of the summer's harvest, they trudged inland for their annual rendezvous with the fat, thick-hided deer. Along the Exploits Valley they repaired or rebuilt last winter's fences of saplings and deadfall — sometimes thirty miles long — and fixed fresh snares in the gaps. Soon the migrating animals, seeking a way through such barriers, would be trapped in pounds or snares. Then they were slaughtered and butchered for the meat, hide, sinew, bone, and horn that would supply Beothuk families with the necessities of life through the damp, chilling Newfoundland winter.

In Beothuk camps near the fence gaps, or close to the caribou's favourite fording places, there was time for story-telling. And although none of their legends has been preserved, we may be sure that in the latter days a recurring theme would have been the Beothuk's early encounters with the European, told and re-told

to caution each dwindling generation against any contact or dealings with the intruder.

Lacking any record of these tales, it might not be too presumptuous to put words into the mouth of an imaginary Beothuk narrator. The content of what follows is mainly derived from European records of early contacts along the Newfoundland shore. The *style* is based on stories told to the writer by northern Cree in Saskatchewan, describing the first encounters with white men on the coast of Hudson Bay. Thus speaks our Beothuk narrator:

"It was a long time ago. My grandfather and his uncle were there in the Great Fishing Water. My grandfather was just a boy — oh, about ten years old. It was the cod-fishing time.

"My uncle's father saw this great bird on the water, far away — many times bigger than any bird we know —

"I guess that big bird is some kind of manitou. That's what they thought. So they got out of there. They were scared.

"Pretty soon they came to a place where there was cod drying on the shore — but not our way. There was a *mamateek* there, but not like our tents. It was covered with some sort of stuff. But it wasn't bark or hide.

"I wonder what that stuff is?

"There were axes, too, like the ones we find some-

times on the shore. They couldn't understand what that was made of.

"There was lots of fish on the flakes — more than one family could eat in a month. So they were hungry and they ate as much as they wanted.

"There's lots of fish here. Let's take some back to our families. So they took some fish, and wrapped it up in some of the mamateek stuff that was lying there. So they got back to their camp and it was night.

"So it was morning.

"When my grandfather woke up he saw his uncle go out of the tent. He heard loud voices out there — not like our people. And he smelled a different kind of smell. So he was afraid.

"That time he heard a loud noise, like the noise you hear on the coldest day when a tree splits. So he looked out.

"His uncle was lying there with blood on his face. He was dead.

"There were three men there with hair all around their mouth. There was no paint on their skin. One of the men pointed a black stick at my grandfather. He was just a boy at that time. Fire came out of the stick and this noise. My grandfather was hit in the shoulder with this little heavy stone that has bad magic in it. He fell down at first but he got away.

"His brother and sister both got out of the back of the

tent. But they killed his mother and her baby.

"So my grandfather warned me.

"You must always hide when you see those men with the black sticks. If they see you they will kill you."

In the eyes of the fishermen who came in increasing numbers from Portugal, France, and England to fish on the Banks and dry their catch on adjacent shores, the Beothuk were thieves to be shot on sight.

But Bristol merchant John Guy had a happier encounter. Meeting a band of some thirty Beothuk in Trinity Bay, he not only traded successfully with them but arranged to meet them in the same place the following year. The sequel is an historic fact; but let us hear a description of the event as it might have been told by a Beothuk survivor.

"So these Hairy Faces went away in their big canoe. And all the people were sorry.

"So it was winter.

"Pretty soon the ice was gone from the rivers. Pretty soon it was the time of the full leaf again. Pretty soon all the people were camping there on the shore. The canoes were thick on the shore like herring gulls when the smelt spawns. So they waited in that place. All the people waited with their beaver skins. Pretty soon they saw the great canoe of the Hairy Face far away on the water. They were glad when they saw that.

"Soon we will have the axes that cut deep. Soon we will have sharp knives for all the people.

"So the great canoe came close and dropped its big hook in the water. And all the people in their canoes went out on the water, singing and shouting loud songs. For their hearts were big. They could not believe such wonderful things could happen.

"At that time there was this old man, Crooked Pine. He was a great medicine man and conjurer. In his fasting time as a boy he had dreamed of the Great Sacred Bear. So he could not be killed. He went out there with the others. Pretty soon there were holes opened up in the sides of the big canoe.

"I wonder what those hollow black logs are doing there in those holes?

"Pretty soon fire came out of those holes and noise like all the thunder a man might hear in his life.

"So all the canoes were smashed. Men's heads and arms fell off their bodies and all the water turned into blood. So all the people were dead.

"But the Sacred Bear protected Crooked Pine because of his dream. So he lived.

"When you see those Hairy Faces with the black sticks you must hide. For their power is very great. They are not true men. They lie and there is no mercy in them. And their name is Death.

47

"That is what the old man told all the people. For he was a great medicine man. He had the power of the Great Bear. He could not be killed."

Apparently the survivors of this episode never learned the truth. The ship they paddled out so joyously to meet was *not* Guy's ship! It is only too easy to understand how its master, mistaking the noisy welcome for a hostile attack, ordered the guns to be loaded with chain shot and fired at pointblank range.

Yet to the north, and along the west coast, there were successful contacts between the Beothuk and the newcomers. In 1622 Captain Whitbourne found that both the French and the Basques were employing Beothuk helpers at their shore camps, and that the natives displayed "great labour and patience in killing cutting and boiling of whales". This was the small white whale, whose blubber was rendered down for its oil. Both Whitbourne and Guy reported that the natives disturbed nothing that the fishermen left in their shore camps.

The Banks fishermen, however, had a different experience. This could have happened for one of two reasons. According to the sharing practices common to all the hunting people in northern regions of the continent, it was assumed that those in need could help themselves, if they found a plentiful supply of food or goods left unguarded — as the family in our first tale did. This would have been completely misunderstood by the fishermen, who believed that any property was private and not to be taken without permission. Hostilities would naturally follow if the Beothuk violated this concept. But if friendly relations had been established *first*, the fishermen could have made it clear that this kind of sharing was regarded as theft. Thus their property rights would have been respected.

The other possibility is that the theft of the fish and other articles had become deliberate, futile attempts to discourage the visitors, or to exact revenge, without having to face European weapons.

Extermination of the Beothuk

Such friendly relations as had been established between newcomer and native seem to have ended by the early 1700s. Those were brutal times, when criminals in Europe were still being hung, drawn (i.e., disembowelled), and quartered. Ship discipline was routinely enforced by flogging and the even more brutal keel-hauling (which few survived). Slave ships were plying their ghastly trade between Africa and America. Nor were the Beothuk always as shy or gentle as they were sometimes described. Attacked by the fishermen, they fought back. On one occasion they wiped out three French fishing camps, surprising the third and largest by disguising themselves in the clothes of the Frenchmen already slain. Their skill with the bow—they could shoot four arrows in swift succession and with deadly aim—was more than a match for the clumsy, slow-firing arquebus or even the early flintlocks. On the other hand, it is likely that firearms inspired as much terror in the Beothuk as elsewhere on the continent. Heads of slain fishermen were carried triumphantly back to camp for savage rites of triumph. The fishermen were content to rip off their victims' scalps, with ears and face-skin attached, leaving the corpses faceless and bloodily bald. The end approached when eighteenth-century firearms came into use and Micmac were brought in to hunt the Beothuk, matching their skill at surprise and evasion. Nor were the English more humane when they settled the Avalon Peninsula and the outports. As in Australia, hunting the aborigines became an exciting sport in which men, women, and children were equally fair game.

It is logical, therefore, that the little we know about Beothuk culture comes mostly from the few burials unearthed. Some have been found along the shore in shallow caves or other sheltered places, the bodies wrapped in birchbark. Other skeletons have been found under birchbark shields—in one case a flattened canoe—with dirt and rocks heaped over. The burial of a nine-year-old boy included a male doll, possibly a companion for the afterlife. Another body, buried in a sitting posture, must have been exhumed after the initial burial, for the bones were rubbed with red ochre. The most elaborate burial so far found included two miniature canoes with bow and arrows to scale, and bark packets containing red ochre, dried salmon, and dried trout. The whole collection was reddened with ochre and wrapped in a spruce-root fishnet. Iron pyrites found in other graves suggest that an Eskimo method of fire-making was used. In fact, it is difficult to know whether some artifacts should be labelled Eskimo or Beothuk, especially surface finds of carved bone and ivory ornaments or charms. Quite literally the archaeologist has only begun to scratch the soil of Newfoundland.

Throughout the eighteenth century, the numbers of Beothuk declined rapidly. But the times were gradually becoming more humane, and at last governors at St. John's began serious attempts to protect the aborigine. In 1766 an officer sent into the Exploits River country located some 500, but they avoided every effort he made to meet them. In 1811, a Lieutenant Buchan succeeded in surprising a small band in its winter camp. But the heritage of suspicion and mistrust thwarted his efforts. Hostages were exchanged. Then, while the English party was returning to a cache of gifts they had stored twelve miles away, the Beothuk hostages escaped and returned to the band, who killed the English hostages and vanished.

In the early 1820s three women were found — a mother and her two daughters—dying of malnutrition and tuberculosis. One daughter was saved and brought to St. John's, where a young Newfoundlander who had dedicated himself to righting the wrongs done to the Beothuk took her into his household. He hoped that Shawahndidit, as she was named, would learn enough English to become an interpreter for her people. But this hope was never realized. She was able through her drawings to give glimpses of her people's ways, and reported the existence of thirteen other living Beothuk. But efforts to find these failed, and the frail young woman died of tuberculosis in 1829, the last known member of her race.

Life of the Micmac

The failure of the Europeans to establish trade relations with the Beothuk probably ensured their doom. The Micmac escaped this fate largely because the French set a high value on cast-off beaver robes, which the Micmac could provide. And later, when the French-English struggle for supremacy became intense, they were highly valued as expert guerrilla fighters.

The Micmac of the contact period alternated—as we have seen — between village shore camps during the warm months and family bush camps through the cold. In spring and early summer, the gatherings moved from one fish-spawning site to the next. In April, swarms of smelt could be had for the scooping in shallow creek mouths. In May, the gaspereaux spawned. And in June, the fat Atlantic salmon could be speared in pools or trapped in weirs. Weir-fishing went on all summer, and in August and September family groups went clamming. Through the warm months, too, there was offshore fishing: lobsters to trap, and halibut or cod to catch with fresh squid bait. Down the coast and on offshore islands, the great auk nested, and there were countless other seabirds whose eggs were collected in season. With fall came the migration of ducks and geese, pausing to feed in the shore swamps or tidal flats where they could be shot from blinds or speared by torchlight.

For the women, the warm months were busy. Flakes of cod were laid on racks along the shore to dry in the sun. Meat or shellfish that could not be so dried were suspended over a fire to smoke and harden, and then were shredded and further preserved by mixing in fat or oil. All through the summer, the women and children hauled wood and water, tended the strips of flesh or fish on the drying racks, and picked berries and

dried them on bark trays. Some tended the fires, dropping hot stones into the cooking pots to bring the water to a boil and patiently skimming off the fish oil, bear grease, or goose fat. The dried meat and fish and egg yolks were pounded into the consistency of coarse sawdust and stored. There were bark and stone containers to make, of all sorts, shapes, and sizes. Broken clay pots had to be replaced: clay must be gathered, mixed with tempering grit to prevent cracking, shaped, decorated, dried, and fired. Healing herbs for the ailing, and sphagnum moss to keep babies dry, had to be collected in the forests and swamps. And finally, clothes and footwear had to be made or mended — although children ran naked in the summer, and the men nearly so.

Nor was the man's work simple. There was daily fishing in the creek mouths, weirs and fish traps to construct or repair, and hunting excursions inland to vary or supplement the band's diet with beaver, bear, moose, or caribou. To ensure a successful hunt, special rites had to be performed: songs to chant, drums to beat, and sacred dances to perform. And when the men rested by their hearths, there were new stone points, awls, knives, and scrapers to strike and work, new bone or wooden handles and shafts to shape and smooth, and fresh hide and sinew thongs to prepare for binding on 52 points and blades. The wise old men must be con-sulted, too, to find lost objects, settle quarrels, cast out sickness caused by malignant spirits, and make magic to appease offended manitous. And sometimes there were enemies to deal with — wandering bands who coveted the tribal hunting grounds or fishing places.

When the first snows fell, the Micmac loaded their summer's store of food into their round-nosed birch-bark canoes, and paddled and portaged into their winter hunting grounds. There on swift snowshoes the men ran down the moose in deep drifts, or built fences to trap the caribou in snares or pounds.

In their winter camps, the Micmac divided into family groups, each small band returning to its long-established territory to build pole and bark wigwams, banked with brush, earth, and snow. The eye-smarting woodsmoke of the fire burning within — and even the eye infections that could result — was a small price to pay for the snug warmth radiated on a wild wintry day as the wind gusted outside. The earliest memories of a Micmac child might be of storm-bound days within the lodge, relaxing on a moosehair rug while he listened to the tales of the old ones and dipped his fingers in the cooking pot and sucked them clean of the hot moose stew.

But when the moose or caribou mysteriously left their favourite browsing places, and the children lay listless in the lodges for lack of food, there were dark looks around the camp. Who had been so careless as to allow the dogs to gnaw the long bones of the last kill, so that the Source Animal felt the pain and no longer supplied its species to nourish the children of men? And when the aging grandfather's chants and incantations failed to appease the Source Manitou, there were hungry and exhausting days of winter travel: helping the weakened dogs to pull heavily laden toboggans, stopping in the chill twilight to scrape snow from the frozen ground for a warming fire, and improvising a spruce-bough shelter under which to huddle till the cold dawn came. And though the winters were mild compared with those in the Canadian interior, there were always days and nights when damp, bone-chilling blizzards blew. Then adults and children smeared themselves with dwindling supplies of bear grease, tied in the sleeves of their skin tunics, and pulled their beaver robes more snugly around them.

When spring meltwater flooded the creeks and rivers, the trip out to the shore was swift, the portages few. On the more northerly shores, where the floe ice lingered, the hunters could venture far out from land to bludgeon seal pups to death, or stalk and harpoon the adults. Back in camp, while seal meat simmered in the cooking pots, the women laboured interminably, scraping, curing, and smoking the take of hides. But always they kept an anxious eye on the weather, which might bring sleet or fog to the seal-hunters or blow the ice fields and their men far out to sea.

Spring, too, was the season when birchbark was at its best. Like their Algonkian kinsmen throughout the northern and eastern woodlands, the Micmac took advantage of the tough, pliable, waterproof bark in every possible way. It was birchbark that made possible the graceful and versatile Algonkian-style canoe—roomy, shallow of draft, light to carry. Sheets of this bark could be sewn together with spruce root, and the ends bound to peeled sticks to prevent splitting. It could be used for roofing, and then rolled up compactly for carrying or caching. Wherever the paper birch grew, drinking cups, ladles, rough containers, or simple horns for moose calling could be improvised in minutes. The more permanent bark containers were often beautifully decorated with dyed porcupine quills. Or the dark brown inner side of the bark could be scraped to form contrasting yellow patterns. Unlike the more abstract designs of the western Algonkians, Micmac figures were rendered with surprising naturalism — sometimes to identify property, sometimes to maintain the good graces or acquire the power of supernatural beings.

The swiftness with which European trade pots of iron or copper replaced the native pottery is shown by the fact that, although potsherds are found in the exca- 53 vated campsites of precontact Micmac, there are no eye-witness accounts of its use. Blades and points of iron or steel came into use with equal rapidity. Even cloth, though less durable than hide, became more and more preferred for clothing, especially woollen blankets to replace the *castor gras* originally traded off their owners' backs.

From birth, Micmac and Malecite babies were tied to cradle-boards, padded in moss, and laced in with a hide covering. They were fed when they cried, and weaned at their own pace, so that a mother might still be breast feeding after the infant had grown sharp young teeth. Girls helped their mothers at an early age. Boys helped, too, but spent increasing proportions of their time playing at hunting and fishing, or assisting their fathers at the real thing. As each boy approached manhood, he was required to isolate himself in a secluded place for his dream quest. After a week or ten days, he reached the weakened state that lends itself to visions, and a dream finally appeared that revealed to him his personal guardians and taboos. Sometimes, too, such dreams would predict future events. Yet he did not become a man until he had slain, unaided, his first deer or bear. To win a wife, he had to spend a full season helping to provide for his prospective in-laws.

Each family head was both household shaman and chief provider. As he grew older, his hunting prowess declined but his status continued to grow. The younger men would turn to him for guidance in matters of ritual, or in a crisis that faced them all. In the larger bands of the summer villages, one old man was usually respected more than any other for his wisdom and experience. And Europeans mistakenly assumed that he was a "chief" who had the power to make treaties for the band. When some of the band disregarded such a "treaty" (never having been consulted about its terms), the Europeans assumed that this was an act of treachery. For a decision to be binding, the opinions of every male adult in a band had to be heard: the so-called "chief" was merely the one whose word had the greatest weight in the band councils.

The respect for old age among the Micmac extended to women, too. And, in addition, their authority was dominant under the roof of the wigwam. Through forceful personality, or proven wisdom, a woman in her old age might achieve high status. Such older women, too, were respected as midwives, for their knowledge of healing herbs, love charms, and potions, and sometimes, for their power to cast spells on personal enemies.

But the most powerful shamans were usually male. Regarded with fear as well as respect, the chief shaman was called upon to perform healing rites in critical

54

illnesses, or to appease malignant or offended deities, who were believed to be the cause of tribal misfortunes.

When death came, the body of a Micmac was sewn in birchbark wrappings and buried in a shallow grave. In winter the corpse would be cached in a tree until it could be carried out in spring for a shore burial.

As the trading and bush-fighting partners of the French, the Micmac effectively harassed the British. Even after the Acadians were expelled in 1755, the Micmac faithfully continued to wage guerrilla warfare on their new rulers, until the British brought in the Mohawks to hunt them down just as ruthlessly as the Micmac had hunted down the Beothuk in the previous century. The Micmac survived, but their old life was gone.

The handful of Micmac man-hunters who stayed in Newfoundland after the Beothuk slaughter mingled more and more with European stock until their identity was lost. In the other Atlantic provinces, both Malecite and Micmac maintained a lingering identity on the lands reserved by government treaty. Gradually, they became more and more dependent on a paternalistic government and slowly lost their special skills and most of their material culture. By the middle of the present century, these skills were reduced to such home industries as basket-making and the shaping of axe-handles. Micmac find occasional employment in tourist areas as guides, but for the most part work as itinerant farm labourers or domestic servants.

Nevertheless, the present writer, familiar with the Cree and the Ojibway of the continental interior, has been astonished to discover how closely the Micmac resemble their distant cousins far inland, after nearly four centuries of exposure to the values and attitudes of Europeans and their Canadian descendants.

5 Farmer-Warriors of the Lower Lake Region

The Walled Town of Stadacona

In the summer of 1534 two French ships, commanded by Jacques Cartier of St. Malo, anchored in Gaspé harbour. Here they encountered forty canoes of mackerel fishermen. Cartier noted that these natives "have not the same character as the first ones we have seen [on the north shore of the Gulf]. . . . They have their heads completely shaven, except for a lock of hair on top of the head which they allow to grow as long as a horse's tail, they tie it to their heads with small leather cords."

Cartier learned from their gestures that these people had come from a village far to the west. It was too late in the season to follow them there, but he persuaded their chief — Donnaconna — to allow his two sons to visit France, promising that on their return they would bring with them all sorts of gifts for his people. It was a risky procedure, for on a later voyage nine of the ten aborigines that Cartier took back with him died in France. But this first arrangement turned out well. Donnaconna's sons returned with Cartier on his second voyage, guiding him to their native village of Stadacona and acting as interpreters. Their return was living proof that the Frenchmen could be trusted.

The joy with which their return was celebrated by the villagers astonished the Europeans. As their boats came ashore they were showered with gifts including "much of the bread, made with large grain, which they threw into our boats in such quantities that it seemed to be falling from the air." Already, in describing his first contact in the Gaspé, Cartier had mentioned "a kind of grain as large as peas" which the women pounded into flour in "mortars of wood". Then, he tells us, they "gather it into dough, make it into cakes, which they place upon a large hot rock, then cover it with hot stones." Here in Stadacona he observed that "they plough their land with small sticks half as large as a little sword." Nor did they limit their farming to corn. Cartier lists "melons, cucumbers and gourds, peas and beans". They also cultivated a plant for which they had a curious use: "they dry it in the sun and carry it in a little pouch around their necks, with a horn of stone or wood; they make this grass into powder and put it into one of the ends of the horn, then place a hot coal on the top of it and suck at the other end, filling their bodies with smoke so that it comes out from their mouth and nostrils as from the pipe of a chimney." The sailors tried out this strange practice, but too tentatively to experience anything more than a slightly scorched tongue.

These villagers, Cartier explains, "are not nomadic like those of Canada and the Saguenay." The "Canada" he refers to was on the north shore of the Gulf of St. Lawrence, to the west of the mouth of the Saguenay River, and the word applied to the territory of only one Amerindian tribe. These "Canadians" were probably Montagnais, and were certainly Algonkian-speakers. They were trading partners of the villagers and when Cartier came in 1535, a group of them, along with other Algonkian-speakers, were scattered in camps along the shore beneath the cliff on which Stadacona was built. It was probably the situation of these camps, below the village, that made Cartier say that "the Canadians are subject to [the villagers] as are eight or nine other tribes living on the banks of this river."

Certainly when the French sailors stared at Stadacona from their offshore anchorage, they saw the most impressive human habitation in all their voyaging in the New World. Here, surrounded by miles of waving corn and commanding a wide view, was a walled town of at least a thousand people. The wooden ramparts rose thirty feet above the ground — as high as many a European fortress wall—constructed of "three rows of timbers [i.e., heavy upright stakes] in the shape of a pyramid, crossed at the top, having the middle stakes perpendicular, and the others [leaning] at an angle on each side, well joined and fastened in their fashion." Within the walls were scores of multiple dwellings, each housing a dozen related families. Cartier gives us no figures, but from other sources we know that a single lodge might contain as many as 20 families and that some stockades might enclose up to 200 lodges.

But the broad "River of the West" beckoned the explorer upstream. Perhaps *La Chine* (China) could be reached before winter set in, and in a month or less he and his men would be anchoring within sight of the 57 fabulous cities described by Marco Polo. To his surprise, his new friends began to raise all sorts of objections to the proposal that the French go up river to Hochelaga. When all else failed to weaken Cartier's determination to go on, the shamans took over. The Frenchmen had barely set out on their way upstream when three sinister figures paddled out from the shadows of the shore to block their progress—"devils" threatening direst misfortune to anyone who went up river. Cartier, however, was not impressed: "they dressed up three men as devils with horns as long as the arm, and they were covered with the skins of black and white dogs. Their faces were painted black as coal, and they were placed in a concealed canoe." A few days later the Frenchmen were welcomed by the Hochelagans. Swarming down to the shore from their palisade, the villagers "received us as well as a parent does a child, showing great joy."

Soon the French explorer stood on the summit of the newly named *Mont Réal*, peering westward. There, snaking majestically into the blue distance, lay the road to China. There, too, roared the formidable rapids whose name, Lachine, is all that remains of Cartier's dream. When he proposed to go on, he was told of ferocious Agouianda "armed to their fingers ends" at

war "continually, tribe against tribe". These tales might have been an accurate picture of the wars of the inland Iroquoians before the formation of the League — or an exaggeration, or fabrication, to discourage Cartier from taking his gifts elsewhere.

The awesome vista of great volumes of water plunging down the channel of the Lachine rapids was probably enough to discourage a salt-water sailor from going further, even if he had not been daunted by tales of ferocious tribes upstream. Lingering only briefly at Hochelaga, Cartier returned to Stadacona, where he anchored offshore from the village, having decided to winter there rather than face the equinoctial storms of the North Atlantic.

Now he had leisure to satisfy his curiosity about Iroquoian life. They stored their corn, he learned, in "lofts or granaries" within each lodge. They also had "large vessels in their houses, like casks" — probably made of bark — "in which they place their fish, which they smoke during the summer and eat during the winter." Hardened though the sailors were to rough seafare that would become mouldy and maggot-ridden by the end of a long voyage, they found that the saltless native food "was not to our taste, having no flavour". In later times a Jesuit Father complained that the bread the French gave their dogs in Europe was more palatable than Iroquoian corn cake!

It proved to be a grim winter. By early December, an epidemic was raging in the village, creating suspicion of the French and discouraging contacts, so that the sailors confined themselves largely to their ships, frozen into the ice perhaps a mile away. They subsisted on ship's food that lacked the vitamins essential to health. By early spring Cartier's men were dying off like flies. Then Cartier discovered that the villagers had a remedy for the disease his men were suffering from. The cure so impressed him that he probably exaggerated the speed of his sailors' recovery and the quantities of spruce-bark brew they consumed. There is a mystery here. What were the villagers dying of? It could not have been scurvy, since they had a cure for it. It seems far more likely that they picked up an infection from the sailors, possibly the plague then rampant in Europe. Whatever the disease, it is clear the villagers blamed the Europeans for it. Their growing hostility added to Cartier's reasons for weighing anchor to sail home as soon as the ice went out.

The possibilities of a lucrative trade with the "Canadians" must have counted more in Cartier's plans thereafter than dreams of reaching China. Even on his first voyage, his men had been lured ashore in the Bay of Chaleur by natives signalling that they had furs to trade. No doubt Spanish and Portuguese ships had already nosed their way northward, and traded knives and axe-heads for furs to protect the sailors from the unaccustomed cold. Cartier's third and final voyage was designed to set up a trading post at Tadoussac, at the mouth of the Saguenay, in order to winter with the Canadians and collect their furs in the spring. But the expedition was a failure.

The Iroquoians

Three-quarters of a century were to pass before another French explorer—Champlain—sailed up the St. Lawrence. By the time he arrived, the villages of Stadacona and Hochelaga had vanished, a mystery historians have been at a loss to explain to this day. Some maintain that it was the north-shore people—Cartier's "Canadians"—who used the weapons they got from European traders to drive the St. Lawrence Iroquois inland. Yet an equally good case can be made that the epidemic Cartier had witnessed at Stadacona had been transmitted to Hochelaga, and that the survivors had fled the whole region. Whatever the reason for the desertion of the villages, the villagers could have gone

59

in one of two directions: up the Richelieu River to Lake Champlain, where the Mohawk lived, or up the Ottawa River and across to Georgian Bay, where the Huron had their villages. In either case, they would have been among people of the same cultural family. The villagers that Cartier had met belonged to a large group of tribes sharing the same life style, and the term Iroquoian is used to describe them all. They included the *Huron* in the vicinity of Georgian Bay, the *Petun* just to the west, the *Neutral* and the *Erie* just to the north of Lake Erie, and the group south of the lakes that is known in history as the *Five Nations*: the *Mohawk, Oneida, Onondaga, Cayuga,* and *Seneca.*

Champlain arrived at a critical moment in the early fur trade. To the south, the Dutch and then the English had established so successful a trade with the League of Five Nations that the region south of Lake Ontario had been cleaned out of prime beaver. The Five Nations, taking on the role of middlemen, had pushed north and come into conflict with the Huron. The Huron, however, had had a long-established partnership with the neighbouring Algonquin, exchanging farm produce for forest products. Thus they had become middlemen for their bush neighbours, who had access to large fur supplies. And it was these supplies that the Five Na-

tions were after. Naturally, as the threat of the Five Nations increased, the trading alliance between Huron and Algonquin became a military one.

Champlain, in order to solidify a trading relationship with these allies, agreed to join a foray into Five Nations territory on the shores of Lake Champlain. Thanks to the fear and havoc created by the French firearms, the Iroquois League was routed in this first encounter. But a pattern was established which ensured permanent hostility between the Iroquois League on the one side, and the alliance of Huron, Algonquin, and French on the other.

Champlain's second expedition, aimed at the Five Nations' heartland south of Lake Ontario, earned him only an arrow wound and a snow-hampered retreat overland to Huronia. Here he spent the winter of 1615-16, waiting for the spring break-up and a safe return to Quebec by way of Lake Nipissing and the Ottawa River. So he had the leisure and opportunity to observe at first hand the Iroquoian life style.

An Iroquoian Village

It will be useful, therefore, to picture Champlain making his notes on parchment with a goose-quill pen in the smoky light of a Huron lodge. A companion translates the strange tongue and dramatic gestures of his hosts, who squat around on corn-husk mats, or loll in the background on a sleeping platform.

Looking around under the arched cedar-bark roof, he can count a total of nine fires, each shared by two families, spaced evenly down the hundred and twenty feet of living space. There are entrances at either end of the lodge. The ceiling is supported by twin rows of stout poles that serve also as legs for the wide sleeping platforms, and as props for wooden storage racks and bark-covered shelves. Some shelves sag under the weight of bark or plaited baskets filled with nuts, beans, dried berries, or parched corn. Here hangs a haunch of freshly killed venison or a brace of gutted hare; there, suspended on a rawhide line, are ermine skins drying on wooden stretchers, or a pair of handsome wolf pelts. Dangling from the rafters, stowed under the platforms, or suspended from projecting poles, are the miscellanea of daily living: snowshoes, winter caps and robes, piles of sphagnum moss for the babies' cradle-boards, freshly smoked and tanned deer hides, coils of spruce roots or rawhide rope, bunches of dried herbs and medicinal roots, fish spears, bows and quivers of arrows, fire-drills — the variety is endless. Round-bottomed clay cooking pots with castellated 61

rims hang over the fires, or stand in a bed of coals, while the contents simmer and the women stir. Odours of fish and dogmeat broths or stewing beans and corn are mingled with the smell of smoke-tanned hide, of overripe meat or rancid fat, of human sweat and children's accidental droppings.

The trader-explorer's eyes wander now, from the stolid seated figure of a nursing mother to a crippled old grandmother crouching over her cooking fire, to a young girl tightening her lips over a garment-sewing task. He sees the young boys race between the fires, or crouch tensely under the platforms as they play at hunting or fishing—and the older youths flirting with a group of girls whose eyes dance and bodies shake with giggles at the boys' suggestive humour. Champlain's eyes return then to the men around him, half-naked in this smoky, draughty hall: the wrinkled impassive face of an elder here; a younger, sensuous face there; another to his left that lightens with humour and intelligence — or darkens momentarily — while the conversation rises and falls around the now familiar guest. The conversation is punctuated by silences or shouts of laughter, accented with eager assent or silent denial, and the moaning near by of a recently widowed woman, her tear-streaked face unwashed since her bereavement, a great gap in the hair of her head where she had cut or torn out a huge lock in mourning.

In May, when the fields lie ready for another crop, the women will loosen the soil with their digging sticks, and with hoes made from the shoulder-blades of deer, to plant the corn, beans, and squash that form their staple crops. As the cornstalks grow, the bean vines will twine around them, and the broad leaves of squash or pumpkin will discourage weeds. Through all four seasons, as the need or urge arises, the men will hunt deer, bear, beaver, and porcupine, or fish with net, line, and spear. In summer and fall there will be wild turkey, geese, and ducks in abundance, and the sky will sometimes darken with flocks of passenger pigeons. Throughout a normal year it will be a rare day when there is not a full cooking pot from which each helps himself as appetite urges.

Daily throughout the year the women and girls will draw water from the near-by spring, or walk weary miles to forage in the woods for firewood, carrying it home in great bundles on their backs. As twilight falls in the warm months, the girls will linger in the woods where the boys hide, to mock, or make advances. With the approach of womanhood, the older girls may live in turn with each of two or three men in a sort of trial

The life of the mature Iroquoian woman centred around work and child-rearing.

marriage, until they choose the father of their future children and settle into the long drudgery of toil and child-bearing that is the adult woman's lot. Yet the opinions of Iroquoian women could be heard at the council fire, and among the Five Nations the rank of *sachem* could only be inherited through the mother's side of the family.

Year after year wood-gathering will take the women farther from the village, and the surrounding soil will gradually lose its nutrients. Ten or fifteen years after the village was built, the women's pleas will bring a final nod from the elders. Yes. It is time to build a new village.

Already in their hunting forays the men have located a number of alternate sites — each on strategically defensible rising ground, close to a spring or stream, with easily worked soil, and not too heavily wooded. Choices will be discussed and a decision made, influenced no doubt by the distance that must be travelled back and forth as the old village is dismantled and the new one built. And so, week after week, the whole band will toil at the new location. Tough hardwoods are girdled with fire, and charred and chipped till they fall, to be trimmed for posts or burned to clear the land. Some build the stout palisades, others the lodge frames to be roofed with slabs of elm bark, while others carry still-useful poles and materials from the old site to the new. In the spring, the women will plant corn, squash,

and beans in the soil between the standing stumps, while the men complete the building—and the whole village will move into its new quarters.

Festivals, Games, and False Faces

For all the Iroquoian tribes, life was measured by the festivals that marked the passing seasons. Among the most eagerly anticipated were those that celebrated the first green shoots of early summer, the fall harvest, and the winter solstice. Then all else would be neglected while all the villages feasted, day after exciting day. Age-old chants and rites were revived to the music of the water drum and the six-holed flute. Gambling fever gripped the adult males. Plumstones blackened on one side, or pottery discs, were tossed like dice in a shaking bowl. Valuable possessions — even wives — were won or lost.

Between festivals, story-telling was a favourite entertainment. Time stood still in the long winter evenings as young and old gathered around the skilled story-tellers, listening avidly to legends of their ancestors. New variations of old stories, with sly references to village characters or budding romances, set the audience rolling on the ground with hilarity. Thus children learned what their elders felt was good, brave, or

intelligent. And they also learned that ridicule would greet examples of cowardice, meanness, or dishonour. To be laughed at was to be shamed, so that ridicule was a major means of preserving village discipline.

In warm weather or cold there were always games to play. At intervals all the able-bodied men of two villages would meet for a contest of lacrosse, throwing themselves with such zest into the rough-and-tumble that by sundown there were more than a few broken bones and cracked heads, with no penalties called. Women, too, found time to play rough field games. The young men had their tests of strength and skill, like the hurling of a wooden "snow snake" down an iced slide nearly a mile long. Indeed, this contest survived, to be played by their descendants four centuries later on the banks of the Grand River in Ontario, just as Mohawk craftsmen living near Montreal in the 1970s would still be making lacrosse sticks.

Secure as the Iroquoians seemed to be in their food supply, life could be hazardous. Misfortune, they believed, could result from breaking tribal rules, from spells cast on them by enemies, or from offending the mysterious forces of nature that could ruin a crop with an early frost, or create unpredictable shortages of fish or game. Enemy raids might burn the ripening grain, or enemy magic visit disease on a whole village.

Only the shaman knew the complicated rules that must be followed to placate the hostile influences. At his best, such a man was spiritual counsellor and physician combined. His wisdom and experience, supported by tribal customs and rites, and a sometimes uncanny intuition, were probably quite effective in reducing despair among his people. Yet each person was to some extent his own shaman, guided by the visions that had come to him in his puberty fast. The older people, too—especially the women—knew the barks, leaves, roots, and berries that could be brewed into effective remedies for some forms of sickness, particularly vitamin deficiencies.

But when death approached, the people turned to the highly specialized doctors of the Society of Faces. Hideous masks were carved to symbolize evil beings known as the False Faces. Merely a glimpse of such a being might strike the beholder with instant paralysis. And so, fighting fire with fire, this society of doctors created and displayed hideous masks to drive away the evil beings who were bringing death to the village. Brought into the presence of the dying man, this magic was believed to ward off all but the most malignant power, and the death of the patient was accounted for by mistakes in rendering the chants, or loss of power in the charms and rattles used in the ritual. A bone tube was applied to the part of the body where the malignant power was believed to be most active, to suck it out bodily. Sometimes, indeed, the patient's belief in the treatment carried him over the crisis, and undoubtedly the Society of Faces cured many a psychosomatic illness.

The Recollet Fathers were impressed with the Hurons' attitude towards death. "These good people are not like many Christians, who cannot suffer death to be spoken of. . . . When the recovery of anyone is despaired of . . . they even prepare in his presence all that is necessary for his burial." Dying persons might even go to the length of permitting themselves to be wrapped for burial and then "hold a feast of farewell for their friends, during which they sing, sometimes without showing any apprehension of death . . . considering it only a change of life very little different from this."

The first burial was a temporary one, lasting at the most a dozen years. Every decade or so—perhaps just prior to moving a village — a Feast of the Dead was celebrated, at which all who had died during the period (as many a thousand persons) were carefully dug up and prepared for re-burial. The families of the dead scraped

the bones free of any putrid skin and flesh remaining without any signs of disgust, clothed the skeletons lovingly in their richest furs, and carried them reverently on their backs to the common burying pit. A passage in the *Jesuit Relations*, written by an eyewitness, describes how a woman unfolded the wrappings of her father and her dead children for a last farewell, how she combed her father's hair and "touched the bones of one after another with as much affection as if she would have given them life." She put bracelets on her children's arm bones, "and bathed their bones with her tears." Ghastly as these practices may appear to twentieth-century readers, the Jesuit fathers who witnessed them were deeply moved by the human tenderness and religious solemnity with which the rites were conducted.

Foundations of a Civilization

Of all the native peoples of Canada, with the possible exception of the West Coast cultures, the Iroquoians showed the most promise — but for the European invasion — of developing a major Amerindian civilization. For they already had four essentials. These included the capacity to maintain peaceful inter-tribal relations and to organize, when necessary, a common military front. More significantly, the Iroquoians had agricultural skills, a widely accepted medium of exchange, and a means of keeping records.

A kind of currency and a form of picture-writing existed among the Iroquoians through the use of beads shaped out of the core of the whelk. Cartier left a curious account of how the Stadacona villagers collected this small white shell by making incisions in the thighs and shoulders of slain enemies, then letting the bodies down on the river bottom for half a day. When the bodies were raised to the surface, the whelks were found in the open cuts. This *wampum*, Cartier states, was extremely white and "more valued than gold and silver". Two centuries later it was used as money among the New England colonists. An even more valuable "denomination" was made from the purple part of the quahog shell.

Such white and purple beads were combined into patterns which recorded accurately the text of agreements or other ancestral records. In addition, symbols carved on wooden "Condolence Canes" recorded in picture-writing the names of all the chiefs who had agreed to the treaty by which the League of Five Nations was established. Picture-writing was also carved into the stripped trunks of trees to record the outcome of a raid, or a simple trail message.

Currency and a system of record-keeping were useful in trading, and all the Iroquoians were avid traders. This was especially so among the Huron, who created a trading empire that was, in many ways, unique in North America. Throughout the winter, Champlain   69 noticed, "the women grind corn for summer travelling for their husbands," and Brébeuf reported that during the summer "the Country is stripped of the men, who have gone trading, some one way, some another." The income of this trade supported Huronia, and it was not until 1906 that the population of the area was as large as it had been during the time of Champlain.

It is likely that Huron trading skills developed very early, from the time when Iroquoian bands settled in pockets of arable land in Algonkian hunting territory. From the beginning, the corn and tobacco they grew was attractive to the Algonkians, while the latter had dried meat, hides, and birchbark articles to trade for them. By the time the French had arrived, the Huron were trading far into the interior and they naturally became the dominant fur middlemen from the Saguenay River to Lake Superior, and northward to James Bay.

During the winter, the Huron would stock up on their trading provisions, gathering corn, tobacco, and hemp from the Petun and the Neutral, and processing some of these items into manufactured goods: sacks, fishnets, and "collars" of nettle fibre. When spring came, they would pack bales of tobacco, bags of corn-meal, and bundles of manufactured goods into their canoes and set off on trading journeys that could take them the entire travelling season to complete. The longest of these annual journeys covered a circuit that, at its furthest point, was over a thousand miles from Huronia.

Across to the Ottawa, up to Lake Temiscaming, and then east to Grand Lake they would paddle, trading as they went. From Grand Lake they went east to the headwaters of the Bell River, and thence by a chain of lakes to the St. Maurice, where they could cut south to Three Rivers. So regular were these trips that the Jesuits used them as postal routes from Huronia to Three Rivers.

But some of the Huron, instead of cutting south, would continue north and east to the Saguenay River district, where they arrived for an annual rendezvous with tribes from the James Bay area. An Algonquin who saw such a meeting further to the west described them as great fairs, where tribes would gather and trade in numbers too great to count. Numerous items would be traded here. The Papiragan of the James Bay district, for example, traded for birchbark: their hunting territories were too far north for the birch to grow, and thus they had to depend on outside supplies for the raw material of their canoes.

After meeting the James Bay tribes, the Huron followed the Saguenay south to Tadoussac on the Saint Lawrence, and paddled *west* to Quebec, where they exchanged fur for French trading goods. And now they headed home, arriving in Huronia in time for one of the most important rendezvous of all, the annual trade with the Nipissing. The winter was spent re-stocking supplies from the Petun and the Neutral, and trading across the ice with the Algonquin on the islands of Georgian Bay.

As long as the Huron nation existed, it controlled the trade of the whole country north from the St. Lawrence River to James Bay, and very little came to Quebec that did not pass through Huron hands. Beaver, seal, and other furs were stacked at Quebec, Three Rivers, and Montreal, to be sent to France when the ships arrived. And this monopoly of the best fur-bearing territory was a cause of envy among the Five Nations, whose territory had been quickly exhausted of fur. Dependent on the Dutch, and later the English, for European trade goods, the Five Nations saw themselves cut off by the Huron monopoly. When negotiations with the Huron failed to break this grip, the Five Nations decided that war was their only hope of ensuring a continuing supply of fur, and thus of the European goods they could no longer do without.

Like all the Iroquoian, the Five Nations had a highly developed military society. Their young men trained for war from childhood. With a few handfuls of parched corn and dried meat, taken on the run, they could survive for weeks in the woods. Bands of such warriors could descend without warning on their enemies and demoralize them in a swift, ruthless campaign. When one of them was captured, he would sneer haughtily at his enemies as they tore back his scalp to pour hot ashes on his skull, or thrust glowing coals into gaping wounds gouged deep in his flesh. Captive and captor played for high stakes, believing that if a prisoner failed to break down, it would bring disaster on the tribe that captured him.

History records countless examples of such torture carried to incredible extremes and offers ample evidence of ritual cannibalism, where parts of the body of an exceptionally heroic captive were eaten by his captors. Even the torture was sometimes conducted as a ritual, as the chief tormentor pretended to be a loving father "caressing" his son. But historians too often neglect to put such practices in the perspective of the times. For Christian nations were indulging in equally savage practices. In seventeenth-century England, crimes we now regard as petty were punished by tying the prisoner to a post, disembowelling him, and burning his intestines while they were still attached to his living and conscious body. Far worse, a man imprisoned for a political crime might literally rot to death in his own filth in a dark, rat-infested dungeon.

Among the Iroquoians there were undoubtedly sadists whose evil impulses were released by such 71 tortures. But there were also sensitive men, who cheated the torturers by ending the victim's life with a merciful blow, or claiming him for adoption, thus braving their tribe's resentment. All the historical tribes believed that courage and stoicism under torture was the highest human virtue, and that the threat of torture heightened a man's courage. A man might treasure the fantasy of enduring without a murmur every pain that the most fiendish ingenuity of his enemies could inflict. In this way, he would hope to achieve a triumph of the human spirit that was often acknowledged by European bystanders. And, as the wars continued and the Five Nations faced a shortage of manpower, wholesale adoption became a common practice, so that by 1660, according to some, very few of the people in the Five Nations were the original tribesmen.

The proudest achievement of this people has yet to receive the recognition it deserves. The League of the Five Nations (which became the League of the Six Nations when the Tuscarora joined in 1720) so impressed Benjamin Franklin that he wrote: "It would be a very strange Thing, if six Nations of ignorant Savages should be capable of forming a Scheme for . . . a Union [of several tribes], and be able to execute it in such a Manner, as that it has subsisted Ages and appears indissoluble; and yet that a like Union should be impracticable for ten or a Dozen English Colonies. . . ."

The truth is that these "ignorant savages" had solved a political problem that Europeans — with the sole exception of the Swiss—had solved only by force of arms. Here was the model, clearly acknowledged by a pioneer of the American Revolution, for the future United States of America, whose federation set the example for Canada, Australia, Germany, and Italy.

Each tribe of the League of Five Nations ran its internal affairs through its separate council. But, when it came to deciding on any group action, the decision rested with a council of 49 *sachems*, selected from each tribe on the basis of heredity. The meetings of this council were surrounded with ceremony, and discussions were conducted with a kind of parliamentary ritual. Late in August, or sometimes in September or October, the *sachems* met in the land of the Onondaga. Meetings were held around a council fire, with the *sachems* of the Mohawk and the Seneca on the east side of the fire, the Oneida and the Cayuga on the west, and the Onondaga between the two groups, on the north side of the fire. The meeting opened with prayer, and songs were sung by each nation in turn.

Council debate, carried on across the fire, was often long and drawn out. A proposal was introduced, and the discussion of it began the next day. Once the matter had been debated, voting on the proposal took place in pairs. The Mohawk and the Seneca met separately, as did the Oneida and the Cayuga, to see if they could arrive at a common decision. The results were conveyed to the Onondaga. If it was found that any of the nations disagreed with the majority decision, the matter was referred back to the smaller groups, to see if the disagreements could be worked out. If the groups could still not reach agreement, this fact was passed on to the Onondaga, who then cast the deciding vote. If, on the other hand, the Onondaga blocked the decision while the others were in agreement, the Onondaga were forced to go along with the majority. But, wherever possible, the council tried to work out a decision that would be acceptable to all, so that unanimous agreement could be reached.

The Dispersal

It was this council that decided, in the mid-1600s, that the Huron must be destroyed. In the summer of 1648, a band of 1,000 warriors set out for Huronia, and spent the winter hunting in the vicinity, waiting for a chance to strike. It came on a night in early March, 1649, at a time of year when such attacks were unheard of. As the inhabitants of St. Ignace slept, the warriors overwhelmed the few guards on duty and destroyed the village. Only three Huron escaped, and their warning did not save St. Louis, which fell early the next day before a defence could be organized. The Huron counterattacked and drove the warriors off, but Huronia had been demoralized and the fine web of its trading empire broken. The Huron had relied so completely on their trade that they did not have enough food of their own to support themselves in the emergency, and hundreds starved the next winter.

The Huron never recovered. One village surrendered to the Five Nations and was adopted *en masse*. Bands of Huron scattered east and west, and the name of the Huron alliance with the Petun — Wendat or Wyandot—is still attached to the scattered groups who finally settled west of the Detroit River. Refugees showed up at Michilimacinac in the late seventeenth century to raise corn for provisioning fur brigades. Another group established a fishing village on the south shore of Lake Superior, in Shequamegon Bay, that was later to become the cultural focus of migrating Ojibway. One small Huron band survives in the province of Quebec.

Although the Five Nations dispersed the Erie and the Neutral in the year following the collapse of Huronia, their military advance was stopped by more westerly tribes. And, while they terrorized New France, they were shrewd enough not to eliminate the French, whom they could play off against the British, if it served their purposes.

History has exaggerated the hostility of the Five Nations to the French. In 1724, the Surveyor-General of the Province of New York complained that "even our own Five Nations, who formerly were mortal Enemies of the French, and have always lived in the strictest Amity with the English, have, of late, (by the practices of the French Priests) been so far gain'd, that several of the Mohawks, who live nearest the English, have left their Habitations, and are gone to settle near Montreal in Canada: and all the rest discover a Dread of the French Power. . . . And those Mohawk Indians that are gone to Canada, are now commonly known, both to the French and the English, by the name of The Praying Indians, it being customary for them to go through the Streets of Montreal with their Beads, praying and begging Alms."

In 1701, the Five Nations had made peace with the French. It was only later that, in return for an ample supply of trade goods, they became British allies in the long struggle that led to the fall of Quebec. During the American Revolution, although the council of the League originally declared neutrality, the League was gradually drawn into the struggle on the British side.

As early as 1701, the Iroquoian role as middlemen in the fur trade had ended. By this time, the main fur supply was coming from the upper Mississippi country, the watershed of Lake Superior, and beyond. More and more of it had fallen into the hands of the *coureur de bois*, who took his furs to Montreal or Albany, depending on which offered the better price. So when, with the end of the American Revolution, the League ceased to be valuable as a military ally, it met the fate of all Amerindian groups who stood in the way of European settlement. Remnants of the various nations of the League can be found today in reservations scattered on both sides of the Canadian-American border.

As a reward for their service during the American Revolution, one group was given a handsome grant of land in Canada: a half-million acres of prime farmland along the Grand River. The migration of this group, mainly Mohawk, was led by Thayendanagea, known to history as Joseph Brant, and remembered not only as a brilliant tactical general, but as the translator of the Gospel of St. John into Mohawk. Today his people have mixed feelings about their leader. With sole authority to sign treaties with the British, he yielded to the pressures of aggressive and unscrupulous land companies; he and his successors sold off the greater part of the original holdings. By 1950 the original grant of 594,910 acres of Ontario farmland had shrunk to less than 40,000, and the descendants of once-proud allies of the British had become improverished "Wards of the Crown". Today, almost engulfed in the urban sprawl of

Brantford, they till small farms, operate small businesses, or serve in the trades and work as day-labourers. No longer recognized by the Canadian government as an independent nation, the people themselves are divided. "Longhouse" conservatives, determined to preserve ancient traditions, press for restoration of the hereditary system of leader choice, and claim for their people the status of a sovereign nation. On the other hand, an easy-going majority appear to have passively accepted the low economic state in which they find themselves. A third group comprises a small but significant minority. More successful than most at rising to meet modern educational and occupational standards, they are, themselves, divided between those who are content to play important roles in Canadian society and those determined to change the plight of their own people.

Other descendants of the League, driven north by expanding settlement and the American Revolution, moved into Canadian territory. Near London, Ontario, a band of Oneida actually *bought* the land they still occupy, emigrating from the United States in 1849. In spite of this purchase the Oneida of the Thames were reduced to reserve status, although, like the Grand River Mohawk, a minority has preserved the Longhouse ceremonies and traditional council meetings. Two other bands, mainly Mohawk, settled in south-eastern Ontario. A small group acquired a reserve in the Bay of Quinte. A much larger one, assuming they were in Canada, settled just south of the St. Lawrence at St. Regis, near Cornwall. An international commission, however, established a boundary that split the settlement in half. Although the Jay Treaty of 1794 allowed free passage for Amerindians across the border, this right has been recently challenged, and a long, involved series of court contests lies ahead in attempts to uphold it.

Another group of Mohawk, "The Praying Indians", were the subjects of the earliest treaty that concerned native people in Canada. Signed in 1680 by Louis de Buade, Comte de Frontenac, on behalf "of His [French] Majesty in Canada, Acadia and Newfoundland", the agreement granted the Jesuits a tract of land "which would better enable them to entice hither the Iroquois and other Indians and to augment their number, and by this means to spread the light of the Gospel."

Here, at Caughnawaga, on the south shore of the St. Lawrence River by the Lachine Rapids, within sight of the city of Montreal, the descendants of the "Praying Indians" have adapted themselves in a unique way to twentieth-century life. Today they may be found as high-steel workers in every large city of northeastern America, their services as skilled construction workers 75 in wide demand. Returning on long weekends to Caughnawaga from as far away as New York, Buffalo, and Detroit, the men have revived in modern terms their aboriginal practice of long journeys from the home palisades, and the danger of their work continues tribal traditions of male courage. Some families have moved into the cities, where the men can find steady work at their trade, but the more prosperous continue to maintain summer homes at Caughnawaga, returning annually for their holidays.

6 Hunters and Fishermen of the Canadian Shield Woodlands

The Land and the People

The Canadian Shield is a vast horseshoe of rock, water, and forest that sweeps around Hudson Bay from Labrador to the Arctic coast east of the Mackenzie delta. Bordered to the west and the south by the largest lakes in Canada — Great Bear, Great Slave, Athabaska, Winnipeg, Superior, and Huron — it takes in most of northern Ontario and the whole of Quebec north of the St. Lawrence.

All through the Wisconsin ice age the Shield was buried under the Labrador and Keewatin ice sheets. As these glaciers slowly ground their way southward they rounded off rocky pinnacles and bulldozed the crushed debris of ancient, weathered mountains down to the bare bedrock. As they melted back during the long, post-Wisconsin thaw, they left behind them great dumps of glacial till—rock flour mingled with boulders of every size. Complex patterns of clay, sand, and gravel were also left behind — deposits from the streams and pools of meltwater that had formed under the ice. And flat soil beds were exposed, where silt had settled in great freshwater seas that had been dammed up by the retreating ice.

The original drainage systems were so disorganized by the Wisconsin ice that to this day the Shield is a wandering maze of streams and rivers, dammed by obstructions or lost in swamps, that have created lakes of every conceivable size and shape, in numbers no man has ever attempted to count.

The Shield Woodlands are a complex mixture of trees. South of the treeless Arctic prairies stretches the taiga country, dominated by black spruce and the bog known to Canadians by its Algonkian name of *muskeg*.

Southward again the hardy birch and aspen appear, frequently mixed with stands of white spruce and jack-pine. In the southern Shield white pine, elm, scrub oak, and the sugar maple grow. But everywhere the land is laced with waterways.

Over the lonely lakes echoes the loon's wild call. In the swamps, the moose browses, an ungainly relic of great Pleistocene mammals. And in the forests the once numerous woodland caribou still linger. The un-numbered streams and shallow lakes are the beaver's paradise. Black bear grow fat on lethargic spawning jackfish or on the blueberries of an old fireburn. Deep in the forest, lynx pounce upon unwary hare. Otter dive after plump, firm-fleshed pickerel in the deep water below rapids. Marten, mink, and weasel sink their dainty fangs into mouse, mole, or the still-chattering red squirrel. And high above clearwater lakes wheel eagle and osprey, hunting lake trout and sturgeon.

Everywhere swarm the summer flies, to feed small fish and torture large mammals. The blood-letting blackfly, probing mosquito, savagely nipping dogfly, deerfly, moosefly, and the almost invisible sandfly, or "no-see-um"—flies for all occasions and curses, till the first frosts come.

Today, paddling around a rocky headland and gliding beside a sheer wall of glaciated granite, the visitor may still wonder at ancient red-ochre paintings—animals, men, handprints, dream-figures, and strange abstractions — left here by vanished shaman-artists. Their age is yet undetermined, but these modest markings express the faith of generation after generation of men who hunted and fished in these regions. Their struggle for survival, they believed, could be aided by unseen supernatural beings, beings who haunted the hallowed places in these rocky, wooded water-labyrinths.

How did man come to these regions, when did he come, and what was he like? He came initially in the southern part of the Shield even while the ice lingered in the north — mastodon-hunters first, and then men who hunted caribou. By 5000 B.C., the Boreal Archaic people had arrived with their typical woodworking tools of ground and polished stone. During the same period—chiefly in the Lake Superior region—the Old Copper culture emerged. Its tool-makers quarried and cold-hammered the native copper into woodworking axes, gouges, and knives. The forms they created were modelled on those of polished stone tools used for the same purposes. Then, about 1200 B.C., the Old Copper people vanished. During the next millennium, an Early Woodland culture emerged. Grave mounds and middens dating from around the time of Christ are scattered along the southern edges of the Shield, and pottery sherds of this Woodland period still wash up along the beaches. And later, this culture became diversified and the Algonkian-speakers emerged.

Early Contacts

The first definite description we have of these Algonkian-speakers is found in an account by the Jesuit, Father Le Jeune, in 1632. The morning after his ship anchored off Tadoussac at the mouth of the Saguenay, he tells us, "two of them came aboard in a little canoe very neatly made of bark. . . . It seemed to me that I was looking at those maskers who run about France in carnival time. There were some whose noses were painted blue, the eyes, eyebrows, and cheeks painted black, and the rest of the face red; and these colours are bright and shining like those of our masks; others had black, red and blue stripes drawn from the ears to the mouth. . . . There were some who had only one black stripe, like a wide ribbon, drawn from one ear to the other, across the eyes, and three little stripes on the cheeks. . . . All the men, when it is a little warm, go naked, with the exception of a piece of skin which falls from just below the navel to the thighs. When it is cold they cover themselves with furs. . . . I have seen some of them dressed in a Bear skin, just as St. John the Baptist is painted, . . . worn under one arm and over the other, hanging down to the knees. They are girdled about the body with a cord made of dried intestine. Some are entirely dressed. . . . All go bareheaded, men and women; their hair, which is uniformly black, is long, greasy and shiny, and is tied behind, except when they wear mourning. The women are decently covered; they wear skins fastened together on their shoulders with cords: these hang from their neck to their knees." Le Jeune noted, too, that this band was trading with the French "for capes, blankets, cloths, and shirts, there are many who use them, but their shirts are as white and dirty as dishcloths." Significantly, he does not mention the trading of prime beaver pelts for axes, knives, and cooking pots. For these people had already been by-passed by the traders, and, for them, the peak trading period was over.

Meanwhile, following Hudson's discovery of the sea route into Hudson Bay, European explorers were finding their way along the bay coastline and coming into contact with other Algonkian-speakers. Accounts of such first contacts with Europeans still linger, including the one that follows, told to the writer by an old man at Stanley Mission in northern Saskatchewan, 600 miles from the bay. It is written here in the identical words of the interpreter. The narrator got the story as a boy from his grandfather, and there is a ring of authenticity about it that suggests it may have passed down as a record of an early encounter with the English.   79

Perhaps it refers to Button's voyage in 1610, and was kept as a tribal memory, even when the people involved migrated far inland.

"Once upon a time these people were living somewhere along Hudson Bay. They saw stumps that must have been hewn by some sharp tool. They were living in that vicinity—this elder man that people seemed to think could foretell what would happen, and this great-grandfather. They travelled along that bay and saw a house standing. They didn't know what that thing was. But then they saw a door with big iron hinges and a big iron latch sticking out. That man that foretold things, he twisted that iron stick in front of the door and pushed it open. They looked inside and they saw things they didn't know about. They noticed first thing a very black something. That seer spoke up and said that black thing was never supposed to go near fire — that was gunpowder.

"Pretty soon we will see these people coming back in their house and we will see them, what they are going to do.

"Sure enough they saw something in the big, open water coming in—a great big thing. The seer told the great-grandfather to sit tight and not make a move — not be hostile or anything like that.

"And when these men landed from their boats the first thing they did was shook hands with those natives.

The first thing they noticed was how hairy they were. Those men [the natives] must have had their families along. The first thing the white men did, they noticed the kids wearing skins and they were touching—[here the narrator made stroking motions with his hand]—the skins and the fur. They started taking those children's clothing off and changed it for ordinary clothing they brought on the boats—they liked those fur coats so much.

"The next thing they did, they drew a target and they tried to get those natives to point this thing—it must have been a shot gun—to point at the target and fire. After those men showed them how to fire the gun then those men brought cups and poured some whiskey into the cup—but they called it firewater—and gave them that to drink. And when those natives started to get drunk the women started crying—they were afraid of their husbands. But that man that [had] foretold the way things would happen said that this was the strangers' way of saying thank you, and not to worry. Their husbands would be all right in a short while.

"Those men asked for two native boys. Those natives gave their two boys to the men to take back. Next summer they saw the boys again speaking a different tongue. And those kids when they returned, they started interpreting for the men that brought them back again."

Survival in the Shield Woodlands

When the Europeans arrived in Canada, they found that the Shield Woodlands were populated with numerous bands speaking a similar language, to which the name Algonkian has been given. The region they occupied had basically similar conditions throughout, and required the same kinds of skills for survival. And thus the way of life of Algonkian-speakers in the Shield Woodlands was essentially the same, no matter how widely separated the various bands might be.

The *Montagnais-Naskapi* occupied much of the area of present-day Quebec. The *Algonquin* and *Ottawa* were to the west of them, adjacent to Huronia. Along the shores of Lake Superior and the waterways leading into it from the Lake of the Woods were territories that later became the home of the *Ojibway.* The narrator of the above account, however, was *Cree.* Bands of Cree occupied most of the wooded regions draining into Hudson Bay. To the northwest they were referred to as the Woods Cree. Those who occupied the inter-lake district of Manitoba and the taiga and semi-tundra of the more northerly parts of Ontario are sometimes called the Swampy Cree. Those around the fringes of James Bay are known, logically enough, as the James Bay Cree. And eastward from James Bay were the Mistinassi Cree, taking their collective name from the

great lake of that name at the head of the Rupert River.

Let us consider how it might have been with a Cree family making camp in its winter hunting territory in early December, in the same year as the first contact with Europeans described above.

Food that had been plentiful in the fall is getting scarce. Ducks and geese have long since flown south. Bears are hibernating and the beaver houses are solidly frozen in. Moose, for some unaccountable reason, have been getting more scarce each year, and few woodland caribou are wintering in the district. Day after day the man and his son tramp the higher ridges that are still free of deep snow drifts. But game seems to have deserted the whole country and wearily they return to their snow-banked, brush-insulated wigwam, with only a grouse or two. In good winters two or three closely related hunters and their families camped together. This winter, however, the man's brother has led his family westward in search of better hunting. Rarely now do the women find a rabbit dangling in their willow-twine snares. The bags of summer-smoked fish and meat are almost empty, and so are the fishnets under the ice that they visit daily. Once the man wounded a cow moose with a lucky, long bowshot, and then trailed it two days and a night only to find that the wolves had got there first.

He takes out his drum each day and sings a song to *Keewatin*, the north wind that can drift the snow so deep that it hampers the movement of caribou and moose. As he chants and drums, he drops pinches of sweet-smelling herbs into the fire from the precious hoard in his medicine bag.

Then comes a three-day blizzard—perhaps too violent an answer to his prayers. The women and children refrain from eating, so that the little left will give strength to the hunters. They lie in the tent, grown weak and listless from hunger. The baby is fretful at his mother's empty breasts. The old grandmother sits like a stone, conserving her strength to meet the old, familiar winter ordeal, crooning almost inaudibly an ancient chant.

The storm stops.

After eating the few scraps of food saved for this moment, man and boy emerge from the tent, blinking in the dazzle of sun on fresh-fallen snow. They tie on their snowshoes and leave, trailed by their small hunting dog, whose keener nose may find their game and whose scanty meat is their last reserve if this hunt fails. As the grandmother listens to the soft creak of their snowshoes fading into the forest, she thinks of the sinister incarnation of winter, *Wetigo*, who freezes men in their tracks with his howl, and eats their flesh or drives them insane so that they will butcher their nearest and dearest to satisfy a sudden, raging lust for human flesh.

It is growing dark when the grandmother raises her head to listen, then nudges the exhausted mother awake. They hear the creak of a single pair of snowshoes — the boy — and sense an urgency in his approaching stride. He pulls aside the door-flap, enters, and casually tosses down a hide bag of fresh moosemeat, carefully disguising his triumph. They reach for the half-frozen chunks and gnaw at them hungrily while the boy relates how he and his father ran down a big bull in a deep snowdrift, wounded it with a stabbing spear, and cut its throat with a flint knife. Soon everyone is pulling on sleeves and mitts and fur caps and packing their essential belongings. Outside, the toboggan is beaten free of snow and packed with cooking-pots, cooking-stones, hides, fur robes woven from strips of rabbit skin, hunting weapons, fishing gear, woodworking tools, and the best rolls of birch-bark roofing sheets from the dismantled wigwam. Snug in the centre of all this the baby is placed. The boy, mother, grandmother, and an eight-year-old daughter pick up the hauling lines, the two smallest children climb on top of the load, and they are away.

Three hours later the stars are clear above them and the northern lights shimmer in vivid pinks and greens. They traverse a frozen lake towards a faint yellow flicker on the far shore. Soon they are shaking off snow and crowding inside the crude shelter of deadfall and spruce boughs the man has improvised, squinting through the woodsmoke at the choice steaks of vitamin-rich liver and tender rib-meat that sizzle on spits over the fire. The dog sleeps curled in the snow, already gorged with offal and rejected parts of the carcass. But the leg-bones, head, and other butchered parts of the carcass — a week's supply of food for the little band — is cached above his reach. The family reaches greedily, again and again, for the scorched meat until they, too, are gorged.

The grandmother is the last to fall asleep. But first she goes out into the winter silence to gather fuel under a rising moon, with which she will feed the fire from time to time through the long, bitter-cold night. She is satisfied: *Wetigo* has been cheated again.

Such episodes did not always end so happily. And there would be other crises for the family this season — especially in the early spring. Nor was the grandmother alone in dreading the *Wetigo*, variations of whose name were known to all the Algonkian people of the Shield Woodlands. Cannibalism has had its place — religious or dietary — in many of the world's preliterate cultures. Among the Shield Woodland people, however, it was regarded with such abhorrence that its indulgence was taken as a sign of possession by a supernatural power, and whoever ate human flesh became an outcast, and was likely to be killed on sight.

Spring comes to the Shield Woodlands with the 83

cawing of crows and the gentle drip of meltwater. On the lakes the ice blackens and rots, "candling" into vertical slivers until the wind breaks it up on the shores. On rivers it melts first along the banks, or breaks apart under the rising flood into jostling grey ice-cakes. These floes rip the bark from tree trunks high up the shore, or jam at a sharp turn in the river to back up the stream for miles. In May, when the break-up is over, the sun sparkles on blue water, and snow lingers only in spruce thickets on northern slopes, where the sphagnum moss lies deep.

It is June in Ojibway country, on a lakeshore somewhere west of Lake Nipigon. The early summer encampment where a dozen families have gathered to catch jackfish is breaking up. One family has just shoved off from the beach. The man kneels in front, his face weirdly painted for good hunting. There are symbolic markings in red ochre on his bare shoulders and chest as well. His only clothing is a breech clout and moccasins. He will tolerate fly bites with a stoicism he learned to practise from childhood. Bows and arrows, ready for instant use, lie at his knees; drum and medicine bag are stowed in the front of the canoe. Behind the man his ten-year-old son dips his paddle. Then come the daughters; the older is almost a woman, the younger is a five-year lass who plies her little paddle, shaped by her father with a flint knife and scraper only the day before, with short, easy strokes. The mother squats low in the stern, sitting on her heels and calves, her baby's cradle-board propped against the thwart ahead. Charms, including the baby's dried and embroidered umbilical cord, dangle from the lath that curves protectively over the baby's head, and sway in the freshening breeze to catch the attention of the infant's bright black eyes.

The canoe is riding low in the water, for it is laden with everything they will need in the hunting, fishing, and berry-picking paradise they are heading for, fifty miles away. There are hide sacks of shredded, dried pike, fish-skin bags of fish oil, and a birchbark cooking pot half-filled with saltless fish soup, which they will pass around to drink from as the day wears on. The limp body of a rabbit, snared that morning, lies beside a haunch of meat from a white-tailed deer, its red flesh black with flies. Rolls of tanned hide and birchbark (cut early that month when it was at its most pliable stage), reed mats, coils of rawhide line, sewing kits, a bag of partly worked chert, stone axes, fish-spears, and a pack containing the man's neatly folded ceremonial gear, complete the load.

As they approach the first portage, where the lakewater pours into a rocky gorge, a bear appears briefly on the shore. The hunter's heart quickens at this sign of coming success, for is not *Mukwah* his personal guardian, as well as his grandmother's totem? On shore, while his family unloads the canoe, he disappears to drum and chant the song of his dream. He learned this during his boyhood fast, and had been taught by his shaman uncle to record it in symbols on a small sheet of birchbark that he keeps folded in his medicine bag.

"I, Mukwah the Bear. I the strong cunning one. I the one He talked to, giving me his Power"—on and on in endless repetition the chant rises and falls, to the beating of the small hide drum. Returning at last to the portage, he swings the upturned canoe over his head, rests its thwart and gunwales on his shoulders and extended arms, and jogs smoothly up the trail after his family.

Late August finds the family camping on the shores of a wild-rice lake where already dozens of other families have arrived to share the harvest. Wild rice was abundant all through the southern woodlands of the Shield region. It somewhat resembled oats, with grains twice the length of cultivated rice, and grew in four to eight feet of water. The stalk extended another two or three feet above the surface. It was harvested from a canoe with two reaping sticks, one to bend the grain-laden stalks over the gunwale, the other to tap them so the rice would fall into the canoe. The grain was then parched over a slow fire, separated from the husks by foot-tramping, and winnowed in a stiff breeze. Large villages sprang up for such harvesting and the major festival that followed.

The Rhythms of Algonkian Life

For Algonkians, generally, such villages formed briefly around fish spawning grounds, berry concentrations, and other places where food was plentiful. Whatever the reason for summer gatherings, they comprised the peak of the Algonkian year. The ideal site was an island, or a narrow point near a lake outlet or portage, cleared of trees to give full exposure to fly-banishing winds. A wave-sheltered beach, or a flat rock shelf in the lee of prevailing breezes, was necessary so that the fragile bark canoes could come ashore in calm water.

For people who saw none but their own family group through most of the year, these brief weeks of village life were an exciting social event. Old acquaintances met, cross-clan romances budded and blossomed, women gossiped, men boasted and gambled away their leisure hours, and sometimes the whole village played field games resembling lacrosse. All night long the drums sounded, while the shaman's lodges were busy treating the sick, tracking down lost articles, or — literally — dreaming up incantations for clients who wished to improve their hunting skills or love-making powers, or to revenge themselves on enemies with spells that would cause sickness or death. Birchbark song records, engraved with pictographic figures, were used to teach the client the content of the incantation he was purchasing. In historic times, handsome prices were paid for such consultations with the shaman—as much as a great pile of beaver pelts, or a new rifle.

All through the wooded regions of the Canadian Shield, the pattern of brief summer gatherings and months of isolation in winter hunting camps prevailed. Everywhere the white or paper birch provided a pliable, waterproof bark that was put to a hundred uses. Most of the woodland Algonkians built cone-shaped dwellings covered with sheets of bark. Such sheets had endsticks sewn on them with spruce roots, to prevent splitting. But the James Bay Cree and the southern Ojibway favoured hive-shaped lodges, and the latter often used rush mats instead of birchbark for roofing. During winter, the more northerly people sank the tent floor a few inches, and covered the pole and bark lodge with moss, earth, and brush. Frequently, too, a birchbark lining was added to the interior. Everywhere the lodge was banked with snow for extra insulation.

The major value of birchbark, however, was the amazing watercraft it made possible. Most of the factory-made canoes of today — even some of the aluminum models — are modelled after the contours, weight, and proportions of the Algonkian bark canoe. The shape especially preferred is the Ojibway craft, perhaps the most versatile and graceful water vehicle ever devised by man. Wherever there was water — shallow, deep, rough, calm, smooth, or fast — the Shield Algonkian could paddle, pole, pull, or run his craft. In particularly fast water, he could tow it from shore with a rawhide tump line. Only on the larger lakes, when gales lashed the water into waves too heavy for a laden canoe, was he windbound. But the main water routes avoided big water, and followed tortuous ways that were far more profitable for the hunter. The canoe routes of the European fur brigades were an entirely different matter, for they were chosen to cut down on the distance and time required to take goods to distant inland posts or main fur depots.

Where it was necessary to cross a watershed, or pass white water or a falls, the Algonkians preferred to portage. They would seldom risk "shooting" a rapid. Carries were rarely more than a mile in the lake-spattered Shield country, and sometimes, as between the Saskatchewan and Churchill systems at the famous Frog Portage, a mere fifty yards.

Minutes after a party reached the carrying place, the canoe would be on the man's back and its contents on the backs of his family, regardless of age or sex. Rather than make a second trip, each carrier loaded himself to the limit of his strength. But carrying was developed into such an art that it was mere child's play for an adult to pack a hundred pounds. Cases are on record of packs of over eight hundred pounds. The bulk of the weight, balanced from the forehead by a pack-strap, rested on the hips almost at the buttocks. Bundles and baskets were piled on this basic load up to the shoulders, and a heavy roll of hide was jammed in between this part of the load and the head, to make the whole snug and take the strain off the backward pull on the forehead. With his hands free, the carrier would then reach for a top load, which he swung over his head. This added weight further supported the forward thrust of the head. And even this was not all. While one hand might balance this top load, the other could be used to grasp two paddles, or the carrier's hunting gear.

Leaning forward until he felt the push of his load, the carrier trotted in short quick steps, his hips swaying to even out his stride. He could maintain his pace uphill and down, and quicken it as the load became intolerably heavy. With sweat pouring from his skin, borne down by the increasing agony of a heavy load and tormented by the grey cloud of accompanying insects that swarmed in the windless bush, the carrier at last reached open water at the carry's end. The breeze that greeted him was a sweet solace and an ecstasy of relief beyond the imagining of those who have never experienced such agony.

Contrary to European custom, a woman was the steersman of the family canoe. The man, with weapons handy, was poised in the bow, ready to leap ashore at once if game were spotted.

Algonkian hunting rituals were frequently elaborate and intimately associated with a hunter's dream experience. For example, the Montagnais-Naskapi used a symbolic pack-strap in a ritual at the end of a successful bear hunt. The broad headband of this strap was painted or quill-embroidered with the symbols of a bear-hunting dream. Having killed a bear, the owner would burn a little tobacco and lay the animal on its back with forepaws crossed. Then he arranged the portage strap in a given way over it. That done, he would dance around the bear chanting special songs that apologized to the Bear Source for killing the animal, and asked for a continuation of the hunting skill that had made success possible.

But, for all the Algonkians of the Shield region, either the moose or the woodland caribou, rather than the bear, was the bread of life. Rawhide from these animals could be cut into strips and used for stout 87 snares or webbing for snowshoes. Scrapers made of the leg bone helped to clean the skin, which was then "buttered" with a paste made from the brains. The skin was then soaked to break down tough fibres, dried, and worked into softness, and finally smoked so it would not harden after getting wet. Once it was prepared, this hide was made into moccasins or other articles of clothing. It was sewn with sinew taken from along the backbone of the moose or caribou. Even the antlers of a bull moose, taken in spring while still in the velvet, could be cooked and eaten. The lip was a gourmet delicacy. But the skull and the leg bones were left on a large rock or hung in a tree to ensure continued good hunting.

Father Le Jeune has left us an account of what was done with meat that was not immediately eaten. "When the Savages had killed a number of Elks [moose] and passed several days in feasting, they began to think about drying them and laying them away. They will stretch upon poles the two sides of a large moose, the bones thereof having been removed. If the flesh is too thick, they raise it in strips and slash it besides, so that the smoke may penetrate and dry all parts. When they begin to dry or smoke this meat, they pound it with stones and tramp it under foot so that no juice may remain to spoil it. At last, when it is smoked, they fold and arrange it in packages, and this forms their future store." Le Jeune claimed that it was "poor food" — which nutritionists would now deny — but added that "in regard to taste . . . good Elk meat" was "not inferior" to beef.

All the Algonkian bands hunted and fished wherever and whatever was necessary, and travelled as far as was required to ensure survival. The Montagnais-Naskapi occupied the most rugged terrain and endured the grimmest winters. Even today, some bands wander as widely as did their ancestors. One instance is recorded of a family that wintered in the area of Fort Chimo (Ungava Bay), where they trapped arctic fox and subsisted on ice fishing and hunting caribou. Then in the spring, they migrated hundreds of miles south to find employment in mining construction camps near Schefferville. They finally emerged at Sept-Iles on the shore of the Gulf of St. Lawrence in time for the fall eel-spawning. Altogether these wanderings covered over 800 miles — the greater part on foot.

In the early days it was routine for the Montagnais-Naskapi to cover 1,000 miles a year. Their activities were varied, for they adapted to whatever kind of life was required. As caribou hunters in the barrens of northern Quebec, their life resembled the pattern of the Athapascans living in the tundra margin of northern Saskatchewan and the Northwest Territories. As eel fishermen, they were an Atlantic people, sharing the practices of the east-coast Algonkians. And as seal-hunters along the Labrador coast and through the Straits of Belle Isle, they adopted Eskimo traits.

A School for Self-Reliance

Essential to survival in such a rugged life was the traditional Algonkian method of child-rearing, still practised in the remoter regions. A Montagnais-Naskapi baby was cradled in a moss-bag, fed when hungry, and weaned at its own will. Even a three- or four-year-old might still feed from its mother's breast — a practice that, consciously or not, effectively reduced the birth rate. But as soon as the child could toddle, he was given his first lessons in sharing the family's work: encouraged to bring small sticks to the fire, and given light loads for the portages. A harassed mother might give her child a tongue-lashing, or even switch its legs briefly with spruce branches, but a warm, accepting relationship between mother and child — observable everywhere among the Algonkian people — made this a rare occurrence.

Very early the child became aware that everything his elders did had a direct connection with his existence. Not only was he being trained to provide food, shelter, and clothing, but he was being taught about those mysterious external powers whose favour could give him the inner confidence that made survival possible in the blackest of circumstances. So an eight-year-old girl could cheerfully carry water from an ice-hole three hundred yards from camp on the bitterest winter morning. At twelve her brother might be the trail-breaker, ranging far ahead of his family, already skilled at finding his way through unfamiliar country and ready to drop in his tracks rather than give up his proud task. From an early age, too, children learned how to conserve energy when starvation threatened. "When we have no food at all," a Naskapi father told an anthropologist, "children stop play; they will just lie in the tent."

Far from producing the dull, retarded children one might expect, this hard life created bright, fun-loving ones. For their parents accepted them from the first as helpers and companions, smiling rather than frowning at their mistakes, sharing with them the family's fun as well as its tasks and hardships. Among all the Algonkian tribes, it was customary to accept good fortune without undue display. This was probably to make sure that the unseen powers that gave such good fortune did not regret their generosity. But women gave full vent to their grief at the death of a loved one — and infant 89

mortality was high in the north. It was proper for the male, though, to appear stoical. The way to greet material disaster—like the disappearance over the brink of a falls of the canoe containing all one's worldly goods—was with gales of unrestrained laughter.

A boy of the Shield Woodlands cultures who reached puberty was expected to fast in isolation, usually perched in a tree nest, or sometimes under the ledge of a high rock. As he became weaker, a dream appeared that revealed the *manito* that would become his lifetime guardian. And so, when he became a father and starvation threatened his family, the adult hunter was sustained by his faith in the invisible presence of his *manito*. And so he was able to endure privations that might otherwise have sapped his will to survive.

Because self-confidence was so vital to family survival the Algonkians reinforced their identity in many ways. A child's name might be "dreamed up" for him by a gifted visionary. When he became an adult, the hunter might use this name, or adopt a nickname given to him by his family. At the same time, he could have a private name given to him by his dream guardian. Names could be represented pictographically, and thus a leader named Ottertail could sign his name on an early treaty by drawing an otter with an exaggerated tail. Among the Ojibway, a person could also have a totemic identity, inherited from the father. The word *totem* (or dodem) is an Ojibway word referring to the clan one belonged to. Wherever members of a family wandered, they might encounter complete strangers in another band who shared the same totem and therefore would accept them as if they were close blood-relatives.

Even the arts and crafts of the Algonkians played their part in reinforcing an individual's identity. Paintings of personal dream symbols appeared on drums and ceremonial objects, even on the skin of the dreamer. Significant designs were rendered in dyed porcupine quillwork and moose-hair embroidery applied to hide jackets, leggings, and moccasins. The Montagnais-Naskapi used bone or antler stamps to print elaborate designs on their long, tailored caribou-hide shirts. Even bark containers were decorated — perhaps symbolically — with spruce-root stitching, bark appliqué, scraped patterns, and quillwork. Ownership symbols were frequently painted or carved on personal possessions, especially ceremonial ones such as drums, pipes, or pouches.

When a boy achieved his puberty dream, he might learn from his protective *manito* that special visionary skills had been conferred on him. As an adult, he would continue to develop these skills, to achieve the status of a shaman. Women, too, could acquire shamanistic stature through significant dreams.

Visionaries and Midé Masters

In an Algonkian band there might be several kinds of shaman. Most popular was the *jossakeed* who divined the whereabouts of a missing article or person. Within a small cylindrical pole structure, walled with bark or hide but open at the top, the *jossakeed* communed with his *manito* while the tent shook with what witnesses invariably described as superhuman violence. Meanwhile, voices could be heard above the opening — various supernatural beings and fellow shamans speaking from a hundred miles away — "just like a radio", as one informant has explained. Reliable observers have testified to the accuracy of the information obtained by these "tent-shakings". The practice was used not only to find missing articles and people, but also to injure or destroy the enemies of a client.

All the Shield Algonkians practised tent-shaking from the earliest recorded times, and in some remote areas — among the Saulteaux-Ojibway of the Berens River country, and some Cree bands on the Albany River — as recently as 1960.

Nearly as widespread as tent-shaking was the Algonkian belief in mysterious beings with magical power who made their home in solid rock, usually in a high rocky outcrop of the sort found everywhere along the shores of lakes in the Shield. Descriptions of these *Maymaygwessiwuk* (an untranslatable name) vary from region to region. For the Woods Cree they were little people, which Scottish employees of the Hudson's Bay Company confused with the fairies of Europe. In the southern woodlands they were thought to be the same size as humans. Everywhere they were ashamed of their faces: in the northwest because they had no noses, in the east because their faces were covered with hair. They paddled stone canoes and were fond of fish, which they caught underwater, or cut out of a family's nets. In some areas they were said to possess a highly valued "rock medicine" which gifted shamans could obtain by dreaming their way into the living rock where the *Maymaygwessiwuk* dwelt. To this day some northern Algonkians still place tobacco on the ledges of certain rocks to ensure a safe water journey. At many of these sites, mysterious red paintings may also be found, drawn on vertical rock faces close to the water.

Apart from "rock medicine", the Algonkians treated lesser ills with healing or soothing herbs, roots, and tubers. Old people, women in particular, had a wide knowledge of such medicinal plants. When a curative plant was taken from the earth, however, it was replaced with a pinch of tobacco, following the Algonkian feeling that every gift called for a return gift, whether from a person or the mother earth.

For more serious ailments, the shaman took over.

J.G. Kohl, a German traveller who lived with a large Ojibway band at La Pointe in the summer of 1855, gives us a glimpse of a typical Algonkian shaman at work on a child who was critically ill. "The poor little being lay in its father's arms, who looked remarkably sorrowful and grieved. Before him knelt the doctor, who crawled first up and then back again. He gazed fixedly on the suffering child. . . . It was much like a cat playing with a mouse, except that in this case the illness and not the child represented the mouse to be captured.

"The doctor's chief instrument was a hollow, very white and carefully polished bone. This bone, which was about two and a half inches long and of the thickness of a little finger, the doctor repeatedly swallowed, then brought it up again, blew on the child through it, sucked up the skin through the tube and then ejected the illness he had drawn out into a basin with many strange and terrible convulsions."

The most elaborate healing ceremonies were known as the *Midéwewin*. The roots of this Ojibway religion— and of Ojibway identity itself—can be traced back to Sault Ste. Marie as early as 1710. Some time in the early eighteenth century, bands of Algonkians, led by the Crane clan, left Sault Ste. Marie and migrated westward along the south shore of Lake Superior into the upper Mississippi country. It was during this mi-gration that the Ojibway emerged as an identifiable group, and it seems likely that the name of one band of the Crane, the *Ouchipoë*, is the source of the name Ojibway. If so, then the name is derived from a word that means "The Voice of the Crane" and reflects the migration of Algonkian bands into new territory and the creation of a new identity.

Moving into a country with ample supplies of fish, wild rice, and maple sugar, these people formed year-round villages, supplementing their diet with some cultivated crops, and hunting. The transition from bush ways to village life had a profound effect on their religion. Now irresponsible shamans, practising evil sorcery, threatened to break up the new communities, especially when they organized into groups to exploit the villagers. People were afraid to cross these powerful individuals, and cases have been recorded in which a whole village was terrorized by such visionaries, who might cast an evil spell on an individual who did nothing more than say a wrong word, or look at a shaman in the wrong way. And so, to avoid being terrorized in this way, the Ojibway were ready to accept an unprecedented change in their religion.

Late in the eighteenth century, a precocious young shaman named Cutfoot had a vision out of which the *Midéwewin* emerged. The new religion was to be a healing ceremony only, and the willingness of the *jos-* 93 *sakeed* to injure or destroy the enemies of his client was to be discouraged. The *Midéwewin* prescribed dire consequences for those who perverted their *Midé* powers for destructive sorcery. New curing rites and traditions were to be taught, and pictographs on birch-bark scrolls were developed to aid the memory of the teacher in passing on the required knowledge. And so a transition was made from irresponsible, visionary shamanism to health-giving, tutorial shamanism.

Although *Midéwewin* has been translated into English as the "Grand Medicine Society", the translation is inadequate. It does not reflect the important changes that created the religion. Nor does it suggest the full meaning of the ceremonies of initiation, in which Ojibway candidates, male or female, were admitted to the various degrees of the society.

The ceremonies of initiation into the *Midéwewin* took place in a capacious, booth-like lodge, comparable in size with an Iroquoian longhouse. A frame was built and a breast-high wall of aspen brush placed against it. The sides and ends of the frame were kept open, though a roof of brush might be put on for shade. The finished structure frequently looked like an unfinished Iroquoian longhouse, and within it the elders and candidates gathered for the rites. The earliest records suggest that the lodge itself represented Lake Superior, and the degrees of initiation symbolized the stopping-places along the south-shore migration route. Kohl has left us this description of the climax of the initiation rites, in which the candidates received sacred power from medicine bags held by the elders.

"These medicine bags, called *Pindjigossan* in the Ojibbeway language, were made of the skins of the most varying animals: one of the wild cat, another of the bear, a third of the otter, a fourth of the skin of a snake; and all retained more or less the shape of these wild beasts, as head and tail, and in some cases the feet, were left on. They were all filled with valuable and sacred matters, of course not visible. The Indians imagine that a spirit or breath is exhaled from these varied contents of the skin-bag possessing the power to blow down and kill a person, as well as to restore him to life and strength again. ... The *midés* held their bags at the charge, like Cossacks hold their lances in attacking, and trotted up at a sharp pace to the victim they had selected. The drum was beaten powerfully the while, and the rattle of calabashes, filled with peas, was incessant."

The so-called victim was the candidate, who collapsed on being "shot" with sacred power, but was revived by subsequent discharges, and quickly recovered to take part in the ceremonies thereafter as a member of the society. Kohl failed to record that at one point in the ceremony, the initiates appeared to cough

up small *megis* (money cowrie) shells, which were believed to have been shot into the body of the candidate to invigorate him with health-giving power. Although eight degrees of initiation were available, so great an accretion of "manito power" was acquired by the time a candidate qualified for the fourth degree that he (or she, for women were equally eligible) was a person apart, not only widely respected, but feared.

As with medical practices elsewhere in the world, Algonkian healing techniques were not always successful. Kohl's account of the sucking rite, on an earlier page, ended with a visit to the sick child's lodge the next morning. The child was visibly worse and by evening "the hut itself had been utterly removed, the inhabitants had disappeared, the fire extinguished, and all their property carried away. The little being was dead and already buried, and the mourning parents after the Ojibbeway fashion had broken up their lodge, and put out the fire, and gone to live temporarily with some relations."

Some Algonkians wrapped their dead in birchbark and left them with their personal weapons and tools on tree platforms, where they disintegrated with the passing years. Islands were favourite sites for such disposals. It was believed among the southern Ojibway that the dead person could only reach the land of departed persons when, after a long journey westward, they crossed over a stream on a crooked log. The log was believed to be a huge serpent, so treacherous to ride that few children could manage it. So the child must wait until an adult came along to help it over. If no adult death coincided with the child's death, a grief-crazed father might go on the warpath, not only to ease his feelings with the death of an enemy, but to provide his child with the needed escort.

The Legacy of the Algonkian

So rarely were the people of the northwestern Shield Woodlands involved in warfare that the Ojibway of the border country referred contemptuously to their northern kin as "rabbits". The fact is that throughout the northern Algonkian territories, the population was too thinly scattered for inter-tribal friction to develop. As the fur frontier moved west, however, fighting broke out between the Ojibway, who were migrating towards the west end of Lake Superior, and the Siouan-speaking Dakota. This warfare is believed by some historians to have been more bloody and prolonged than the Iroquois-Huron conflict. To the northwest, too, the Woods Cree began to poach aggressively on Chipewyan territory, while the Plains Cree exchanged raids with the formidable Blackfoot.

The history of the Algonkians in the Great Lakes region is confused and obscured. In the seventeenth century they were affected by the Iroquois wars, in the eighteenth by Pontiac's resistance to the British takeover, and in the early nineteenth by Tecumseh's alliance with the British against the invading Americans.

Historians, however, have paid scant attention to the mingling of the French and the Algonkians as a result of the fur trades, even though this is one of the keys to the opening of Canada to Europeans. There are today, on the west shore of Lake Nipigon, blue-eyed, black-bearded men who speak nothing but Ojibway but have French names. For, more than a century before the days of American frontiersmen like Daniel Boone, a remarkable breed of men was growing up along the shores of the St. Lawrence, who gave the word "Canadian" its first strong identity. Here the sons of Breton and Norman peasants and prisoners mingled with their Amerindian half-brothers and blood-cousins, who were born of French fathers and Montagnais, Abenaki, or Algonquin mothers. These *coureurs de bois* learned the bush skills and earned the friendships that were to qualify them as fur traders *par excellence*. Lured inland by a freedom no European peasant had ever know, and speaking from childhood one dialect or another of the Algonkian tongue that was spoken all through the Canadian Shield Woodlands and beyond, the *coureur de bois* was welcomed everywhere in the lodges of the people and in the beds of their daughters. His children were theirs, for he found a wife in every tribe he traded with. For him the aboriginal sharing code became second nature. He knew how to make the gifts, and observe the social rituals, that would oblige the Amerindian to bring in the richest *castor gras*. So the little French colony that straddled the water gateway to the heart of the continent extended its influence deep into North America. And the illiterate "bush-lopers" of mingled French and Algonkian stock, mastering the skills and sharing the sweat of their far-flung kinfolk, laid the foundations of the nation that would one day be called Canada.

It was French-Algonkian friendship, and Algonkian skills in travelling the rough Shield terrain, that ensured the swift expansion of the fur trade to the foothills of the Rockies and beyond. And, in so doing, the *coureurs de bois* established a claim to the Pacific coast and won half a continent for the future nation. It was the friendship between *coureur de bois* and Amerindian, more than any other factor, that reduced the Riel outbreaks to little more than skirmishes, as compared with the savage Indian wars that broke out south of the border.

For four centuries in eastern Canada, and the last hundred years in the northwest, the northern Algonkians established stable fur-trading practices that enabled them to survive almost untouched by the rush of settlement further south. Unlike the Amerindians of the Plains, they were never "herded into reservations", and a few of these bands still hunt, fish, and trap in their traditional territories.

But as railways, lumbering operations, and mining penetrated the north, they began to share the unhappy fate of all the aboriginal people of Canada, as their old skills became less useful. Today the fur trade no longer offers them a steady means of subsistence, and commercial fishing offers a living only to a minority, while depriving the rest of a basic food source. As government schools and hospitals are built in the larger communities, there is increasing pressure to live there the year round. This further weakens old family patterns, while the population expands beyond the food resources of the region. And so, lured to the city by opportunities for education or employment, the more ambitious youngsters rarely return, migrating families face baffling problems of adjustment, and the failures and marginal successes add to the ghettoes of the big cities. These problems and attempted solutions are common to Amerindians across Canada today and will be examined in a later chapter.

7 Bison Hunters of the Canadian Prairies

The Prairie People

The first recorded sighting of the northern prairie is in the journal of Henry Kelsey, a young apprentice of the Hudson's Bay Company, who was sent inland from York Factory in 1690 to persuade the interior bands to send their furs out to the Bay. In August 1690 he wrote, "we pitch to ye outtermost Edge of ye woods; this plain affords Nothing but short Round sticky grass and Buffillo, & a great sort of a Bear wch is Bigger then any white Bear, & is neither White nor Black, But silver hair'd, like our English Rabbit." Kelsey stayed on the prairies only long enough to watch a bison hunt, possibly because the band he was with normally lived in the forests to the east. And he did not give us enough detail to let us imagine the sort of view that startled him three centuries ago.

Climatic conditions today, however, are much like they were then, for the same kind of wind sends shudders over endless prairie fields, and sucks up dust devils around small western towns. Winter blizzards bury the fences, and men still huddle in their homes while temperatures drop to forty degrees below zero. The arctic explorer Vilhjalmur Stefansson, who was raised just south of Saskatchewan, maintained that a winter on the prairies was colder than a winter in the western arctic.

But even in winter, the mountain-dried Chinook winds can drop gently onto the Alberta plains at unpredictable intervals, melting the snow with magical speed. And, as spring advances, meltwater replenishes Saskatchewan sloughs, and floods Manitoba flatlands in the former bed of the ancient Lake Agassiz, creating a duck-breeding paradise for hunters. New grass ap-

99

pears on the drying land, and fresh leaves tremble from the aspens in the parklands that border the open prairie on the north and east. And southward, all the way to the Gulf of Mexico, the fertile prairie sweeps interminably on.

Here bison was once king, roaming in such uncounted numbers that whole herds might pass a lifetime without sight or scent of man. Little is known about the prehistoric feeding or migration patterns of these shaggy-maned, smooth-flanked beasts, and only a little about the men who hunted them. In the lower Bow Valley of Alberta, a few scattered villages have been found of people who raised corn and lived in earth lodges. But all the historic tribes of the Canadian prairies depended almost exclusively on the bison for their existence.

Some forty thousand years earlier, the American camel and the wild horse had grazed on the western plains, to disappear from the continent as the Wisconsin ice closed in. We may never know with certainty whether or not small bands of men out of Asia were already roaming the New World. But we do know that, once the ice receded and the corridor from Asia lay open again, the Paleo-Indian had appeared, wielding the Clovis-pointed spear and slaying the mammoth and the wide-horned, giant bison that grazed on the western shores of ancient Lake Agassiz, or around the margins of post-glacial Lake Regina.

From 6000 to 2000 B.C., the prairies became too arid for grazing herds, and its people were reduced to a food-foraging life somewhat similar to that of the aborigines of the Australian desert. Their diet included berries, seeds, nuts, grubs, ants, snails, honey, ground squirrels, and the occasional antelope.

But the climate became moister and the prairie grasses flourished again. The mammoths had gone, and the giant bison had been replaced by the smaller modern species. The hunters returned, still using the atlatl-hurled dart. Although new bands of migrants were bringing in the bow, throwing and stabbing spears persisted on the plains, where they could be used at close quarters once the bison had been driven into traps, or "surrounds". But gradually the bow, which was fashioned of bent wood reinforced with sinew, and could propel a light, stone-tipped arrow with more deadly power and accuracy than an atlatl, replaced the earlier weapons. However, like the domesticated dog and pottery, the bow and arrow was a relatively late arrival on the prairies, appearing less than 2,000 years ago.

The dominant people of the early historical period, the *Blackfoot*, had their home in the Bow River country of Alberta, though they ranged far south of there. They were closely related to the *Blood* and the *Piegan*, and all three spoke dialects that were basically Algonkian. The Athapascan-speaking *Sarcee*, as they moved out of the northern forests into the plains, developed a culture that was almost identical with that of the Blackfoot.

A second group were Algonkian-speaking bands who moved out of the eastern forests to become a plains tribe. *Plains Cree* occupied the parklands and prairies south of the Saskatchewan River, and merged with bands farther east, the *Bungi (Little) Ojibway*, and the *Saulteaux-Ojibway*, whose territory straddled the easternmost Manitoba prairie and adjacent Shield Woodlands.

A third group—Siouan-speakers—hunted bison in the lands drained by the Assiniboine River, and were called *Assiniboine*.

The Bread of the Plains

Until the arrival of the horse, all these groups hunted the bison on foot, moving their worldly goods from place to place on their backs or on *travois* pulled by women and dogs. La Vérendrye has left us a description of an Assiniboine band he accompanied to the Missouri country.

"The marching order of the Assinboin villagers, especially when they were numerous, is in three columns, the scouts in front, the wings [extending back] to a good rear guard; the old and disabled march in the main body which is in the middle.... If the scouts perceive any herds of buffalo on the way, as often

101

happens, a cry is raised which is quickly heard by the rear guard, and all the most active men join the vanguard, so as to surround the beasts, numbers of which they kill, whereupon each man takes all the meat he wants. As that arrests the march, the vanguard marks out the camping ground and no one must go any further. The women and dogs carry all the baggage. The men carry only their arms. They often make the dogs carry firewood even, as they frequently have to camp in mid-prairie, the clumps of trees only occurring at distant intervals."

A bison herd of thirty might yield enough meat to feed a band of seven or eight hundred, such as La Vérendrye was with for two or three days. In summertime, when the band was on the move and extra meat would quickly spoil, only enough was killed for immediate needs. But as winter approached, large-scale preparations had to be made to surround and slaughter hundreds of animals for a sufficient supply of dried meat and hides to ensure survival until spring. Winter hunting was precarious and gave small returns for much effort. Sudden blizzards or changes in grazing conditions on the winter ranges might lead the herds far away from their customary migration routes threatening the survival of bands who had failed to slaughter a sufficient supply of meat from the fall hunt.

Methods of hunting varied with the season and occasion. Small parties might stalk a herd to get within bowshot, sometimes using animal disguises. In winter the heavy animals could be pursued into deep snow drifts and slaughtered there. Some young men could run down a bison in summertime and kill it at close quarters, though this method was used more as a display of hunting ability than as a useful technique. The chief means used were the various forms of "surround", ranging from the method described by La Vérendrye, to the circling of the herd by a grass fire, leaving a gap at which the animals could be attacked as they poured through.

Probably the most effective form of the surround was the drive, a highly skilled operation that used every human resource in the band. In Assiniboine country, where the valleys were shallow and steep hills rare, the objective was to trap the animals in a large pound, or corral, where they could be slaughtered at will. Farther west, especially where deep coulees, edged with sandstone cliffs, cut through the level plain, a more spectacular form of drive—the "buffalo jump"—was used. In either case the leader of the drive was the "poundmaker", a weather-wise, experienced veteran of many drives and a kind of shaman believed to have mastery over rites that could both locate and lure the herd. Among the Blackfoot he was equipped with a "buffalo stone", the core of a fossil marine shell that suggested the bison form. Well-smeared with red ochre, it was carefully preserved in the depths of the poundmaker's medicine bundle. Whether by conscious manipulation or by sheer intuition based on knowledge of the nature of bison herds, the poundmaker's handling of the stone was often, it is reported, uncannily accurate.

Such a man might have stood with such a stone in his hand in the centre of a Blackfoot encampment of three or four hundred tipis, hidden in a deep coulee a few miles south of where the Albertan cattle town of High River now stands. It is a sunny and almost windless day in mid-October, a thousand years ago. As the tribal ritual nears its climax, the crowd is tense and silent. The venerable poundmaker raises the stone, small enough to be concealed in his fist, and pauses impressively—then lets it fall to the earth. All peer at the old man, who crouches now to study the way the stone lies. Then he grunts his satisfaction, rises slowly to his full height, and points decisively west. There, somewhere this side of the blue foothills that may be seen to the west, his runners know they will find a great herd grazing. These sinewy young men, tradition tells us, can match the pace of a galloping herd and hold it for forty miles. But the head runner knows as he rises to leave that this is no mere chase. With consummate skill and perfect timing, he and his men must guide the herd from its present pasture to the gathering basin, a mile-wide dip in the prairie that slopes gently to the place assigned for the "jump". This must be done without alarming a single beast, and be so well-timed that the herd arrives at the right place on a windless dawn. He himself will control the herd by locating the lead cow and manoeuvring her quietly, always upwind and ever nearer the goal, for 40 to 60 hours, knowing that one false move from a runner, one whiff of smoke or human scent from the hidden village, will ruin the whole operation.

Meanwhile, the poundmaker supervises the building of the corral, so placed below the cliff that it will check the progress of every animal that survives the fall. A seemingly flimsy structure, breast high, made of stones, poles, and brush, its presence alone will be enough to slow down and then stop the short-sighted beasts, who will circle and search for a gap. Should there be a single low spot, one will find it, "tell the others", and all will escape.

On the afternoon of the second day, a fifteen-year-old boy, gasping for breath and desperately trying to conceal his excitement, comes running along the coulee bottom. The herd is getting close. At dusk a runner appears on the coulee crest, signals that all is going according to plan, and disappears.

Few sleep in the village that night, and every fire is quenched. Long before dawn every available member of the band has taken up his appointed position on the prairie around the gathering basin. All are concealed behind piles of brush or stone arranged in a "V", its apex aimed at the jumping place, and the invisible pound below. The brink of the coulee, deceptively camouflaged even in broad daylight by the similar colours and contours of the opposite bank, is invisible from where they crouch. In the coulee bottom, picked slaughterers wait tensely around the pound, silently strengthening it here and there, but pausing mostly to listen, and watch the slow lightening of the sky above the cliff's black crest. Now they sense vague tremors in the ground, and scent the faint smell of the approaching herd.

Suddenly hands tighten on bow or spear shaft as the first faint ululating scream floats down from far over the crest of the coulee. Above, the huge herd has moved unsuspecting into the gathering basin, still grazing. Only the lead cow stops and stirs uneasily at the boy's premature scream. A pause. Now from the far end of the basin, and from either side of the herd, rise other screams. Frightening forms suddenly appear — rarely seen humans, made more unfamiliar and frightening by the noise they make and the hides they wave. The animals at the rear panic, and pass on their terror to the herd ahead. Suddenly the stampede is on, accelerated by new forms leaping out and gesticulating from the narrowing margins of the "V".

Below, the men hear the multiplying shouts, feel the ground shake, see the thin cloud of dust that ascends in the gathering light of the still dawn. Suddenly the head of the foremost cow breaks the horizon.

Sensing her danger, she swings left, while simultaneously a dozen cows follow with their galloping calves. They too have sensed, seen, swerved. For a split second it seems that they may save themselves. But now the whole herd thunders down on them.

Struggling, plunging, desperately clinging to the cliff edge — one by one — slowly — then in a brown avalanche they plunge downward, thud heavily on the talus slope, stagger and roll, eyes staring wildly, panting their fear and pain. Some miraculously recover their footing and rush the corral. But the barrier confuses them and they turn aside. Elsewhere a great bull with a broken back tries to drag his massive bulk forward with his forelegs and a cow tries to limp back up the cliff, stops bewildered, then sinks slowly to her knees, dimly sensing that the whistling sound she hears and the sudden sharp pain behind her shoulder have some connection with the shrieking bipeds who are already stabbing at the animals around her and sending arrow after arrow into the crippled herd that mills around in the pound.

Within the corral now all is confusion and bloody death. Stabbing spears and knives rise and fall and jerk free as the men leap about over the piled mass of kicking, maddened beasts, feet sliding on bloody hides or in the reddening mud of the coulee. A man bends

too boldly to cut the throat of a bull who jerks his head when a great gout of blood spouts forth. The man slips and is engulfed among the thrashing bodies, chanting his death song as his ribs crack. But none notice as they slay and slay in a pandemonium of blood lust.

Finally the last quivering flank is stilled, and the slaughterers wearily make way for the women.

For now there is butchering to do. Bellies are slit and the great hides stripped from the bodies. Flesh is skilfully flensed from the ribs, rump, and shoulders. Bones are shattered with crude stone choppers, and the leg meat peeled from them. All day the women and girls work, but as evening falls they join the feasting men and boys, gorging themselves on delicacies: succulent calves' tongues and sweet marrow from the split leg bones.

The work resumes at dawn until the drying-racks sag under the latticed sheets of dark flesh. The children forage afar for wood from the aspen and willow groves along the coulee slopes, or haul water from the spring nearly a mile away, while the women drop crushed marrow bones into the cooking pots and skim off the precious fat as it rises to the surface. Everyone works without stopping, for time is running out. Even though the October nights are frosty, and the site of the slaughter is shadowed by the cliff through most of the day, the heavy reek of gore and fresh meat will soon be replaced by the gathering stench of decay. And so as much meat as possible must be saved.

But even when the winter store of meat has been hung to dry in the smoke of curing fires, the women's work goes on. For there are still countless hides to cure and tan. The skins are staked out on the ground and scraped again and again until the last vestige of flesh and fat is gone. Then they are buttered with brain-and-liver paste, soaked, washed, dried, pulled, stretched, and worked over and over to a pliable softness. And then selected hides are tanned with wood smoke to be used for clothing.

Once this work is done, there will be leather enough for winter clothes and new tipi coverings, for rawhide ropes and lashings, for buffalo robes and rugs. The finer skins of the younger animals will be sewn into leggings or shirts, while the thicker leather will be cut and sewn into moccasins with bison-sinew thread. As the weather cools, the new winter clothing will be put on. Although the women wear their long-skirted tunics the year round, the men will add shirts to breech clouts and moccasins. Everyone dons leggings, detachable sleeves, and, once the snow comes, buffalo robes. Dyed porcupine-quill work and, sometimes, painted designs decorate such clothing, particularly the tanned sides of buffalo robes, on which are displayed personal or tribal symbols in strictly geometric patterns.

As the preparation of the hides goes forward, the dried and blackened meat is taken down from the curing racks to be processed into pemmican. This light, nutritious food was essential for the winter survival of the bands, and allowed them to make long journeys without stopping to hunt for food. One recipe, described by David Thompson, called for fifty pounds of choice bison meat, twenty pounds of hard fat, and twenty pounds of soft fat. The "lean and fleshy parts of the bison" were pounded between stones into fine shreds, and the "large flakes of fat covering the ribs" were melted into the consistency of butter. The liquid fat was poured into a mixture of dried meat and hard fat "from the inside of the animal", and the whole preparation packed into bags. If desired, saskatoon berries, the fruit of a shrub four to eight feet high, could be added to give a special taste to the pemmican. The fur traders found this food ideal for their long trading journeys, and by the beginning of the nineteenth century the North West Company had established a pemmican-manufacturing centre in the Red River district. Here Amerindian and Métis women were employed to make the food and pack it into standardized bundles.

Although bison was the "bread of the plains", the prairie tribes varied their diet with other meat fare. Bighorn sheep were once widespread on the hills of the southern coulees and the pronghorn antelope sometimes fell prey to the skilful stalker. Mallards, teal, canvas-backs, and other species of duck bred in every prairie slough, while the westernmost tribes made frequent forays into the foothills for elk and sheep, and the northerly ones into the boreal forest for moose. Fruit in season varied the summer diet, or could be dried and mixed with pemmican. Strawberries and the wild-rose haw grew on the open prairie, raspberries, saskatoons, and pin cherries in the coulees, and blueberries and high-bush and low-bush cranberries in the northern parklands. Early explorers found no corn being grown on the Canadian plains, and prehistoric cultivation was rare. The Blackfoot grew a little tobacco for ceremonial use, frequently eking it out with the dried inner bark of the red willow.

A Glorious Time To Be Alive

No one knows for certain how the prairie bands first got horses, but it is agreed that they came from the Spaniards, and spread northwards from band to band until they reached Canada about the middle of the eighteenth century. The effect on the way of life of the plains tribes was revolutionary. Men who had hunted and travelled on foot were suddenly freed, and travel became a joy, not a burden. Women who dragged belongings by *travois* were now mounted on the backs of animals that did the work for them. Bison that were

laboriously driven into pounds and slaughtered at some risk to life and limb could now be surrounded by a circle of riders who, from a safe distance, killed them with bow and arrow. Life became easier and individuals wealthier, better fed, more confident. For the young plains warrior, it was a glorious time to be alive.

An old Blackfoot woman is talking to her granddaughter as they work together on the final smoke-tanning of a prime young bison hide, hung above the smoke of a specially fed fire. With the deftness of decades of experience, the old woman keeps adjusting the loosely sewn hide envelope so that it traps a maximum of smoke while ensuring that the smoky tan is evenly spread over the whole skin. As she works and chats, the young girl is carefully feeding the fire with a combination of green and dry sticks that will provide the right kind and quantity of smoke.

"Soon you will be a woman, my granddaughter. But it will not be the same for you as when I was young. That was before the big dogs came. It was very different for a woman then. Soon you will have your own horse, and ride in comfort while it pulls your folded tipi on the long sticks. Long ago there were only the little dogs for packing. Women carried very heavy loads—a whole tent sometimes, but the tipis were much smaller then. I remember as a little girl we would carry all day long and sometimes I would be so tired that my mother would find me lying there. So she would help me up and we would go on. But my old grandmother died that way."

The girl lays more sticks on the fire. "Grandmother?" she asks.

"Yes, little one."

"When there were no horses what was there for our men to bring back?"

"In those days there were few raids, and only for revenge. It was all we could do to follow the herds. But there were runners then who were just as fast as the big dogs. They could run a whole day without eating."

The reminiscences are interrupted by a horse and rider galloping furiously towards them. They know him from the way he rides, pretending to fall from his piebald pony, only to roll under its belly and swing up on its back from the other side. In seconds his horse is pawing impatiently beside them and the boy rider has flung himself from its back still holding the single rawhide line that is all the rein he needs. He is too young to hide his excitement under a dignified mien.

"My grandmother."

"I see you have a horse."

"My father said I could go."

"It is good. I dreamed that you will take three horses."

109

"See, I have painted my face." He leaps onto the bare back of his restless horse and gallops furiously away.

Grandmother and the girl smile as their eyes meet: "Sun Child has a great name. He will be a great warrior," says the old woman as if she saw his future as a fact.

That night all is quiet in the Sioux camp—twenty tipis unwisely pitched in a coulee where there is good forage for the horses and shade by day from the hot prairie sun. That evening while a little light still lingers in the sky, the Blackfoot party—five men and the boy, Sun Child—have crawled cautiously up to the edge of the coulee, casting covetous eyes on the Sioux horses grazing below. Now, in the pre-dawn darkness, when sleep is soundest, the lad is left with the horses, ready for instant flight, while the men walk quietly down the trail into the coulee, then take to the ground, slithering silently toward the camp.

Soon they are close enough to hear the Sioux horses. The wind is right. The Sioux sleep.

Now knives are out, hobbles quietly cut, and the horses gently herded away from the camp. Then, startling, a dog barks. A horse neighs. The Sioux camp stirs, and is suddenly alive with sharp voices and dimly moving forms.

Leaping on five of the stolen mounts, the Blackfoot whoop and shout at the herd, stampeding most of them up the trail to where their own mounts are waiting. But with the sudden appearance of the panicked herd, the boy loses control of the horses he is holding and has barely enough time to tumble on to his own, before an ominous hooting and whooping is heard below.

Sun Child watches his companions already a hundred yards across the plain, herding the horses away from the coulee. He is turning to follow when the first Sioux head appears at the bottom of the trail.

Should he go — or stay?

But he has captured no horses. His grandmother dreamed of three.

He must stay.

Now he sees three Sioux mounting the trail. No others follow.

Three men; three horses — perhaps those three are all the raid has left them.

Prodding his steed, Sun Child rushes at the foremost man, knocks him from his horse. As the riderless horse turns sideways, blocking the two followers, the lad leaps over to its back, stands upright, and throws himself on the second man, whose horse rears, enabling the boy to thrust his lance into the man's throat. Barely noting that the first man lies inert, his head on a small boulder, the lad leaps to the ground, dives under the belly of the third horse, and thrusts at the confused rider with his knife. With a howl the man strikes at him with his axe, but the lad is too quick. Dodging the stroke and before the Sioux can recover balance, the boy grabs him by the hair, pulls him off the horse, mounts it, and in an instant is driving the other three horses before him up over the crest of the coulee and away, just as the trail fills with running men from the camp.

A day later, as the Blackfoot camp is settling down after celebrating their great triumph, the lad re-visits his grandmother. She is busy smoking another hide. But all he says to her, with the newly acquired dignity of a proven Blackfoot warrior, is six laconic words: "My grandmother, you dream good dreams."

Fanciful as this account may seem, it illustrates the way in which a dream could — so to speak — make itself come true. Nor is our young Blackfoot's adventure so incredible. The world has never known more superb horsemen than these prairie riders, and their skill and resourcefulness in raiding were a byword among their neighbours.

The man with the most prestige in a Blackfoot community was the man able, through his own reputation for daring and skill as hunter and raider, to attract the largest group of vigorous young followers. The followers, in return for the prestige he lent them, would provide the meat — and stolen horses — which their leader could distribute as gifts and thus further build up his status as the one who had most to give away. Much of the alleged treachery of which the Plains people were accused was due to the European's assumption that such a leader could commit his followers to a given course of action. In fact he could not. Any time a follower disagreed with his leader, he could detach himself and take independent action. And thus the English word for this leader — "chief" — was misleading and showed that the Europeans had misunderstood the nature of Amerindian society.

Fearlessness, contempt for pain, and honesty even when boasting, were the highest male virtues among the prairie bands. The favourite symbol of high courage was the white, black-tipped tail feather of the immature golden eagle, sewn into the war bonnet. To get such a prize, the eagle hunter dug a pit on the highest hill in the vicinity and hid there under a grass-strewn willow frame, on which he had laid a piece of meat, attached by a line to his wrist. Patiently — sometimes for days — he waited for the critical instant when he could grasp the legs of the alighting bird with one hand and stab him fatally with a knife in the other. The scars of such an adventure were worn with honour throughout his lifetime. Only the man who had slain a grizzly in a single-handed encounter, entitling him to wear a grizzly-claw necklace, was held in higher esteem.

Like their forest kinfolk, the prairie Algonkians required their boys to go apart and fast until dreams came. Symbols of these dreams were woven into the man's hair, painted on his possessions, and rolled in his medicine bundle. A hawk's foot, a dried toad, and a peculiarly shaped stone, placed in this bundle, might signify a guardian being or a special power gained in the dream. Each band, and even each tribe, had a medicine bundle for the whole group. The privileged keeper of this bundle had to chant without error a song for each of the many items it contained. If he made a single slip, it was believed, the bundle's magical power would leak away, bringing misfortune to the whole group.

Rib-Stones, Signs, and Spells

Very little is known of the earlier beliefs among the prairie people. In eastern Alberta and southern Saskatchewan, the first settlers found hill-top boulders — most of them of flint-hard quartzite — that had been carved in peculiar ways. Some which had parallel grooves running out from a central groove were dubbed "rib-stones". Others were covered with twisting labyrinths of grooves that seemed to have no plan. All such stones were generously pitted, perhaps to represent the impact of hailstones, which may have

symbolized the rain their makers desired, and yet other boulders of softer stone were carved in a different style, with mask-like human faces. So far nothing reliable has been learned about who carved all such *glyphstones*, or when, or for what purpose.

But from the time of the first European contact, there was a widespread belief all through the plains in a powerful sun-manito, for whose favour elaborate ceremonies and a special dance were held each summer. The bands believed that self-inflicted torture would ensure the sun's continuing favour, and the youths thought that the greater the pain they endured without flinching, the greater would be their lifelong share of the manitou's power. So the young men had wooden skewers thrust through their breast or back muscles, and then attached these skewers by thongs to the top of a sort of Maypole. As they hung suspended, they gazed open-eyed into the sun until they went into a frenzied trance and tore themselves loose.

The fluctuating movement of the Plains tribes promoted inter-tribal contacts and trade over wide areas. These were aided by a sign-and-gesture language, which probably developed out of long-distance signalling in the clear prairie air. Sign language made fluent conversations possible even between persons who had no knowledge of each other's spoken language. In the historical period a form of record-keeping took shape: the *pictograph*, drawn or painted on hide surfaces.

Originally, such symbolic communications, including those in quill embroidery, were drawn in geometrical abstractions that only a person specially trained could "read". But with the sudden blossoming of the "horse cultures", pictography took a surprising turn, becoming more and more naturalistic and communicative. In its most developed form, it recorded the history of a band or of a prominent individual in what is called the "winter count". This was a pictorial summary of the events of each succeeding year, drawn in a growing spiral of picture-writing on the broad surface of a bison hide. This first groping toward a system of writing fell far short of the sophisticated *Midé* engraving on birch-bark of the Ojibway. But the spirited drawings of horses and individual conflicts painted on some hides, or carved in the sandstone walls that bank the Milk River in southern Alberta and adjacent Montana, express the verve and power of Plains life in its final phase.

Few of these pictographs seem to have been related to dreams, or to the acquiring of supernatural power, as was the case with the Ojibway. But magic and the casting of spells played a major role in the religious life of the prairie. One could cause an enemy to go mad, it was believed, by placing bits of his hair or nail-parings in a little bag and tying it to a treetop. As the wind spun it dizzily about, so the victim's mind would spin insanely. And it probably did in many cases, if the victim heard of the act, for belief in the power of such magic was strong. And sickness was thought to be inflicted by hostile spells, so that a shaman was hired to neutralize them.

All the prairie people had a strong belief in an afterlife. The Sarcee slaughtered a man's favourite horse over his grave to be his companion in his new life. The Blackfoot wrapped their dead in hide and placed them high on scaffolds or trees, or in the sandstone caves that frequently occur in the eroded walls of many western coulees. Their greatest leaders might be sewn in their tipi covers, along with their personal possessions, and the body heaped over with stones to form a cairn. Other stones were sometimes arranged in radiating lines from such a cairn, each line pointing in the direction of one of the leader's distinguished exploits. The Assiniboine, however, burned their dead. Among them a man's burial was related to his importance, and many who had outlived their usefulness and their immediate relatives might lie unburied on "the lone prairie", meat for the raven and the coyote.

The Unique Prairie Peoples

The glorious days of the mounted bison-hunter and the raider lasted barely a century. By the third quarter of the nineteenth century, the flow of settlers into the American plains was under way. This stream of land-hungry men was little concerned with the sanctity of treaties, or the conservation of wildlife. With them came the professional buffalo hunter, who slaughtered bison to provide meat for railway construction crews, and buffalo robes for winter coats on the eastern market. Inevitably friction developed between newcomers and natives. The Plains people, seeing their lands being taken over and their food supply reduced, struck back savagely. Even when U.S. federal troops were sent west, the Plains tribes resisted so effectively that they could only be subdued by the deliberate destruction of their food supply. At the height of the slaughter that followed, thousands upon thousands of bison were wantonly killed by professional hunters, who often did not even bother to collect the tongues that were in wide demand as a delicacy. Free enterprise let loose, and deliberate government policy, resulted in the destruction of two and a half million bison for *each* of the years from 1870 to 1875!

At the beginning of the nineteenth century, fur brigades of two-wheeled Red River carts were occasionally held up on the prairies by a herd of bison that took two days to pass. "At such times," one report tells us, "one might stand on an eminence, and for a belt many miles wide and as far . . . as the eye could reach, the prairie was hidden by a vast, moving black mass. And when such a herd had passed no running fire would leave the prairie more dry, dusty and destitute of grass." A century later, a count was taken of wild and captive bison in Canada: there were 41 in parks and zoos, and a mere 600 still wandering north of the fringe of settlement in Alberta. The fact that these herds were saved, and are now in the increase at Wainwright and in Wood Buffalo Park, is one of the few bright spots in the history of wildlife conservation. But such concern came too late to save the food supply of the Plains people.

North and south of the border, guerrilla warfare, smallpox, measles, and illicit whiskey peddlers spread havoc among the prairie tribes. In Canada, when the fur trade was threatened by the independent traders from the United States, the North West Mounted Police was formed, and put an end to frontier lawlessness in the Canadian West. It was the "Mounties", too, who enforced the treaty rights of the native people against the rapacity of the settlers. This, and the influence of a few individuals the native leaders had learned to trust, prevented the powerful and discontented Blackfoot and Plains Cree bands from throwing their weight behind the *Métis* in the Northwest Rebellion of 1885.

The *Métis* (Mayteece) were a unique group of Canadians formed by the intermarriage of French, Scots, Siouans, and Algonkians. The French had come west with the fur brigades and, as *coureurs de bois*, had been the backbone of the trade. Settling down along the Red and Assiniboine rivers at the end of their fur-trading days, they had taken Amerindian wives and raised families, supporting them by bison hunting, the manufacture of pemmican, and some marginal farming. Slightly later, Scottish crofters were brought to the Red River vicinity by Lord Selkirk, and the remnants of this community had mingled with the Amerindian and the French.

The result was a unique *Métis* community, combining the cultural streams of French and Scottish with those of Siouan and Algonkian. As the bison herds dwindled, they turned more and more to tilling the prime land they owned. French in speech and Roman Catholic in faith, they formed a prairie melting pot of racial heritages for whom no other name can be found than Canadian. Here and there across the prairies, along the river banks near the older trading posts, small islands of such people appeared, forming a bridge of transition from the old free life of the prairies to the farming communities of the future. It was a tragic historical accident that outside settlement pushed in before this relatively painless transition from a hunting to a farming economy had completed the conversion of the restless prairie tribes.

Lack of consideration for their land titles and the arrogance of English-speaking politicians in eastern Canada led the *Métis* to rebel against the Canadian government. In 1885, delegates from Louis Riel approached the Blackfoot and Plains Cree and asked them to join the rebellion. Many warriors were anxious to do so, for their people were starving on the reservations. Government money and farm implements could not replace the vanished bison, and desperation was enough to make proud men ready to go to war.

But Crowfoot, the wise old leader of the Blackfoot, realized the consequences of joining the rebellion and turned down Riel's emissaries. His nephew by a half-sister, Poundmaker, held back the main body of the Cree and influenced neighbouring tribes against war, even though he could not restrain his young men from taking part in minor skirmishes. But the efforts of both leaders moderated what might have been a far bloodier business.

As it turned out, the Canadian Pacific Railway brought troops to the scene more quickly than the *Métis* had expected, the rebellion was crushed, and the *Métis* patriot Riel was hanged. Quebec was politically alienated, and the language and the faith of the Métis were swamped by Ontario Orangemen and English-speaking farmers, too dominated by religious and racial prejudice to accept the *Métis* as social equals. Nevertheless, French-speaking communities survive on the prairies to this day, and the *Métis* remain a substantial—though severely depressed—element in the populations of Manitoba and Saskatchewan. It is a sad fact that the descendants of the settlers who came from eastern Canada and Europe to farm the prairies show little understanding and less appreciation of the vital role played by *Canadiens* and *Métis* in the founding of the West.

By 1900 the native people of the prairies were resigned to marginal farming and fairly successful ranching. While adopting the ways of the settlers surrounding them, and depending partially on government aid, they clung to their ancient identity. Sun Dance ceremonies had been discouraged by missionaries and banned by the government, but with the new century, restrictions were relaxed, and modified forms of the old ceremonies were revived. In recent years, the more educated native youth have been leaving the reserves to join the mainstream of Canadian life. But many have encountered attitudes and values they could not adapt to, and have returned to their home communities to reinforce tribal conservatism. Pride of identity survives strongly among the Blackfoot of the lower Bow River, the Stonies in the foothills west of Calgary, and the Plains Cree centring around Old Battleford. As might be expected, leaders of national importance are still emerging from the stock that bred men like Crowfoot and Poundmaker, and some are leaders in the recently formed National Indian Brotherhood. The Indian Association of Alberta, in particular, has been aggressive in demanding the full recognition of aboriginal rights.

8 Fishermen and Hunters of the Cordilleran Interior

A Land of Contrasts

No other region of Canada offers so wide a range of climate and terrain as the interior of British Columbia. For us today, gliding swiftly by trestle or tunnel on steel rails, driving smoothly along the engineered grades of paved highways, or rivalling the speed of sound thousands of feet above the highest peak, it is next to impossible to imagine the physical contrasts experienced by those who lived in daily contact with this variety.

No one has left a more eloquent description of these contrasts than Alexander Mackenzie in the journal he kept of his return trip from the Pacific. In an entry dated July 26th, 1793, he recorded how he and his heavily burdened Canadians, after a 3,800-foot climb up the west side of the Coast Range, had camped "in such an extremity of weariness, that it was with great pain any of us could crawl about to gather wood. . . ." Yet so impressive was the view—even to a man who had spanned a whole continent—that Mackenzie forgot his fatigue to write: "Nor was it possible to be in this situation without contemplating the wonders of it. Such was the depth of the precipice below, and the height of the mountains above, with the rude and wild magnificence of the scenery around, that I shall not attempt to describe such an astonishing and awful combination of objects; . . . Even at this place, which is only, as it were, the first step towards gaining the summit of the mountains, the climate was very sensibly changed. The air that fanned the [coastal] village we left at noon, was mild and cheering; the grass was verdant, and the wild fruits ripe around it. But here the snow has not yet dissolved, the ground was still bound by frost, the herbage had scarce begun to spring, and the crowberry bushes were just beginning to blossom."

In a mere half-day of climbing the explorers had travelled from midsummer weather to the beginnings of spring. And, to cross the Coast Range on the way home they would ascend into an icebound wintry region, traversing tundra as bleak as anything in the barrens of the high arctic.

But Mackenzie's overland route lay far north of the most striking contrasts. In the Okanagan Valley one may drive eastward in an hour from semi-desert, where sage and cactus grow, to lush forests clothing upland slopes. The western side of the valley, and the whole plateau through which the Fraser and its tributaries rush to the sea, lie in the rain shadow of the Coast mountains. Here the descending air is too dry for forests, but ideal for grasslands. Eastward, the moisture picked up in the Fraser plateau condenses more and more frequently to nourish woodlands of aspen, poplar, spruce, and red cedar to the east. All through this region the wide range of altitudes and varying

exposures to rain-bearing winds from the Pacific create a great variety of local environments. And even time itself seems altered, for on the higher ranges glaciers linger from ages past, still grinding their slow, implacable way toward the foot of their hanging valleys.

In summer, clear, green meltwater cascades a thousand feet to fill a basin below with the unbelievable milky turquoise of a mountain lake. Quietly the water flows from the lake's lip, only to pour boiling through a rocky gorge, pausing and plunging a hundred times on its impetuous way to the sea. And incredibly the game salmon fight their way up each roaring cataract, to spawn in the lakes where they were born.

But when winter comes the roar diminishes in every mountain gorge, and each thinning waterfall is lined with fantasies in ice. Below, in the forests of the mountain slopes and across the valleys the snow lies deep. Along the upper fringes of the forest, the caribou feed and the hardy Bighorn and agile Rocky Mountain goat paw for forage. Deeper in the bush the elk, moose, and mule deer find winter shelter and ample browse. Grizzly and black bear and marmot may hibernate for a while, but under roofs of frozen mud and sticks the beaver munch on aspen bark and breed the young that will be born when the weather warms. And beneath lake ice, the salmon fry find their food, preparing for the day when they will seek the sea.

With spring the mountain streams will leap into life, flooding and jamming as they tear away their banks and loosen slides of clay and gravel. Far above, a hanging snow field may plunge in a sudden avalanche, and half a mountain side of solid rock may unpredictably roar down on the valley below, breaking into boulders big as a house, the violence only spending itself halfway up the opposite side of the valley.

Some ten thousand years ago, another kind of spring came into this land, as it lay silent and invisible under its burden of Wisconsin ice. Slowly the Cordilleran glaciers began to yield to the warming climate until by 7000 B.C. green fingers of life made their brief appearance along the wider valleys. But another thousand years or more were to pass before men came: hunters, fishermen, and food gatherers, to live in the interior valleys and plateaus of the land we now call British Columbia.

The protein diet of these earliest men consisted mainly of deer, salmon, and freshwater mussels, and they carried on a small trade with the coast people of the same period. The men who followed them were

119

skilled at striking off thin, razor-sharp micro-blades from cores of volcanic rock, but how they fixed them on handles, or what they used them for, we can only guess. The atlatl dart and spear were their favourite hunting weapons until early in the Christian era, when the bow and arrow began to replace them. Around 1500 B.C. the first villages appeared, consisting of earthen dwellings of a type that was still being built in the early historical period.

When the first records were made of the peoples in the Cordilleran region, there were three distinct groups: the *Interior Salish*, the *Kootenay*, and the *Déné*. The Kootenay spoke a language distantly related to Algonkian, and occupied the southeast corner of what is now British Columbia. The Interior Salish were divided into a half-dozen tribes that lived in the central third of the region: the Lillooet and Thompson people, the Shuswap, Lake, and Okanagan tribes, and a few bands of the Nicolet (Nicola), who failed to survive early European contact. The Déné roamed over the northern two-thirds of the region, and were almost as numerous as the Interior Salish. They included the Tahltan and Tstesaut in the north, the Carrier in the geographic centre of present-day British Columbia, and the Chilcotin to the south. And all these tribes,

except the Kootenay, depended for their sustenance on the life cycle of a magnificent food fish, the Pacific Salmon.

The Salmon Eaters

In the spring, after three years of feeding and maturing in the Pacific Ocean, the salmon would swarm upstream in incredible numbers, driven by an ancient urge to mate and spawn in the headwaters of the Pacific rivers. Neither swift rapids nor cascading falls discouraged their upstream thrust. By midsummer the rivers of the interior were teeming with their threshing bodies, providing a rich harvest of fish-flesh for Salishan and Déné alike. Yet so numerous were the salmon that there were ample survivors to find the mountain lakes and streams where they were born and in which they would spawn and die.

A glimpse of a Carrier village at the height of the salmon run will serve as a sample of how the Déné lived in the most exciting months of summer.

Around the bend of a tributary of the Fraser River, youngsters appear, carrying baskets of freshly caught salmon. They drop them by the water's edge, along a little shelf, where the women are gutting, beheading, and splitting the salmon open. More youngsters take the gutted fish up the high bank, where a dozen rectangular pole-like structures, surrounded by flat drying platforms, stand. Here dozens of women are at work, spreading the gutted salmon out to dry, or ripping away the backbones and attached ribs of half-dried fish and spreading them flat with wooden skewers, or carrying the flattened fish into the lodges to hang them for a final drying. It is all they can do to keep up with the steady stream of youngsters that still appear around the bend, while from upstream there comes the busy roar of a falls.

Beside the falls, two men are lifting a big dip-net, filled to the breaking-point with kicking salmon. Above them, one salmon after another bounces down a screen of sapling poles set obliquely into the falls, to land in a trough below. As fast as they arrive, small boys fling them ashore, where others throw them into baskets. On a rocky ledge over a deep pool above the falls, an expert spearman stands, his two-pronged fishing spear poised over the water.

"Hah!"

The spear blurs suddenly downward. The man jerks back the shaft, which comes loose from the head of the harpoon. He drops the shaft, grabs the two lines that hold the fish, and yanks a thirty-pounder over the ledge into the expectant arms of his son, who clubs it senseless, wrenches out the harpoon-like, barbed toggles, and hands them back to his father to be refitted into the shaft head. In seconds the salmon-hunter has re-coiled his lines, ready to strike again.

Far upstream, men and boys are repairing a weir of poles and brush that will guide fish into a huge basket trap. Mackenzie describes this trap as "a cylindrical form fifteen feet long, and four and a half in diameter; one end was square, like the head of a cask, and a conical machine was fixed inwards at the other end [with] an opening of about seven inches diameter. This machine was certainly contrived to set in the river, to catch large fish, and very well adapted to that purpose; as when they are once in it, it must be impossible for them to get out."

He had found this "machine" in an unoccupied summer fish camp, inside a multiple-family dwelling. The lodge, thirty feet long by twenty wide, had five-foot walls supporting a roof ten feet high along the ridge pole. Spruce bark, lashed in place with cedar bark fibre, formed the roof and siding. Mackenzie remarks of this Carrier lodge that "it was the only Indian habitation of this kind I had seen on this side of Mechilmack- 121

ina," where he had seen bark lodges built by a fugitive band of Huron.

Such confirmed fish-eaters were the Carrier that they had neither snowshoes nor toboggans for winter hunting trips, preferring to supplement their summer stock of dried salmon with suckers netted under the ice. At other seasons, or when fish ran short, they varied their diet with caribou, bear, beaver, rabbit, and marmot or "whistler"—the last a large grey-furred version of the eastern groundhog. Another article of diet was the inner bark of the spruce. "This," Mackenzie says, "is of a glutinous quality, of a clammy sweet taste, and is generally considered by the Indians as a delicacy, rather than an article of common food." As we shall see, it was a favourite with the Coast people.

The winter dwellings of the Carrier were built with cedar slabs in the Coast style and they traded their skins and moccasins with the Coast people for cedar cooking-boxes and Chilcat blankets. Mackenzie deduced that some wooden tombs he observed were used over and over again. Remains of former occupants were removed for a final burning rite, and the ashes suspended from poles in bark containers. The Carrier earned their peculiar name (they called themselves Takulli) from the unique practice of their widows, who were said to carry the charred bones of their husbands on their backs for the rest of their lives. Among the Carrier, Mackenzie noted, "Age seemed to be an object of great veneration . . . for they carried an old woman by turns on their backs who was quite blind and infirm, from a very advanced period of her life."

Like the Carrier, the Interior Salish also traded extensively with the Coast people. The Lillooet exchanged goat's wool, dried berries, hides, and bark for shells, slaves, and an occasional dugout canoe. As a result, tribal customs were altered. The Shuswap, for instance, had a class system, with defined grades of social rank. Whether or not the idea of the cooking-pit came from the Coast, the Interior Salish found it the ideal way of cooking two roots of which they were extremely fond: the wild onion, or lillooet, and the blue-flowered camass lily. The latter was dug up with a sheephorn-handled digging stick while its flower was in bloom, to prevent it from being confused with the poisonous white-flowered variety. After the cooking bed had been heated with red-hot stones, the stones were removed, the bed filled with alternate layers of leaves and lily bulbs, and the whole covered with stones, more leaves, earth, and hides. The result—a dark, sticky and delectable vegetable mass—could be eaten hot, or dried and stored for winter.

The houses of the Interior Salish were basically the same as prehistoric dwellings dating back to 1500 B.C., but were totally unlike those of any other Canadian tribe. The floor was sunk some five or six feet into sandy, well-drained soil and covered with spruce 123 boughs. Above this a low, stout, conical framework of poles was raised, with an opening in the centre that served as both smoke-hole and doorway. The beams were then covered with spruce boughs, over which earth was laid. Weeds quickly took root in the earth, so that by midsummer the whole dwelling, seen from above, was a green mound, with paths leading to the entrance. The descent was made by steps notched in a stout, slanting pole, and the person entering shouted down to the women below so they could whisk any food away from the accompanying shower of dirt.

The technique of making waterproof cooking baskets out of watape, though borrowed from the Déné, was brought to its highest pitch of perfection by the Lillooet and Thompson women. Winding the split roots of either spruce or cedar in a spiral from the base, they bound each strand so tightly to the next that, when the basket was water-soaked, it became completely leak-proof. The fineness of the weaving, enhanced by dyed patterns, created an object of beauty unexcelled by basket-makers anywhere in the world.

All through the mountain interior, often in places that are difficult to get at, can be found strange abstract paintings on rock faces. Many of these are known to be the work of Salishan youths and girls as part of the required ritual for their puberty dream-fast. Some of the symbols represented special tasks they were required to perform while they were secluded. Girls, for example, were expected to spend day after day endlessly plucking needles from spruce branches, or digging shallow trenches, in order to train the nimble fingers and develop the strong backs they would need as grown women.

In spite of their digging skills, the Interior Salish made no graves for their dead. Indeed, they seemed unconcerned about the prospects of life after death, for they buried the corpse with apparent carelessness under rock slides, as if it did not matter if they were found by hungry coyotes or ravens.

A unique watercraft, either invented by the Interior Salish, or brought over from Asia by their remote ancestors, was the "sturgeon-nose" canoe, described by Mackenzie as "a small, pointed canoe, made after the fashion of the Esquimeaux". Constructed of wood and bark, it bore a remarkable resemblance to watercraft used by the Amur River people in faraway Siberia. Because this strange canoe was adopted by the eastern neighbours of the Interior Salish, it is sometimes known as the "Kootenay canoe".

The Kootenay

But the Kootenay, living just west of the Rockies, followed an entirely different life style. Essentially they followed prairie ways, and it seems likely that they migrated from the Plains to escape raiding from the powerful Blackfoot early in historical times. Speaking a language rather remotely related to Algonkian, they lived in tipis covered with buffalo hide, treasured medicine bundles, practised the Sun Dance, and trapped golden eagles — Blackfoot fashion — on hill-tops. Their use of bison hides was so extensive, and their craving for bison meat so strong, that they made excursions over the Rockies in early summer and fall, and sometimes even in mid-winter, to hunt on the plains. They used dogs to pack heavy loads, and, like most hunting people in Canada, travelled on snow-shoes in winter.

Prairie hunting practices were adapted to their new environment. A Duck Chief organized autumn hunts in which whole flocks of ducks were driven into nets strung on tall poles above their feeding grounds. On the Lower Kootenay River, the village population spread through the woods in a giant horseshoe to drive deer toward an ambush of waiting bowmen. Kootenay bows were widely known for their propulsive power, and so efficient that the Piegan preferred them to flintlock firearms, which were clumsy to load and heavy to carry by comparison.

Kootenay costumes were almost identical with Plains ones, except that the women had some touches of elegance the prairie women lacked. They wore knee-length leggings under the usual skirted tunic, and carried fringed handbags. As a result, perhaps, of European influence, they perfumed themselves with a preparation of beaver musk and flower petals, in a grease base, and powdered their babies' buttocks with fine wood punk. Only in minor details did their tipi furnishings differ from those of the Plains. The floor, for instance, was covered with rush or grass mats instead of buffalo rugs.

A distant link with the eastern woodlands is suggested by a simplified variation of the tent-shaking practice. In place of the small vertical tent into which the Algonkian shaman disappeared, the Kootenay version was a hide stretched over a line between two uprights. Initially the shaman summoned his spirit aides in full view of the audience, and only after the blanket began to shake would he duck behind to converse with his supernatural informants.

Outside of this, Kootenay religious and magical patterns followed Plains models. Some reports suggest that they shared the carelessness of their Salish neighbours in the way they buried their dead. But the dislocations of the fur trade came too rapidly to make it possible to reconstruct an accurate picture of Kootenay life before European contact.

A Changing World

Once Thompson had smuggled guns through to the Kootenay, they were able to hold off Piegan raids. Having made a partial transition to local hunting and fishing, they were not as hard hit by the disappearance of the bison herds as were the Plains tribes. Their isolation, too, worked to their advantage. Never having committed themselves deeply to the fur trade, they turned more easily to horse raising and trading. Today Kootenay horse and cattle ranchers hold their own with neighbours of European stock more successfully than any other tribe of the Cordilleran interior.

In the nineteenth century, epidemic diseases wiped out more than half of the Interior Salish. The Cariboo gold rush of 1858, followed by sporadic rushes to any part of the interior where the gravel beds of a mountain stream revealed traces of pay dirt, brought the influence of the worst elements of the invading society to every interior tribe. And while the Salishan tribes of the Fraser plateau have had some success in establishing marginal ranches, a majority hire out as ranch hands, or do seasonal labour as pickers in the fruit districts.

In the north some bands of Déné still make an adequate living off the land, aided by trapping in years when the price of furs is adequate. Others subsist more precariously on freighting, lumbering, or guiding. Each year, however, the bush skills of the Déné are losing their value, as mining and forest industries invade the remotest valleys. And new problems are multiplying for the oldest peoples of the Cordilleran interior.

9 Salmon Fishermen and Whalers of the Pacific Coast

The Incredible Coast People

"We no sooner drew near the inlet, than we found the coast to be inhabited; and three canoes came off to the ship. . . . Having come pretty near us, a person in one of the last two stood up, and made a long harangue. . . . At the same time, he kept strewing handfuls of feathers towards us, and some of his companions threw handfuls of red dust or powder in the same manner. The person who played the orator wore the skin of some animal, and held in each hand something which rattled as he kept shaking it."

So run the opening words of Captain James Cook's account of his first contact in March 1778 with the Pacific Coast people of North America. Anchoring here in Nootka Sound to take on wood and water and to refit his rigging, he had two weeks in which to observe these unusual people. Canoe visitors, he found, "generally went through a singular mode of introducing themselves. They would paddle with all their strength quite around both ships, a chief, or other principal person in the canoe, standing up . . . hallooing all the time" and flourishing a weapon. "Sometimes the orator of the canoe would have his face covered with a mask, representing either a human visage, or that of some animal; and, instead of a weapon, would hold a rattle in his hand."

Then the trading would begin. Cook was well aware that he was not the first European to visit those shores. The villagers "were more desirous of iron than of any other of our articles of commerce, appearing to be perfectly familiar with the use of that metal." 127

Among the wide variety of furs they offered were superb pelts of the sea otter. "But the most extraordinary of all the articles which they brought for sale were human skulls, and hands not yet quite stripped of the flesh." Cook speculated that "the horrid practice of feeding on their enemies is as prevalent here as we found it to be at New Zealand and other South Sea Islands." Visiting the native houses, he found the women making bark cloth "which they executed exactly in the same manner that the New Zealanders manufacture their cloth."

From Cook's time to ours some students of the Coast cultures have continued to point to such striking parallels. Surely, they argue, independent invention can scarcely account for the fact that peoples on opposite sides of the Pacific have so many traits in common: rectangular gabled wooden houses, high-prowed canoes capable of traversing the high seas, a social caste system, pit-cooking, ritual cannibalism, bark cloth, unison chants, and sophisticated styles of tattooing and wood-carving.

Regardless of this controversy, most authorities agree that the earliest human migrations to reach the Canadian West Coast had come from Alaska down ice-free corridors in the interior to emerge on the coast. Here they established a fishing and shore-gathering economy. Evidence is accumulating that at a much later time, Eskimoan people found their way from Alaska down the coast as far south as Vancouver Island. This would account for the widespread use among coast peoples of the harpoon, and of techniques for hunting sea-mammals, particularly the whale-hunting skills of the Nootka. The merging of Eskimoan and earlier peoples, in different proportions and at different times, has been suggested to explain the fact that six separate languages and a dozen dialects developed in so small a geographic region. It is a remarkable fact that in spite of the ease of sea communication, more language differences occur between the mouths of the Fraser and Stikine rivers than in the whole of the rest of Canada! And it may not be a coincidence that the only two Amerindian peoples of Canada who have shown an extraordinary talent for sculpture are the Eskimo and the Pacific Coast peoples.

We don't know how the Coast people lived just prior to European contact, since they had been trading for European goods long before Cook arrived. And yet there are few records of such contacts. Cabrillo and Ferrelo approached the vicinity as early as 1543, and Drake came close a quarter-century later. Some

Spanish expeditions might have got farther north, and we know that Russian fur traders had introduced European goods as early as 1741.

When Cook arrived, there were six linguistic groups on the Coast. The most northerly were the *Haida*, who occupied the Queen Charlotte Islands and the southernmost archipelago of the Alaska Panhandle. Occupying the adjacent mainland were the *Tsimshian*. At the extreme south the *Nootka* lived along the west coast of Vancouver Island, while on the east side of the island and the opposite mainland were the *Coast Salish*. The coastal fringe between the northern and southern tribes was occupied mainly by the *Kwakiutl*, with Salish-speaking *Bella Coola* villages sandwiched in the middle at the heads of the deep inlets of Dean and Burke channels.

No cultures anywhere in boreal North America emerged against a more magnificent setting, or enjoyed as varied and abundant a food supply. Coastal villages were built on a rugged, picturesque shore against a background of lush forest growth and towering mountain ranges. A labyrinth of island-studded channels and deep, protected inlets swarmed with sea life. Sea mammals abounded: seal, sea-lion, sea-otter, and whale. Halibut and black cod were plentiful

The setting in which the Coast cultures emerged.

offshore, as were the mature salmon. In season the rivers were choked with salmon and the oily eulachon. Mussel, clam, scallop, sea-cucumber, and edible sea-weed awaited the shore forager.

In winter, warm, moist Pacific air was carried by the prevailing westerlies up the slopes of the Coast Range, where it drenched the region with Canada's heaviest rainfall, and gave it the nation's mildest winters. This was the home of the huge red cedar whose straight-grained, easily split wood could be cut and shaped for a thousand uses, even with Stone Age tools, while its bark provided fibre for cloth and rope. The inner bark of the spruce and hemlock was a source of food. And other vegetable foods abounded, bushes loaded with wild fruit in the clearings of old fire-burns, and edible roots in forest and mountain meadows. Or, if the native wished to vary his sea-food and vegetable diet, he could seek his meat on the mountainside, hunting the bighorn sheep, caribou, and Rocky Mountain goat.

Abundance from the Sea

Salmon was the basic food of all the Coast tribes, ex-cepting the Nootka and the Haida. No doubt the Car-rier learned their techniques of gutting, splitting, and hanging the salmon to dry from their Coast neigh-bours. At any rate, these techniques prevailed every-where on the coast. But if salmon was the bread of the people, eulachon oil was the butter, cooking-fat, and cream. The eulachon was so saturated with oil that its dried body could be used as a torch, and hence this small cousin of the salmon is often known as the candle-fish. On the Queen Charlotte Islands there were no large river mouths where the eulachon could swarm, so the Haida made do with black cod oil. The Nootka rendered down whale blubber for the same purpose, but both tribes eagerly traded with their neighbours for the precious oil of the candle-fish.

Through April and May the permanent villages were empty, for every inhabitant had moved to a nearby river to await the eulachon run. When the fish came, amid shouts from excited children, screams of wheel-ing gulls, and the croaking of ravens, every daylight hour would be busy with the oil harvest. Men and boys waded back and forth between shore and fish-choked traps which were set in the gaps of a pole-and-brush weir set across the river. Others raked the swarming fish directly into their canoes, or scooped them out of tidewater traps along the shore. The air reeked with the stench of dead fish, heaped near the fires to ripen and rot for rendering, and with the stink of this rotting mass boiling in huge cedar cooking-boxes, into which the women dropped hot stones, skimming off the pre-cious oil as it floated to the simmering surface.

There were prayers and rituals for each step of the 131

process. For the Coast people the flesh they were boiling was merely the "clothing" of the Great Fish Being. This Being didn't really mind what was done with the "clothes", as long as It was treated with the proper respect. So careful were the people not to offend that the women — smeared with filth from the rotting eulachon—feared to wash themselves until the last drop of oil had been collected. For if the Great Fish Presence were offended by such a gesture, the candle-fish might never run here again.

Fishing, however, was not limited to the runs of eulachon and salmon. Throughout the year, offshore salmon, cod, and halibut were caught with hook and line. Fish-line was made from yarn spun out of the fibres of spruce root, cedar bark, or nettle. The hook was ingeniously contrived out of wood by a steaming and setting technique. One group of Kwakiutl, fishing for halibut, addressed the fish as "Old (meaning revered) Woman" and called the hooks their "Young Brothers". Bait for cod and halibut was a strip of octopus tentacle, and the hook was kept at the proper level by a small seal bladder or wooden float. Cod were sometimes speared after being lured to the surface by a wooden "wobbler" that had been pushed down by a long pole, then released.

All the Coast people — but especially the Haida — hunted the sea-lion and the seal for their hides, meat,

and fat, and the sea otter for its magnificent fur. The Nootka were the sole whale-hunters, venturing far out to sea in their Chinook canoes, which were fifty feet or more from stem to stern.

Long before whaling time in May, the Nootka harpooning chief went through long ceremonies with his wife to ensure success in the hunt. Singing their magic whale-enticing songs, they imitated all the while the spouting and diving actions of the great mammal. So the chief prepared himself for the critical encounter. Sighting his quarry, he manoeuvres his men to within striking distance. At the critical instant, he thrusts the mussel-headed harpoon deep into the whale's side, near the head and away from the huge flukes that could make matchwood of the boat with a single stroke.

"Hold firm my line, Noble Whale Being!" he shouts and chants as the whale sounds deep, and fifty feet of whale-sinew line whips out of the bow, followed by hundreds of feet of inch-thick bark rope humming over the gunwale.

Feasts, Status, and Slaves

In every Coast village winter feasts were the reward for summer's unceasing toil. Such orgies of eating were so lavish that if spring came late the villagers might actually run out of food and starve. Nowhere else in the northern part of the continent did aboriginal feasts

have comparable menus. Characteristic "appetizers" might include salmon, halibut, octopus, sea-cucumber, and clams. These might be baked, boiled, or broiled. A sort of bread might follow, made of the white inner bark of hemlock or cedar, pounded into cakes. Then fern roots and camass lily bulbs, steamed to succulence in a cooking-pit, might be served. As eating ardour grew, the festive villagers might turn their enthusiasm to roast mountain goat, steamed venison, or boiled and smoked blubber, served with sticky cakes of dried fruit. Finally, to a chorus of satisfied belchings, the dainties would appear: crab-apples pickled in eulachon oil, or bark bread and oil beaten with snow into a kind of ice cream. And what sighs of gastronomic ecstasy arose if the supreme delight appeared — soap-berry froth! This was prepared by soaking crumbled, dried seaweed overnight, adding salal-berries, and whipping the combination into a thin foam. The result was flicked into the mouth with a special horn spoon.

Coast villages faced the water, usually in sheltered island coves or on channels near a river mouth, although sometimes they might be found on a river bank well upstream. Along the beaches lay graceful dugout canoes, covered when not in use to prevent the sun from warping their sides. Above the beach ran a terrace where the village work was done. Rows of houses faced on this, the chief's in the centre, the nobles' on either side. At either end of the row, and sometimes in a second or even third row behind, lived the ordinary people — "the ones who have nothing to give away".

Buildings varied in style from tribe to tribe, but all used enormous planks of red cedar for the walls and roofs, with massive beams that sometimes spanned 120 feet. Inside, great house posts supported the beams, which were carved with ancestral motifs. Waist-high partitions separated family apartments, each with its own fire-pit. Smoke from all the fires normally found its way out by a common vent, except in good weather when the roof boards could be pushed back. The wall boards, too, could be removed when light and air were wanted. In historical times, tall, carved "totem poles" stood outside. Although clan symbols were included in these carvings, much more was involved in the carvings on the totem than the popular word suggests. For, in a very literal sense, the poles were "family trees", recording the rank and achievements of the owner, and of his ancestors.

Among coastal peoples, rank meant more than tribal status. The nobles owned the rights to fish, hunt, or gather in specific places, and commoners could only share these rights at a price. Otherwise, they had to be content to find their food in less favoured localities. Titles and wealth were inherited through the mother's side, so that women might exercise considerable power and be accorded higher status than males of less exalted families. Even women of low rank were not required to perform the humble tasks of hewing wood and drawing water, for all the heavier drudgery was assigned to slaves.

All slaves were male, captured in inter-village raids or inter-tribal warfare. Owned body and soul by the nobles, they had no rank, although a captive might once have been the chief of a large village. Even the life of a slave was precarious, for his owner might order half a dozen slaves to celebrate the completion of a new sea cruiser by lying across the runway from which it was being launched. Their broken backs were an eloquent indication of his wealth.

He Who Has Most To Give Away

Through the warm months, everyone, free and slave, worked hard to produce wealth and thus raise his status, or that of the village and its chief. At the top of this social ladder stood the proud person who could truthfully boast that he had more to give away than any other. To make good his boast he might hold a potlatch (from the Nootka word, *patshatl*, or "giving"). This was an elaborate giving-away ceremony in which the host tried to humiliate a social rival by giving him more than he could afford to return on a future occasion. Since the rival was expected to give even more wealth away on a return engagement, a spiral of inflation was created that tended to make the rich richer and the poor poorer. As the practice became more and more elaborate, the value of the highest measure of wealth — the elaborately sculptured shields known as "coppers" — soared from hundreds to thousands of Chilcat blankets.

A wealthy chief might invite the whole population of a rival village to a pole-raising potlatch. After presenting his guest, the chief of the visiting villagers, with pile after pile of blankets, carved chests, and jade objects, he might pretend he was chilly and order his slaves to bring in a huge box of the precious eulachon oil. As the oil was poured on the flames, the fire flared until its heat began to singe the visiting chief's robe. He, however, made no effort to move, merely making sarcastic remarks at how stingy his host was being with the oil! At the climax of the potlatch, the host might order his most famous copper to be brought forward. Casually he would recount its fame and its price. Then, to the gasps of the audience, he would rise haughtily, break the copper into pieces, and fling it disdainfully into the fire as a mere item of his incalculable wealth.

All eyes would not turn to the guest, who might remark that he *had* heard of this particular copper, but it was probably the only one his host had, and it was a pity he should reduce himself to poverty in a contest he   135 couldn't possibly win. All the time, however, the visitors were watching the display with alarm and calculating how much time and labour and scraping together of resources it would take to accumulate the wealth that their chief would have to give to his rival, or destroy before his eyes, in order to outdo him. For the status of the chief reflected the status of the village, and such a potlatch was a challenge that could not be ignored.

War was sometimes the only solution. For the slave was the ultimate measure of wealth, and with an ample supply of captives to trade for coppers and other forms of affluence, a chief might meet a challenge that was otherwise too formidable.

Yet wealthy nobles felt their responsibilities as well as their status and power. What they feared most of all was a mean or miserly name, and it was they who fed— and frequently housed as well—the needier families, widows, and orphans. Nowhere else in the world has such a fantastic combination of capitalism and communism prevailed.

Smaller potlatches were given by all who could afford them, on every important family occasion. They might celebrate the naming of an infant, his re-naming in later childhood, the end of a girl's preparation for womanhood, the initiation of a youth into one of the secret societies, or the completion of a new house or canoe. Above all, a potlatch was held when an heir

became head of the household and was expected to justify his rank by sharing the wealth he had inherited. And, from 1850 onwards, individuals who became wealthy in the sea-otter trade placed great carved totem poles before their dwellings, as an additional sign of their wealth and family status.

Master Craftsmen of the Coast

However, long before the totem pole became fashionable, the technical skill required to fell and carve huge cedar trunks had been developed in the construction of great dugout canoes. Using stone axes, jade adzes and gouges, and shell-scrapers the Coast people built the largest ocean-going vessels known to prehistoric North America. The Haida, masters of the boat-building craft, produced graceful seaworthy canoes capable of carrying forty men and two tons of cargo.

A huge red cedar was chosen and girdled with fire, which slowly ate into the trunk as the charred wood was chiselled out. On the ground the huge log was hollowed by the same charring and chipping technique, the fire controlled with damp sand. When the sides had been gouged and scraped down to a two-inch thickness, they were steamed and stretched apart, the ends bowing upwards into an elegant curve. Stern and stem pieces were then fitted on. The whole was smoothed down with sharkskin and the sides painted with strik-

ing symbols of the owner's rank and family. All through the process, as in every procedure of Coast practices and techniques, the head carver practised special rites, their intensity peaking as each critical phase of the operation was reached.

The finished boat might be a small fishing canoe such as Mackenzie saw at Bella Coola, or a 60-foot Nootka whaler. The Haida, who had access to the huge, clean-limbed red cedar of the Queen Charlotte Islands, made the largest dugouts, some exceeding 75 feet in length. Such a craft, paddled by sixteen slaves or more, with as many armed freemen erect beside them, was a proud and formidable sight. Toward the bow, the shaman habitually crouched, clutching his power-charged ceremonial rattle. The chief stood amidships in his richly ornamented, fur-trimmed, bark-fibre robe, his haughtiness increased by a strange tall hat, while he swung his jade-headed war club to the beat of the crew's deep-throated unison chant. As the sleek painted vessel rounded a point into sight of the enemy village, the mood of the chant changed — savage now, and impetuous. Paddles flashed in quickened rhythm and the sea foamed higher on the prow as the tense warriors strung their bows for the imminent encounter.

But there were gentler songs than the war chants. Vancouver relates how he was soothed to sleep by the soft melodies of Nootka crews circling his ship through the night (probably to reduce the threat of the strangers' magic). John Meares, who sailed these waters in 1788, has left an enthusiastic impression of Coast music. "We listened to their song," he writes, "with an equal degree of surprise and pleasure. It was, indeed, impossible for any ear susceptible of delight from musical sounds, or any mind that was not insensible to the power of melody, to remain unmoved by this solemn, unexpected concert. The chorus was in unison, and strictly correct as to time and tone; nor did a dissonant note escape them. Some times they would make a sudden transition from the high to the low tones, with such melancholy turns in their variations, that we could not reconcile to ourselves the manner in which they acquired or contrived this more than untaught melody of nature." The sight of the singers, he said, impressed him as much as the sound: "at the end of every verse, or stanza, they pointed with extended arms to the North and the South, gradually sinking their voices in such a solemn manner, as to produce an effect not often attained by orchestras in our quarter of the globe."

John Jewett, an Englishman captured by the Nootka just after the turn of the century, described Nootka headwear as "a cap or bonnet in form not unlike a large sugar loaf with the top cut off. . . . The one worn by the king, and which serves to designate him from all the others, is longer and broader at the bottom; the top, instead of being flat, having on it an ornament in the figure of a small urn. It is also of much finer texture than the others, and plaited, or wrought in black and white stripes, with the representation in front of a canoe in pursuit of a whale, with the harpooner in the prow prepared to strike." All the Coast people wore variations of this hat, some merely as rainwear; but among the Nootka the high crown reached its literal peak, its height an indication of the wearer's rank.

Cedar-bark rain capes were frequently worn in rough seas or during heavy downpours. Men were barefoot the year round and went completely naked indoors, or in the warm weather. Women usually wore a short apron. When moccasins were needed for hunting in the mountains, or for winter wear among the more northerly tribes, they had to be bartered for with the interior tribes who made them. Although upper-class Haida wore tanned hides and fur robes, the standard Coast garment was a robe of woven cedar fibre, worn over one shoulder with the more active arm free. It was sometimes girdled at the waist, and those that could afford to trimmed it with fur.

On ceremonial occasions the aristocracy donned the magnificent Chilcat blanket. Although the weaving was simple, the preparation of the yarn was quite complex. The wool of three mountain goats, freed of all guard hairs, was gathered for a single blanket. Part of this was then twisted into a fine yarn, and the remainder mixed with finely shredded cedar bark and spun into a heavier, thicker yarn to give the cloth more body. The yarns might be dyed in black, yellow, and cerulean blue, then woven into striking designs abstracted from the forms of animals, birds, fish, and men. Most of the supply of yarn came from the Tlingit of the Alaska Panhandle, who had learned how to make it from the more northerly Tsimshian.

Tattooing was common along the Coast, but it was the Haida who brought it to the level of high art. After submitting to weeks of painful skin-piercing and rubbing, men and women of rank would display designs, based on ancestral symbols, that completely covered their backs, breasts, arms, and legs. In addition, they pierced the lower lip and inserted a plug of wood or stone (labret) that was increased from year to year until, in some, the weight pulled the lip down over the chin. All the Coast people pierced their ears — Haida nobles in as many as six places—and most of them also inserted plugs in their nasal septum. Sea shells, animal teeth, jade, and copper were favourite materials for dangling or insertion. And the Kwakiutl and Nootka even altered head shapes. The former bound their infants' heads to elongate them and the latter used a board and pad to produce a similar result.

Great attention, too, was paid to face painting. Jewett once watched Chief Maquinna of the Nootka spend hours striving for effects and wiping them off time after time to start all over again. Black and red ochre were the commonest colours, applied on a greased skin. Kwakiutl women were particularly concerned with their appearance on festive occasions: combing and replaiting their hair, using deer tallow as a cold cream, wiping off the surplus with a soft cedar-bark pad, then carefully lining-in eyebrows and decorative strokes with small, flat paint sticks. Red ochre was sometimes added to the hair, accounting for early reports that there were redheads among the Coast people.

The giant kelp provided a sort of soap, and a rinse of urine followed by fresh water was sometimes used to remove grease from the skin. Cleanliness was cherished for religious rather than social reasons. Preparations for initiation, healing, or other rituals which required close contact with supernatural beings invariably demanded elaborate washing procedures. And the Coast people seem to have been the only Canadian aborigines who made special provision for the disposal of their faeces. Mackenzie noted, while touring a Bella Coola village, that "at the end of the house that fronts the river is a narrow scaffolding, which is also ascended by a piece of timber, with steps cut into it; and at each corner of this erection there are openings, for the inhabitants to ease nature."

The Healers

The shaman was both doctor and priest in Coast societies, and often shared wealth, status, and power with the upper classes. Marius Barbeau, the Canadian pioneer of West Coast ethnology, discovered a Tsimshian shaman still practising his craft at Hazelton in 1920. According to this shaman, "the fees for doctoring might be ten blankets, prepaid, for each patient, or it might be as little as one blanket. But if the doctored person died afterwards, the blankets were returned. The fees depended on the wealth of the family calling for services, also upon the anxiety of the relatives of the sick person who wanted to urge the doctor to do his utmost. Should a *halaait* or *swannasu* refuse to doctor a patient he might be suspected of being himself the cause of the sickness, or of the death should it occur. In this eventuality, the relatives would seek revenge and kill the one suspected. This was the hard law of the country. But the doctors were not known to decline any invitation to serve the people in need."

Another of Barbeau's informants, describing how the shaman acquired his calling, had this to say: "This power came unexpectedly. Whomever this power struck became very ill and would be near death. He [or she] would go into many trances and have visions in which the different [spirit] aides appeared that the medicine man would have. His songs and amulets would be shown to him in a vision. These he would henceforth use as his own."

This extreme trauma was not experienced by shamans of other Canadian tribes, but is strikingly parallel to the apprenticeship of Siberian shamans far to the northwest. Otherwise, however, healing practices followed the same general lines as elsewhere in boreal America. Bella Coola shamans, though, used a whole "orchestra" of singers, who sat in a row beating a large sounding-board as they sang. A conductor, alertly watching the healer at work on the patient, synchronized the percussion and chanting with the healing ritual. "Back and forth he sways," writes the observer, "followed by the beating; nearing the climax, he treads mincingly, whereat the noise rises to thunder-pitch, then jumps twice, and as he strikes the ground all the sticks come down with a final ear-splitting crash. Throughout the whole the women drone 'iiiiiiii — '.

"Meanwhile the functioning shaman is gurgling and chattering through half-closed lips. At last he rises from the sick person, holding his hands carefully cupped together as if he held something within them that might escape. It is the sickness!"

The class system tended to divide shamans, too, into higher and lower ranks. Among the Kwakiutl, for example, a group of shamans belonging to a highly organized secret society accepted only nobles as its members, and in turn made its services available only to the upper classes.

A whole book would be needed to describe adequately the initiation rites, social functions, and practices of the West Coast secret societies. Of these, the most dramatic were known as the "Cannibal Societies".

A youth who has been accepted as a candidate in such a society has spent months alone in the forest, fasting, praying, and facing many self-imposed hardships. Finally he reaches a state of mind in which he is convinced that he has captured the spirit of "First-to-eat-a-man-at-the-river-mouth" — the Supreme or Original Cannibal. One terrifying morning, the word flies around his village that he has returned, transformed into this monster.

Everyone vanishes, to peer in fearful fascination from under furtively lifted wall boards as the youth appears on the terrace or between houses. He dances and grimaces horribly, rushing ferociously at anyone unfortunate enough to be caught outside, and biting chunks of living flesh out of the victim's arms or breast.

But now "The Healers" come to the rescue, shaking death's-head rattles at the youth. He stops to glare and threaten, but gradually calms down. There is a pause, while the men wait for the proper moment. Then they rush and overwhelm him, carry him down to the water, and extinguish the remnants of his frenzy with repeated duckings. Thus the spell is broken and a round of festivities begin. Dances, ceremonies, and feasts continue for days until the youth has paid fines for each bite he has inflicted.

Some ethnologists believe that this symbolic biting was the modified residue of true cannibalism, and that in prehistoric times the "monster" was appeased by being offered the flesh of slaves.

Treatment of the dead varied widely from one Coast tribe to another, although all believed in an afterlife. When a man's wife died he might live and eat alone for months. Some tribes had elaborate funeral feasts at which the dead man was seated in his coffin, like the corpse in an Irish wake. One tribe might bury its nobles under their war canoes, after the latter had been "killed" by knocking a hole through the bottom. Another tribe entombed its high-ranking corpses in wooden coffins set on carved posts. But among all, a chief's death was the occasion for a great potlatch,

when his heir would stand for hours reciting from memory the deeds of his ancestors for several generations, together with the sacred names they had inherited or won. And, to uphold their honour, he held a potlatch giving away or destroying vast stores of accumulated goods.

Life After European Contact

European contact was, at first enormously stimulating. After Cook had discovered a fabulous market in China for sea-otter pelts, there was a sudden influx of wealth to the Coast villages, boosting potlatch ceremonies to new levels of greed and extravagance. Art — already embedded deeply into every aspect of life — flowered uniquely. Totem poles proliferated, appearing in villages where they had not been known before, and towering to new heights to match the arrogance of their owners. Pigments, originally limited to red and yellow ochres, black, and blue-green copper oxide, now ranged through the whole spectrum of European trade colours. A new aristocracy of woodcarvers and sculptors emerged. And "Coppers" increased in value up to six and seven thousand blankets, though these were now Hudson's Bay blankets instead of the Chilcat product.

From the 1780s on, ships from North Atlantic nations swarmed in the waters of the Pacific Coast. Soon

the trade was dominated by Yankee clippers. These would drop anchor off one of the larger villages to trade iron, copper, blankets, muskets, and ammunition for sea-otter pelts. Then they sailed for China, where they sold their furs and filled the ships' holds with tea for the equally profitable home market. As floating trade posts, they left no mark on the land and in a few decades destroyed their own success by the swift depletion of the sea-otter.

It went otherwise with the North West Company and its successor, the Hudson's Bay Company, for both traded in a wide range of furs. For a time Haida and Nootka "trading chiefs" rivalled the Canadian companies, collecting furs from their neighbours and re-selling to the Americans. The Kwakiutl followed this example and, to the north, the Tsimshian and Tlingit expanded their ancient trading role with the interior tribes. The latter came into open conflict with the Hudson's Bay Company, and on one occasion wiped out an outpost in a surprise raid.

But the brief flare-up of hostilities died with the arrival of the epidemics from the east. By the middle of the nineteenth century, the pride and power of the great coastal chiefs was on the decline. War and disease had nearly halved the population, the sea-otter were gone, and settlements were collecting around the more successful trading posts. Salmon fisheries, lumber mills, and sporadic gold rushes increased the impact of the invading culture.

Nevertheless, the old ways continued for another generation, especially in the more isolated villages. These yielded reluctantly to the degrading effects of whiskey, prostitution, and venereal disease, and to the increasingly efficient fishing and lumbering techniques of the newcomers, who had less and less need for native skills and labour.

In the villages, commoners might now earn more than nobles, creating new social problems as their potlatches poured shame on ancient and honoured families. Missionaries added to the confusion. Completely misunderstanding the heraldic symbolism of Coast art, they insisted on the destruction of totem poles and house posts, or influenced their converts to abandon their traditional village sites and ways. The government outlawed slavery and banned the potlatch, and with them disappeared two of the bases on which Coastal society had developed. By the end of the century, the West Coast culture had collapsed. Even the flourishing Haida communities of the Queen Charlotte Islands crumbled before the onslaught, and their population dropped from 6,000 in 1835 to 588 in 1915.

Yet nowhere in Canada — with the possible exception of Caughnawaga in the east — were such impressive efforts made by the churches to cushion the impact of the invading culture. In 1862 William Duncan, a lay catechist for the Church Missionary Society of England, persuaded a large band of Tsimshian at Fort Simpson to move away from the degrading influence of white settlement and build a Christian village at Metlakatla. Within fifteen years the village was an impressive community of over a thousand souls. Persuaded by Duncan, these descendants of the most class-conscious tribe on the Coast abandoned their ranking system, along with almost every last vestige of their aboriginal culture. At its peak the town had a sawmill, sash factory, carpentry shop, brickyard, blacksmith shop, salmon cannery, weaving house, bakery, and store, and was described by a visiting Commissioner as "one of the most orderly, respectable and industrious communities to be found in any Christian country".

An almost equally successful community was organized by the Methodists at Fort Simpson, and it seemed as if a solution had been found for the problem of Amerindian transition to European society. But neither community survived the pressure of economic changes that followed, and the churches and their leaders were powerless to insulate their converts.

Undoubtedly Christianity made a strong appeal to people whose faith in themselves and their own religious traditions had been profoundly shaken by the collapse of their social structures. But these conditions were also fertile soil for native saviours. One outstanding "Messiah" was the Coast Salishan, John Slocum. In a dream-vision, he had died and gone to heaven, but was refused admission on the grounds that he had been chosen to return to earth and lead his people to salvation. Early in his religious career, he fell critically ill and his wife was seized with a fit of shaking at his bedside. When Slocum recovered, his wife's shaking fit — a form of chorea — was credited with healing power. Thereafter, a quasi-Christian cult emerged in which fits of shaking among the faithful were incorporated into the healing rites of the new church. The "Shakers", as they are popularly known, are still active, and their church has adherents on both sides of the international boundary.

The treaty rights of the native peoples of British Columbia have been a source of controversy ever since 1858, when Chief Factor Douglas of the Hudson's Bay Company was appointed the first governor of the new colony. As a Company servant he had already persuaded a number of bands to make treaties for land transfer. Now, he was instructed by the British government to pay compensation for the land transfers out of the colony's funds. Thereafter, Douglas's successors were reluctant to recognize *any* native title to the land. When British Columbia entered Confederation, the province and Ottawa had reached no agreement on the matter. British Columbia insisted that existing settlements were sufficient, while Ottawa demanded (almost at gunpoint during one critical period) that far more generous land allowances and compensation should be paid, in line with treaties that had been made with the native peoples in other parts of Canada.

In 1906, Tsimshian leaders from Nass River began to agitate for a revised settlement. Ten years later they were joined by Coast Salish and other southern leaders, and the United Tribes of British Columbia was formed. A delegation from this body went to Ottawa and then to London, to lay its case before the Privy Council. In 1927 a Special Joint Committee of Senate and Commons declared a settlement that awarded an extra annual payment in lieu of past claims. The agitation died down. Today, however, the whole treaty structure of the province is under pressure from native organizations, with some federal support, to reach more equitable agreements.

In recent years, the numbers of the Coast peoples have been increasing, and since 1950 the native sense of identity has been reviving. One reason for this has been worldwide recognition of the unique art of the Coast people. Long before Canadians awoke to the treasures of the Coast cultures, prime examples of house posts, poles, and other forms of religious and ancestral art had been collected by the world's great museums. Some of these collections surpass any to be found in Canada. But this neglect has been partly compensated for recently, and native sculptors have been encouraged to revive aboriginal art, notably small sculptures in argillite and massive reproductions of poles. The late Mungo Martin, of Kwakiutl ancestry, designed and carved original totem poles in early tribal styles, and his work is impressively represented on the campus of the University of British Columbia, where he and a number of assisting craftsmen and apprentices reconstructed a section of a Haida village.

10 Hunters and Fishermen of the Taiga and Northwestern Woodlands

The Setting

The Athapascan homelands ranged northward from the Peace and Churchill rivers to the tundra and the Arctic Coast. To the west rose the lofty ranges of the Cordillera, to the east lay Hudson Bay. All through the heart of this region, drained by the great Mackenzie River and its tributaries, stood the sombre forests of the *taiga* — a Russian word that describes similar terrain in Siberia.

Stands of black spruce dominate the taiga flatlands. Where shallow lakes have been overgrown by swamp grasses and filled with decayed vegetation, the sphagnum moss takes hold, forming hummocks loosely held together by the roots and branches of water-loving shrubs: Labrador tea, leather leaf, and yellow berry — the last a sort of watery low-bush raspberry whose taste has given it the popular name of "bake-apple" berry. And so one may emerge from close-growing thickets of spruce into what looks like a green meadow but turns out to be the kind of bog known to Canadians by its Algonkian name of *muskeg*. So treacherous is this swampy terrain that, for every mile the wary traveller crosses, he can count on at least a dozen misguided steps, as a seemingly solid hummock gives way and he plunges anywhere from calf to thigh deep in the black muck beneath.

In southern Athapascan lands deciduous trees begin to appear: trembling aspen, white birch, and swamp alder gradually replace the conifers until, in the parklands of the Peace River country, poplar groves alternate with open prairie. To the west, the taiga merges into foothill forests, while to the east it thins out into the treeless tundra.

Through the wide plains of the Mackenzie Valley, shallow, willow-bordered streams meander from swamp to swamp, where the moose seeks summer relief for his fly-tortured flanks, and browses on underwater roots and weeds. Here, too, the beaver builds his dams and lodges, favouring vicinities where aspens grow, their bark providing him with his preferred food. In the drier uplands, on winding sandy eskers—the sediments from sub-glacial streams—and in the scanty soil of the northernmost Shield Woodlands, stands of jackpine alternate with open areas, where the caribou moss grows. This hardy lichen forms a grey carpet an inch to three inches thick, characteristically crunching underfoot in dry weather, but soft and spongy after a rain. Both the woodland caribou and its smaller barren-land cousin thrive on this seemingly unappetizing fare. This grey lichen dominates the vegetation of the tundra, providing forage for the hundreds of thousands of caribou and the once large herds of musk-ox that roamed the "barren lands". The musk-ox was so hardy that it could survive the fierce winter winds of the open tundra, but the caribou migrated south and west to paw for forage in the soft snow of the taiga forest.

It is not known how long ago bands of ancestral Athapascans crossed over from Asia into Alaska. If, as many believe, they were the last immigrants to enter North America, it is likely that they moved into taiga country that had yet to be occupied. Certainly enough time passed for some bands of Athapascan-speakers to penetrate as far south as New Mexico and become ancestors of the sophisticated Navajo and Apache tribes. Others—the Chilcotin, Carrier, and Tahltan—moved into the western mountains and adopted a salmon-fishing culture.

It might have been as early as 1612 at the mouth of the Churchill River that men out of Europe first heard the clucking gutturals that so clearly distinguish the Athapascan language. With the establishment of the Hudson's Bay Company posts at York Fort and Churchill (later Fort Prince of Wales) in 1682 and 1688 respectively, the fur trade flourished. Within a decade the *Chipewyan*, who occupied a Shield Woodlands region north of the Churchill River from its mouth to the shores of Lake Athabaska, had become middlemen in a trade that reached far inland. Northward, the *Yellowknife* were hunting in the taiga and tundra in the vicinity of Great Slave and Great Bear lakes.

Four tribes roamed the taiga of the Mackenzie, Athabaska, and Peace rivers. In the far north were the *Hare*. From the shores of Great Bear Lake southward to Great Slave, the *Dogrib* roamed. To the south again,

the *Slave* occupied the whole of the upper Mackenzie plain, and the *Beaver* people ranged over the Athabaska and lower Peace River country.

To the west, in more rugged lands, were three tribes: the *Kutchin* in the lower Yukon Valley and the Peel River country, the *Nahani* on the upper Yukon and Nahani rivers, and the *Sekani* on the upper Peace River as far west as the Cassiar Mountains.

Survival in a Harsh Land

It is from Samuel Hearne, a trader with the Hudson's Bay Company, that we get the earliest recorded impressions of these remarkable people. In 1770 Hearne was ordered to investigate reports of copper on the Coppermine River, and was able to obtain, as his guide, the leader of a band of Chipewyan and Yellowknife known as Matonabbee. On the return trip, his party encountered a Dogrib woman who had escaped from captivity and was making her way, alone and unaided, back to her people. Her story illustrated many of the hardships faced by the Athapascans and their ingenuity in coping with them. This is Hearne's account:

"On the eleventh of January, as some of my companions were hunting, they saw the track of a strange snowshoe, which they followed; and at a considerable distance came to a little hut, where they discovered a young woman sitting alone. . . . On examination, she 149 proved to be one of the Western Dog-ribbed Indians, who had been taken prisoner by the Athapuscow Indians."

She so impressed Hearne that he pronounced her "one of the finest women, of a real Indian, that I have seen in any part of North America". Before her capture no one in her band had seen any iron. They had heard of it, but hostile neighbours had blocked their access to Cree traders. And so they were still using caribou-antler ice chisels, beaver-tooth knives, and stone tools. A raiding Slave party had slaughtered all in the camp except this woman and three others, who were spared to become extra wives for the raiders. This she had accepted as the custom of the land, but when the Slave women killed her baby, she resolved to escape. A whole year passed before she could get away, and then all she could take were two small pieces of iron she had acquired, a little bundle of caribou sinew, and the clothes on her back.

She tried to retrace, on foot, the canoe route by which she had been brought into the Slave country. But long detours around swamps and open muskeg finally confused her, and she realized she was lost.

Weeks passed and winter was closing in. Finding some pyrite in a rock outcrop, she doggedly struck two pieces together until, at last, a feeble spark "took" in a nest of wood punk. Gently she fanned the spark into a flame and kindled a fire that she had nursed all through the winter. Rabbits, snared with the sinew, had kept her alive, and she saved every skin until she had enough to sew herself a neat, warm winter suit. The two tiny pieces of iron she had saved were put to good use; from one she made an awl that served as a sewing needle; the other she fashioned into a tiny knife blade. When she ran out of caribou sinew, she discovered that the tendons of the rabbits' hind legs would serve for thread. Hearne's hunters found her cheerfully constructing a fish net out of several hundred feet of willow-bark twine that she had already prepared.

Hearne's male companions were so taken with her resourcefulness, courage, and youth that the whole evening passed in wrestling matches to decide who would take her for his wife. Such contests were not unusual. Elsewhere Hearne comments that boys practised wrestling from an early age so they could keep their wives once they had acquired them. But he went on to say that he had never known anyone to be seriously hurt in such contests.

The thing to do was to get a good grip on an opponent's hair. "It is not uncommon," he wrote, "for one of them to cut his hair and grease his ears, immediately before the contest begins. This, however, is done privately; and it is truly laughable, to see one of the parties strutting about with an air of great importance, and calling out, 'Where is he? Why does he not come out?' when the other will bolt out with a clean shorned head and greased ears, rush on his antagonist, seize him by the hair, and though perhaps a weaker man, soon drag him to the ground, while the stronger is not able to lay hold on him."

Wrestling was by no means the only way of winning a wife among the Athapascan tribes. Among the Kutchin a more usual way of wooing was for a man to take a stick on which a wad of moss had been tied and poke it through the tent flap of a girl's home. Such a proposal was rarely refused, lest the frustrated suitor cast an evil spell on the girl.

In Athapascan society, a woman's life was beyond her control and almost always arranged to the male's advantage. Survival in the taiga made such heavy demands on her labour that polygamy was the rule rather than the exception. A superior hunter might need eight wives or more to dress the caribou hides his following would require. This was especially so among the Chipewyan and the Yellowknife, who made long summer forays into the arctic prairie to hunt the small, barren-ground caribou.

With some exceptions, the caribou was as important to the Athapascans as the bison was to the Plains tribes, for its flesh provided food and its hide was used for tents and clothing. But caribou migration patterns were unpredictable and some years they might not appear in their usual wintering ranges. Then the Athapascans would have to turn to their other food resources and the margin of survival might be dangerously narrowed.

All the Athapascans were fishermen, stretching their nets beneath the ice of frozen lakes or rivers and hauling out any fish caught by the gills. Small game, such as ptarmigan and hare, would be sought and, if the hunter was lucky, a moose might be killed. And, if beaver lodges were near by, a beaver hunt would be organized.

As a good fur trader, Hearne was particularly interested in how the beaver were captured. Much to his disgust, the Athapascans quickly learned how to play off one European trader against another, in order to get the best price for their beaver pelts. And the beaver of the taiga produced the best pelts in North America.

Beaver were often hunted in winter, when their fur was longest and their meat in prime condition. Once a beaver lodge was located in the middle of a frozen lake, pond, or river, the hunters used ice chisels to search along the banks for the holes into which the beaver would scatter once their lodge was attacked. Pounding on the ice at the edge of the water, the hunters listened until the sound of their pounding told them they had located a vault dug into the bank beneath the ice. They

151

then cut a hole in the ice, and marked the location by sticking a branch of a tree or some other marker into the hole. Once all the hiding places in the bank were discovered, the women and children broke open the lodge, frightening the beavers and driving them into the hiding places. As soon as the motion of the water in the holes showed that the beaver had entered the hiding places, the hunters blocked up these vaults with sticks and hauled the beaver out by hand, or with a hook on the end of a pole. The hunter who discovered each vault was entitled to all the beaver caught there, and disputes were settled by referring to the tree branches that had been used to mark the ownership of each hiding place.

The Athapascans hunted in bands. A number of these bands might gather at a good hunting location, or meet temporarily for trade or canoe-making. But the Athapascans were constantly on the move, following the annual migrations of the caribou and other game animals, and supplementing their diet with fish, beaver, or whatever else came to hand. Much of this travelling was done by foot, and canoes were made small and light, so that they could be carried from one fording place to the next. Hunting territories were fluid, and raids upon neighbouring bands were frequent.

The Balance of Life

From the writings of Mackenzie, Hearne, and other early explorers, we can make an intelligent guess as to the cause of one imaginary, though typical, raid. At the same time, we can get some idea of what it must have been like to live in Slave country in the period just before contact with Europeans.

Along the bank of a small river stand dark ranks of spruce, here and there relieved by the white trunks of birch or aspen and the green of their budding leaves. Against this background we can count seven dwellings, standing on a grassy knoll. One looks like two tents pitched together sharing a common door and hearth, but its covering is a grey tattered patchwork of skins. The others are gabled pole houses, roofed with thick thatches of spruce boughs. Outside the nearest hut a woman and girl sit, working at a smoky fire. Above the fire hangs a watape cooking-basket suspended from a pole tripod that has drying racks attached. The woman stirs the fire and, using a split stick, deftly picks up a hot stone from among the coals and drops it sizzling in the pot. Within is a dark gluey mess of lichen — the leafy "rock tripe" to which northern people turn when food runs out. The woman's hair has a ragged look, dirty and

153

unkempt. When she is not tending the fire, she sews a hide legging with a fishbone awl and split-sinew thread. But the legging is old and torn, and the sole of the attached moccasin is worn through. We notice then that the first joint of her left middle finger is missing and that the skin over the stump looks angry and infected. A small, gaunt dog slinks close, eying the other moccasin-legging that hangs, inside-out and apparently just washed and mended, well out of his reach on the drying rack. He turns listlessly then, to sniff at fragments of bleached bone that lie about, from which the last particle of nourishment has long since been extracted.

There is an unusual silence over the camp. Both the women and a group of men who stand in the background keep turning to glance upstream. The swift, muddy water holds no threat, for it has dropped a good six feet below the peak of the spring flood, whose highest point is marked by fresh ice scars on the tree trunks of the opposite shore. Overhead a big raven flaps heavily, wheels, and silently alights on the spike of a dead spruce that stands above the nearest cabin. The men exchange quick, dark glances and peer upstream with fresh expectancy.

Now a bark canoe appears around the bend. Its sole occupant approaches with swift strokes, and beaches his craft expertly beside a stranded log of driftwood on the near bank. Still no one speaks. All watch the strange figure, his head encased in the snowy skin of an arctic owl, his bare arms and shoulders raw with half-healed gashes, his face streaked with red ochre. Without a word or a glance in their direction, he throws his paddle on the bank, steps stiffly out of the canoe, and pulls it high out of the water. Now he crosses the narrow sward to disappear up a path into the thicket of spruce. Only then do we discern through the trees the reddish brown of a weathered spruce-bough roof. The waiting figures listen, unmoving, until they hear the low beat of a drum and the wavering high-pitched chant of a shaman's song, coming from the hidden hut. Now the men move quietly up the path, five in all, to be joined by two others who have been watching and listening from one of the farther dwellings.

All afternoon the sounds of drumming and chanting come from the shaman's lodge. An hour before sunset, the seven file silently back to their huts and, soon after, re-emerge. Each now wears his own peculiar headdress of feather, fur, or horn. All are fitted with bone nose plugs. Ochre has been freshly rubbed over their tattooed cheeks, and their long hair has been bound in a bundle behind the head, in preparation for bush travel. Two carry wooden shields, and one wears a crude breastplate of willow withes. All are carrying hide-encased bows and arrows, sharp stone knives, and clubs of caribou antler—except the boy, who is armed only with a pronged fish leister. As silently and swiftly as they appeared, they are gone.

The woman with the ragged hair rises heavily, and walks slowly into the bush. Soon she comes to a pole structure set back from the river, like a long, low dog-kennel. She stands there a moment, till the stench of the body decomposing within reaches her. Now she throws herself moaning on the ground, making motions of grief and despair, tearing at her hair and scratching her face till the blood comes. Rising at last she glances towards two heaps of branches that mark two other burials, then turns and walks slowly back to camp.

The man in the grave-house is Raven, and the boughs cover his second and third wives. The woman is Minkfoot, his oldest wife, whom he had married when he was eighteen and she twelve. The second had been won in a gambling game, and the third had been spared when a raiding party, led by Raven, had destroyed a Nahani band in a distant western valley. All three had died of the same sickness, a high fever during which strange red spots appeared all over the body. Another member of the band had also died, and only Minkfoot and the shaman had escaped the illness. Clearly, the band was under a powerful spell, for though the shaman had been protected by his own power, it had not been enough to save Raven. In spite of the foreign objects the shaman had been able to suck out of the sick man's body, and the incantations chanted over the patient, Raven had died. And so the best provider of the band had been lost.

Minkfoot could recall other hard winters, but none like this. Summer and fall had been almost rainless; then winter set in without warning. Between freeze-up and the first mid-winter thaw, only one moose and seven caribou had been snared. The meat was barely enough to feed the band, and the hides were only sufficient to outfit and shelter a single man until spring. For days, fires were kept burning over the beaver houses in the surrounding creeks and ponds until the frost was driven out and the hunters could break through the mud-and-stick roofs with antler chisel and stone axe. But all the beaver meat and the summer hoard of dried meat and fish were soon gone. So were all the dogs but one. The ptarmigan and hare seemed to have vanished from the whole country. Ice fishing had been good for a few weeks, more than enough for the dogs—but then days would pass without a single trout in the net. Plainly the little band was under a deep, malignant spell.

The nights were getting shortest when two infants were born. Both were strangled at birth, to save the remaining scraps of food. But the old and ailing 155 shaman's mother was still given her share of the scraps. Had she not, the shaman might have put his curse on the others.

The infants' deaths seemed to ease the bad luck, for shortly afterward the men had taken two caribou. But it was on that same hunting trip that they had met a man from another band, who spoke of a strange new sickness he had seen in a camp far to the south. All its people were dead. And it was said that there was a whole race of shamans appearing in the south, who carried fire and thunder in long sticks. Twelve days after the men came back, the spots broke out on Raven's second wife.

Somehow the survivors had lived through until the spring break-up. But there was no more food. Soon they would be boiling every scrap of skin, including the tattered hide tent, to get what meagre nourishment it contained. The surviving dog had barely enough meat to give one hunter the strength he needed for a day's journey.

And then, ten days ago, the hope of the band had been revived by the shaman's abrupt departure to his place up the river. His old mother revealed that he had gone to fast and lacerate himself, until he gained the power to overcome the spell. And now that he had returned their spirits rose high. As the men armed themselves and painted the symbols of their dreams on bodies and weapons, they told their women what the shaman had said. It was a Nahani sorcerer, the dream told him, who had cast the spell—and he had failed to break it because of *Raven's Nahani wife.*

Now they could act. For they knew of a small Nahani camp of three lodges, a mere twenty miles distant over the hills. Unknown to the women the shaman had fed the raiders from a secret hoard of food, kept for such an emergency, and so they would have strength for the task. Tonight they would travel under a full moon until they reached their stations around the sleeping camp. With the first grey light of dawn they would strike. The Nahani men, groping for their weapons, would die first, then the screaming women and sleep-heavy children, till the last babe lay quiet in its own blood. Then the distant shaman, wherever his magic might take him, would learn that his power had been broken. And the dreadful power of their own shaman would grow, increasing the sinister reputation of all Slave shamans who—as everyone knew—were feared the world over.

In the events that followed, it would seem to the little band that this savage raid had been justified. Inevitably spring would come, releasing the icebound streams, thawing the frozen beaver lodges, wakening the hibernating bear. Spawning fish would swarm, berries would ripen, and babies would be born who would grow to replace the victims of disease and winter scarcity.

Six of the band had died and a dozen of its Nahani neighbours in the next valley had been slain. Quite unconsciously, the band had followed an inexorable law of nature: that when game is over-hunted, the human population must decline — by disease, starvation, or warfare. In this instance, all three alternatives had operated and drastically tipped the ecological balance. Next winter, barring unpredictable natural disasters, there would be food enough and to spare for all the survivors.

The Slaves were widely feared for their sorcery, but it was the Kutchin who were reputed to be the most implacable raiders. Proud of bearing and picturesquely attired, they were said to have taken the war path in so fierce a mood that they systematically slaughtered every living creature they encountered on the way. If the report is true, this slaughter was probably a kind of ritual to build their confidence for the raid. Here is how Hearne describes a raid by a group of Chipewyan and Yellowknife, led by Matonabbee, on an Eskimo camp on the Coppermine River.

"Finding all the Eskimaux quiet in their tents, they rushed forth from their ambushcade. . . . The poor unhappy victims were surprised in the midst of their sleep, and had neither time nor power to make any resistance; men, women, and children, in all upward of twenty, ran out of their tents stark naked, and endeavoured to make their escape; but the Indians having possession of all the landside, to no place could they fly for shelter. . . .

"The shrieks and groans of the poor expiring wretches were truly dreadful; and my horror was much increased at seeing a young girl, seemingly about eighteen years of age, killed so near me, that when the first spear was stuck into her side she fell down at my feet and twisted round my legs, so that it was with difficulty that I could disengage myself from her dying grasps. As two Indian men pursued this unfortunate victim, I solicited very hard for her life; but the murderers made no reply till they had stuck both their spears through her body, and transfixed her to the ground. They then looked me sternly in the face, and began to ridicule me, by asking if I wanted an Eskimaux wife; and paid not the slightest regard to the shrieks and agony of the poor wretch, who was twining round their spears like an eel!"

The raid had been carefully planned, and after the Eskimo band had been destroyed, the Athapascans conducted an elaborate cleansing ritual that probably indicated the seriousness with which they had undertaken the attack. None of those who had killed, said Hearne, were allowed to cook anything either for themselves or for others. They would eat out of no dish but their own and, before they ate, they used a red ochre to paint their cheeks and the space between their nose and chin. This ceremony continued before each meal, even after they returned to their families. Nor would the raiders kiss their wives and children, as they considered themselves in a state of uncleanness. After winter set in, all those who had shed blood made a fire some distance from the encampment and threw into it "all their ornaments, pipe-stems and dishes". Only then were they cleansed of their act.

Family Roles and Skills

But these were grim men, and they lived in a grim world, in which the margin of survival was narrow. This may explain why it was that on such occasions the milk of human kindness could turn so sour. Stories are told of the old days when an Athapascan woman would pause beside the trail to deliver her baby unaided, then hurry along to rejoin her band in camp at nightfall. In such a situation she would brace each foot against a tree and her back against a third to assist in bearing down. More normally, however, she would have the help of two women, one of whom sat behind to support her, the other sitting in front so the mother in labour could pull on her shoulders. As we have seen, an infant born

in critical times might be strangled; but when food was plentiful, children were wanted and loved with the typical warmth and tolerance of Amerindians everywhere.

Babies were carried by the Kutchin with the help of a broad band of caribou skin, elaborately embroidered. Yellowknife, Dogrib, and some Kutchin adopted the custom of their Eskimo neighbours and put their babies inside tunics that were made oversize for the purpose. In either case the baby's effluents were looked after by a generous wad of sphagnum tied to its bottom. A majority of the northern Athapascans used soft leather moss-bags to carry their infants, for the cradle-board appeared only in lands bordering Cree territory. All Athapascan women were extraordinarily skilful basket-makers, expert at sewing tailored garments, and talented at moosehair and porcupine-quill embroidery.

The only colour in a woman's life of drudgery — outside of the satisfaction she got from her special skills — was the excitement of being snatched from her husband by another man. But this was unlikely unless —as in the case of the "Dog-ribbed" woman—she was young, resourceful, and childless. As she aged and weakened, to the point where she could no longer keep up with the moving band, she could be left to die on the trail, like a wornout moccasin. And women aged

*Survival in a grim world: swimming caribou were
sometimes hunted from canoes.*

rapidly in this strenuous life, hauling wood and water, carrying heavy loads or dragging them in winter, and endlessly scraping the caribou hides that were in constant demand for a hundred purposes.

Mackenzie gives us a glimpse of Beaver women on the trail. "Except for a few dogs, they alone perform that labour which is allotted to beasts of burthen in other countries. It is not uncommon, while the men carry nothing but a gun, that their wives and daughters follow with such weighty burdens, that if they lay them down they cannot replace them . . . so that during their journeys they are frequently obliged to lean against a tree for a small portion of temporary relief." Even in bereavement, while the women tore out handfuls of hair and cut off fingers at the joint, the men merely gashed themselves superficially with beaver-tooth knives.

Yet Mackenzie also pays tribute to the strenuous nature of the male role. "These men," he writes, "are excellent hunters, and their exercise in that capacity is so violent as to reduce them in general to a very meagre appearance." In some tribes, too, the man's duties extended beyond hunting. Among the Slave people it was not considered shameful for a man to help his wives with carrying and lifting, and Kutchin males actually took over the cooking! Nor did the woman's hard lot brutalize or degrade her to the extent that we might expect, for Kutchin women brought the art of quill embroidery to the highest pitch of perfection achieved in any tribe in Canada.

Mackenzie admired the ways in which the Athapascans used hide, roots, and fibres. "They have snares made of green skin," he said, "which they cut to the size of sturgeon twine, and twist a certain number of them together; and though when completed they do not exceed the thickness of a cod-line, their strength is sufficient to hold a moose-deer. . . . Their nets and fishing lines are made of willow bark and nettles; those made of the latter are finer and smoother than if made with hempen thread." Above all, he was impressed with the baskets they made from split spruce roots, or *watape*. "Their kettles are also made of watape, which is so closely woven that they never leak, and they heat water in them, by putting red-hot stones into it." Another type of cooking vessel, in which hot stones were also used, was made of spruce bark. This, too, was the bark employed by the Sekani in constructing canoes up to eighteen feet long. Later they adopted the more durable birchbark.

Magic in Life and Death

Few other people on the continent lived in such constant fear of bewitchment. Any unusual sickness or death was explained as the sorcery of an enemy. And it was up to the shaman to track down its source and take appropriate counter-measures. Hearne offers us some striking examples. Sceptical of Chipewyan medical practices, he once spied a shaman privately shaping a short board with an unusual end-piece. The following day, the same man announced that he would shove a long board with an identical end-piece down his throat. Watching closely from a privileged position, Hearne saw the naked shaman seemingly push the long board an incredible distance down his throat. Although Hearne was positive that somehow, in the uncertain light, the six assistants had managed to substitute the shorter board for the longer, he had to concede that he was completely baffled as to how they had done it.

In this case, the shaman was attempting to cure a patient who "had been hauled on a sledge by his brother for two months. His disorder was a dead palsy, which affected one side, from the crown of his head to the sole of his foot. . . . He was reduced to a mere skeleton, and so weak as to be scarcely capable of talking." For three days and four nights, the five men and one old woman who assisted at the swallowing rite continued to "suck, blow, sing and dance, round the poor paralytic", without taking any food or even drinking water. At the end of this period, Hearne was astonished to see that the patient was able to move the toes and fingers of his paralysed side. Three weeks later he was walking, and at the end of six weeks he was hunting for his family. Frequently thereafter he appeared at Fort Prince of Wales, although Hearne felt that "he never had a healthy look afterwards and at times seemed troubled with a nervous complaint."

Equally remarkable is Hearne's account of his own dabbling in sorcery. Matonabbee had always been convinced that Hearne was a shaman, but was too sly to admit it. He kept urging Hearne to show his power and, at the same time, to get rid of an enemy of Matonabbee's. The persistence of his guide finally wore Hearne down, so that he agreed at last to try. On a sheet of paper, he drew a figure to represent the enemy, and one of himself pointing a bayonet at the enemy's chest. In the background of his drawing, he added a tree with a large eye drawn on it and a hand protruding to one side. The delighted Matonabbee took the paper with him on his next inland trip, showing it around wherever he went. When he returned with his furs the next year, he informed Hearne that the enemy "was in perfect health when he heard of my design against him; but immediately afterwards became quite gloomy, and refusing all kind of sustenance, in a very few days died."

A single death might set a whole band to making extravagant demonstrations of grief. Mackenzie came across one band of Beaver "who were absolutely starving with cold and hunger. They had lately lost a near relation, and had, according to custom, thrown away everything belonging to them." And if it became clear that the shaman was powerless to deal with a crisis, a

161

kind of collective despair might settle over a whole band. Individuals would meet the ailments of old age and the prospect of death with this same kind of passivity. But when death was slow and food was scarce, an old man might put a noose around his own neck and calmly wait for a close relative to jerk it tight.

In a land where long migrations were often necessary, and the ground was frozen for nine months or more of the year, a corpse might be covered with nothing more than some snow and brush. For less important members of the band, like Raven's two wives, no more than this was done at any time of the year. The central Athapascans placed their more important dead in grave-houses or cached them—Algonkian style — in trees. The Kutchin, and perhaps the Sekani, burned their dead. When this was done, the ashes were put in bags and tied to the tops of painted poles. But more notable persons were placed in tree coffins, to be taken down and burned after the flesh had rotted away.

From Pelts to Petroleum

The huge territory over which the Athapascans roamed was the ideal beaver habitat, and at an early date became the prime territory of the fur trade. Even today, although beaver has lost its primacy, the superior quality of all northern furs, and the remoteness of many bands, supports a trapping economy for many Athapascans. Fort McPherson, for example, is still a centre for prime muskrat that are trapped in the multiple channels and numerous backwaters of the nearby Mackenzie delta.

Despite the fact that the Hudson's Bay Company had sent Hearne in the early 1770s to establish contact with the inland Athapascans, fur traders from Montreal soon gained dominance in the heart of Athapascan territory. Reacting to this, Hudson's Bay traders established rival posts at select locations and competed with the men of the North West Company for the prime pelts of the southern Athapascans.

As had been the case elsewhere, contact with the Europeans transformed the lives of the Amerindians. Smallpox decimated the bands, and trade guns altered their territories. Once the Beaver got guns, for example, they held back Cree attacks from the east, and pushed westward into Sekani territory. And so, when Mackenzie went up the Peace River, he had great difficulty in contacting the Sekani, who had become demoralized because of Beaver attacks. And yet Sekani weapons were probably sufficient to repel the Beaver raids, as these tough mountaineers used Russian trade iron to tip their arrows and had bows of sinew and wood that were strong enough to slay the grizzly bear. The noise and flash of the trade guns, however, had convinced them that they were doomed.

When the North West Company and the Hudson's Bay Company amalgamated in 1820, the southern Athapascans could no longer profit by playing off one rival trader against another. In the meantime, an Athapascan economy that used to be based on independent hunting had become centred on trapping and European trade posts. Polygamy declined, and the bands tended to develop more permanent settlements. And yet, until recent times, much of the territory of the Athapascans was too remote to feel the full impact of industrial society.

Interest in northern copper had been one of the major reasons for Hearne's explorations in the early 1770s, and the Yellowknife had been named after the copper knives which they traded to neighbouring tribes. In 1898, the discovery of gold in Kutchin territory had brought a rush of miners to the Dawson City region. But until the advent of aircraft, it was not possible to confirm many of the early reports of major mineral bodies in the far north. Since 1928, when the Northern Aerial Mineral Explorations Company sent its first bush planes into the arctic, air travel and transport has been opening the whole land to industrial exploitation. And recent interest in the undeveloped mineral and oil resources of the world has accelerated plans for developing the resource potential of the far north. The presence of major mineral bodies and oil fields has recently been confirmed, and modern technology makes it possible to establish a mining community anywhere in the far north.

Roads now creep northwards, accelerated by the shifting of the administrative centre of the Northwest Territories from Fort Smith to Yellowknife. Since the Second World War, the Alcan Highway to Alaska has crossed Nahani territory, while plans for oil and gas pipelines call for the opening of a resource transportation system through the heart of Athapascan homelands. But both environmentalists and natives fear that the ecology of the region could be disrupted, for it is known that a single tractor trail can erode the soil down to the permafrost level, upsetting the growth cycle of the lichens and moss of the adjacent tundra and muskeg for decades. And so even the most remote Hare, Kutchin, Nahani, and Chipewyan bands have not long to wait before they are confronted with the most rigorous test of tribal adaptability they have faced in all the thousands of years they have survived in their harsh homeland.

11 Sea-Mammal and Caribou Hunters of the Arctic Coasts and Interior

A Merciless and Unpredictable Land

Near the north shore of Ellesmere Island, a bare 580 miles south of the North Pole, there lies a body of water roughly twice the size of Lake Nipissing — Hazen Lake. Here an archaeologist working for the National Museum of Man found evidence of an Eskimo tragedy that took place five centuries ago. Under the gathered tent stones of what had been a summer dwelling, he found the remains of an Eskimo hunter. On the stone sleeping platform of a winter dwelling site near by, he found all that the arctic wolves had left of a woman's skeleton. If there had been children, no trace of them remained.

Around A.D. 1400, this couple had ventured far inland from their usual summer hunting grounds on the east shore of Ellesmere, to discover for themselves an uninhabited fishing and hunting paradise. Even now the outlet of Hazen Lake is open throughout the winter, offering an abundance of fat arctic char for the taking. And in 1400, the climate was somewhat warmer, so that a valley over the nearest ridge offered a winter haven for musk-ox and caribou. To the man and his wife, as they cleaned out and rebuilt a house site already a century old, it must have seemed a wondrous place.

But they lived in a merciless and unpredictable land. The man died—as to how or why no clues were found. His wife buried him under the stones and lived on alone for a few months or a few years. Finally in the darkness of an arctic winter, the flame above the moss wick of her soapstone lamp flickered out. With neither oil nor fat for food, nor fuel with which to boil the skins she might have spared for food, she was doomed. And so she died, knowing no help would come—but knowing, too, as the cold slowly numbed her senses, that death would be gentle with her.

But the survival of this family for so long, in a seemingly impossible environment, is more significant than its eventual death. The Eskimo — or *Inuit*, as they prefer to call themselves—are an eloquent witness to the incredible adaptability of the human species. No people elsewhere on this planet have faced and overcome — even at intervals *enjoyed* — the living conditions of so harsh a land.

Throughout a nine-month winter, the million square miles of the high arctic is a bleak waste of snow, ice, and rocks, swept by winds that are drier than the air of the Sahara and blizzards that are more dangerous to man than a desert dust storm. In September the sun barely skims the southern horizon, in October twilight falls over the white wastes, and by January the only lights that relieve the long darkness are the pale glow of the full moon and the fitful, rustling glimmer of the Northern Lights.

Yet when spring returns and the sun reappears, the exact reverse occurs, so that even at night there is no real darkness, and by summer the sun never sets. Then, as the weather warms, the slow thawing of the permafrost provides ample moisture for the grasses, sedges, mosses, and lichens of the treeless tundra. Along the watercourses the willows, and dwarf varieties of a few other tree species, root in the shallow soil. Briefly, in the arctic meadows, a profusion of arctic flowers blooms. And over great stretches of gravel-strewn terrain, as well as on the exposed bedrock itself, a hardy lichen known as "reindeer moss" provides the basic food for vast herds of caribou. Here, too, the sturdy musk-ox grazes—a lingering relic of the Pleistocene mammals that roamed the tundra of the Ice Age. The herds of both caribou and musk-ox have dwindled, but geese and swans still nest in countless numbers on the shores of innumerable shallow lakes. And the icy meltwater, as it rushes and pauses on its way to the sea, teems with whitefish, lake trout, pike, grayling, and arctic char. Nowhere in the world are ocean shores inhabited by so many species of sea mammals: white whale, narwhal, walrus, polar bear, and five kinds of seal, while the sea-cliffs are white with the droppings of millions of sea-birds. Inland, the arctic fox still preys on hare, lemming, mouse, and ptarmigan, while the wolf of the tundra trails herds of arctic deer, alert for the faltering straggler.

The Ancestors

Investigations into the prehistory of the arctic are complicated by the likelihood that evidence of early sea-mammal hunters, who may have camped along ocean shores, are now under many fathoms of water. For during the Wisconsin Ice Age the coastline extended far beyond its present limits, and in post-glacial times the rising water probably drowned out many significant sites.

Present knowledge suggests that early arctic cultures, known as *pre-Dorset*, were found on the arctic coast of the Yukon as early as 3500 B.C. Bands of pre-Dorset people arrived in the eastern arctic some 2,000 years later, and developed a *Dorset* culture unique to the region. One of the features of this culture was a semi-subterranean house, built by clearing stones to make a depression in a rocky area and stretching a skin roof over this. Viking records talk of people who "lived in caves or holes in the ground", and some Norse scholars have suggested that the intermarriage of such Dorset peoples with settlers in Greenland created the next culture to emerge in the high arctic, the *Thule*. But remains of a Thule culture have been found in Alaska, and the date given for the site is 100 years before the Vikings arrived in the Canadian arctic. It is currently thought that the Thule culture originated in Alaska, and arrived in the east about a century before the last Greenland settlements of the Vikings disappeared.

It is not certain where the events took place that are described in the *Saga of Eric the Red*, and they may, or may not, be records of Viking contacts with Canadian Eskimo. The first unmistakable record of European contact comes from Martin Frobisher in 1576. He met nineteen natives on the Labrador coast who were "like to Tartars, with long black hair, broad faces, and flat noses, and tawny in colour, wearing seal-skins". Farther north, in the bay named after him, he "perceived a number of small things floating in the sea far off, which he supposed to be porpoises or seals, or some kind of strange fish; but coming nearer, he discovered them to be men in small boats made of leather." Five of Frobisher's men went ashore to visit an Eskimo camp and were never seen again, and this suggests that any previous contacts with strangers, whether Icelandic settlers or ancestral Naskapi, had taught the Inuit to distrust aliens. According to Peter Freuchen "the cry of 'Indians!' in an isolated Greenland settlement could throw the inhabitants into a state of senseless panic, and this was true even though the word had lost its meaning to them hundreds of years before!"

Such an extraordinary statement becomes somewhat less incredible when we recall Hearne's harrowing account of the Coppermine raid. But the fear was not all one-sided. In 1789, as Mackenzie was descending the river named after him, an Athapascan told him that the Eskimo "are very wicked and will kill us all, that it is but two summers since a great Party of them came up this river and killed a number of his Relations." In 1834, Captain Back was told the same kind of thing. Later, when Back passed an Inuit camp on the lower stretches of the Great Fish River, the women and children of the Eskimo began to "howl with fear", while the men came down to the shore making threatening gestures. Even after they had passed the camp without making any attempt to land, the shaman of the band followed them "imitating the growling and motion of a bear, bending himself and walking on his hands and knees, thinking, no doubt, to charm us away".

New Perspectives on an Ancient People

The *Mackenzie Eskimo* were the westernmost Canadian group, living on the shores of the arctic in the neighbourhood of the Mackenzie River delta. To the east were another coastal people, the *Copper Eskimo*, in the area of Coronation Gulf and Victoria Island. Baffin Island, and the adjacent islands of the Arctic Archipelago, were the homelands of the *Central Eskimo*, while, as we saw in the opening paragraphs of the chapter, the *Polar Eskimo* crossed over from Greenland to spend the summer hunting on Ellesmere Island. South of them, on the mainland of North

America, were the *Labrador Eskimo*, ranging along the coastline from James Bay through Hudson Strait and down the Atlantic seaboard as far south as Newfoundland and the interior of Ungava. The only Inuit who spent most of their time inland were the *Caribou Eskimo*, who ranged the arctic prairies north of present-day Manitoba, between the treeline and the arctic coast, west of Hudson Bay.

Life in the high arctic has astonishing variety and abundance, both on sea and on land. But living here is precarious, for abundance can be followed by scarcity. Survival would have been impossible for the Inuit without the presence of two animals and the help of a third: the seal and the caribou, whose meat, fat, and hide fed, warmed, and clothed him, and the dog, whose keen scent aided the search for food and whose endurance and obedience made possible the long winter treks on which the Eskimo's survival depended.

But so much emphasis has been put on the Inuit ability to survive an arctic winter that the popular image of an Eskimo stresses igloos, sled dogs, and winter wastes. And when the Eskimo is not imagined cracking his whip over the backs of his huskies, he is seen paddling a kayak among the ice floes, in pursuit of seal or walrus. If the word "Indian" suggests feathers and war paint, the word "Eskimo" calls to mind ice, snow, and seal blubber.

Like all popular images, this picture is distorted. In his public lectures, the arctic explorer Vilhjalmur Stefansson continually emphasized the fact that Pacific air currents moderated temperatures in the western arctic, so that minimum winter temperatures there were no lower than on the Saskatchewan and Dakota prairies where he grew up. Igloos were unknown to some bands, and were used only for winter travel by others. Far more typical was the caribou-skin tent that all the bands used in summer. And while the majority of Inuit were coast people, depending for their food on sea-mammal hunting, they moved inland during the summer to hunt the caribou, one of the most important natural resources of their way of life.

Arctic survival required light, warm clothing, and the hide of the caribou was ideal for this. When the tough, light-weight hide was sewn into clothes with the hair inwards, the slivers of air trapped within each filament provided excellent insulation. As a bonus, a caribou carcass produced meat, sinew thread, and a kind of spring salad of half-digested green fodder that was found in the stomach. This latter food was an Inuit delicacy that he could get in no other way, for the high arctic provides few edible plants.

If starvation threatened a band, caribou hide could be eaten. On one occasion, Stefansson reported, his party had nothing to eat but a bag of seal oil, which they had difficulty keeping down and which had little effect on their hunger. To give it "body", they tried various combinations: tea leaves, ptarmigan feathers, and caribou hair. "Most commonly," he said, "we took long-haired caribou skin [boiled with the hair on], cut it into small pieces, dipped the pieces in oil, and ate them as a sort of salad." "Fresh raw hide," he added, "is good eating, it reminds one of pigsfeet if well boiled." And the Anglican missionary, Bishop Bompas, is celebrated for having survived one crisis by eating his boots!

So the summer months were spent inland, for an Eskimo family required many caribou hides to survive. The way an Inuit family lived then can be glimpsed by following one group into the caribou grazing grounds of the arctic hinterland.

It is near the end of June. All through the "night" the orange ball of the midnight sun has skimmed the northern horizon. Now it is slanting its way imperceptibly higher above the broad expanse of ice that stretches beyond the grey horizon of Foxe Basin, touching with pink the bleached hide of the caribou-skin tent pitched behind the gravel ridge above the boulder-strewn beach. There is no sign of life, except for a single dog that has risen from his slumbering fellows to sniff in a desultory way at the circle of stones that holds the tent cover to the ground. Hours pass before the tent flap is flung aside and a stocky, middle-aged man emerges, hawking and spitting to clear his throat of the night phlegm, sniffing the air, scanning the sky expertly, and nodding his head. A good day to travel.

Leisurely, through the following hour, but with easy efficiency, poles and hides are rolled into long, stiff bundles. The grandmother packs the few precious possessions that cannot be improvised at need: the oxhorn spoon, flint ulus and skin scrapers, bone awls, and needles and thimbles, and a few strands of dried caribou sinew that were all that remained of the previous summer's supply. The mother, while her baby nurses at her breast, chews the stiffness out of the uppers of the sealskin *kamiks* she has just finished for her eight-year-old daughter. The little girl is greedily drinking the last of the fish stew from the soapstone cooking pot as her grandmother waits patiently for her to finish, so that she can wrap the pot carefully in softened caribou hide and pack it in a skin bag. The girl's brother, only two years older, is tightening the pack on a dog as big as himself. The man gathers together his hunting bow, quiver of stone-tipped arrows, and bone-handled stone knives, a bag of partly worked flint blanks, and a new fishing leister that he had finished in the light that was still ample for the task the "night" before. His daughter and son-in-law, both still in their teens, pile the rocks higher over the cache in which the family's winter equipment has been stored.

169

Soon the family is moving over the tundra: the men ranging ahead with their lighter loads, alert for the first signs of caribou, the heavily laden women, dogs, and children following. Hour after hour they tramp south-westward, wading the ice-bottomed pools, fording swift, shallow streams, climbing the occasional gravel ridge of an esker that breaks the flat landscape. Far ahead now, as the sun slopes westward, the hunters spy the wide, boulder-strewn stream they planned to reach. Arriving, they repair a stone fish-trap in the rushing, crystal-clear water, and by the time the family has arrived a dozen silvery grayling lie gasping on the ground. Now the hunter strikes sparks from two pieces of pyrites into a nest of dry arctic cotton, whirls the smouldering fluff in his hand at arm's length, and as it bursts into flame tucks it quickly under a handful of dry twigs he has snatched from nearby shrubs. The women add larger sticks that they have gathered along the way, and the fire blazes up, crackling cheerfully.

As the sun lingers over the horizon to the north and the air chills, the family sits close to the little fire, taking the edge off their hunger with partially cooked fish while the rest boils in the skin pot, heated with stones from the fire. There is laughing as the little girl draws streaks of black charcoal across the baby's face in imitation of the mother's cheek tattoos, and jokes flow freely. Tonight they smell again the sweet wood smoke of the tundra shrubs. And tomorrow, perhaps, they will sight the first distant grey forms of the migrating caribou.

To such families the annual migration patterns would be well known, and the fording places or narrows between lakes where the caribou swim across would be populated with relatives and friends, some of whom they might not have seen for two or three years. Such groups worked together, piling stones to guide the herds into pounds, or ambushing the animals and slaying them with arrow or spear at the crossing places. While the herds passed there were long days of slaughter, butchering, feasting — and the eternal scraping and curing of green hides that would be converted into new tent coverings, sleeping bags, and warm winter clothing. And, as the herds moved on, the camp was moved in pursuit and a growing burden of hides weighed down the band.

Even if fuel had been plentiful in their wood-scarce land, the Eskimo would still have needed to eat a proportion of the fish and flesh raw, for the vitamins the uncooked meat contained. Wild fruit was scanty, and the main source of vegetable vitamins was the half-digested lichen in the caribou's stomachs, for which the Inuit had an uncontrollable craving in the spring. Cooked or raw, frozen, fresh or ripe, meat was the staple diet. When there was plenty, the Eskimo gorged himself into a stupor. When food was scarce, his seemingly inexhaustible good humour sustained him as he searched for new supplies.

Mid-August brought the first snow-flurries and some respite from the hordes of hungry mosquitoes — even more predatory than their southern cousins — that plagued the warmer days. Soon the caribou would be moving south and the long wedges of migrating geese would be passing overhead. Waking one morning to find a skin of ice over a nearby pond, the hunter would know that summer was gone and he must lead his family across the whitening plains toward his cache on the coast.

Winter on the Arctic Coast

By December in the high arctic only a faint glow on the southern horizon would hint that the sun still existed. But even under the low sun in the brief hours of daylight, the arctic air is so clear and dry that light reflected from the snow can be too intense for the unshielded eye. Hence the Eskimo protected himself against snow-blindness with a wooden device that fitted over the nose and eyes with mere slits to see through.

The arctic night can be black indeed, and yet through the long winter the stars are brilliant: northern lights cast their weird, shifting light, and the moon remains above the horizon for more than a week.

As winter deepens even the ocean disappears under a thick crust of ice, and snow merges land and sea together into one endless desert of white. At sea the new ice cracks and buckles into rough, high pressure ridges, with huge up-ended ice blocks confronting Eskimo dogs and sledge. Or the slow tides beneath and changing winds above may open up wide "leads" with treacherous speed, into which an Eskimo may watch his sled and dogs with all his worldly goods vanish. As the days lengthen and the ocean slowly warms, a mile-wide ice floe may split off from the shore ice without warning, to drift far out to sea, bearing an unlucky hunting party to its doom.

In this perilous world the Eskimo was as much at home as the urban Canadian is on his highways and city streets. Far out on the frozen ocean an Eskimo village of sixty souls might shelter and feed themselves through months of sub-zero weather. For under the ice swam and fed the warm-blooded seal, emerging at intervals through the hole it kept open in the sea-ice to breathe and rest and nourish its young on a ledge under a dome of snow. While blizzards raged and nights were day-long, it lived an untroubled life until the hunter and his dog located the breathing-hole.

In summer and fall the Eskimo hunted the sea-mammals from his kayak in open water. In this watertight, decked-in skin craft, propelled by powerful strokes of a thin-bladed double paddle, he could stalk the seal, walrus, and beluga whale. Once he had buried the head of his harpoon in the animal, he could use the attached line to play it like a fish until it tired or bled enough for him to tow it to the edge of the shore or a floe, kill it, and drag it out of the water for butchering.

Meat from such a kill could be hauled to camp in the roomy *umiak*, an open skin boat. When it was necessary to move camp, the *umiak* could transport a heavy load of children, dogs, women, and goods, and was paddled by the women and boys while the hunters fanned out ahead in their kayaks.

In the north an early nickname for Eskimo was "Husky", a name that now refers only to the Eskimo's dog. The original husky dog was a powerful animal, frequently interbred with the wolf; it could be treacherous in inexperienced hands but was managed expertly even by the Eskimo child. Always hungry and often abused, it none the less hauled the Eskimo sled, and its keen nose, rather than the eyes of the hunter, was more likely to locate the hidden breathing-hole of the seal. And then the patient hunter would remain poised and motionless hour by hour behind a snow windbreak until the slight movement of a delicately poised twig, thrust through the snow, revealed the seal's arrival. Then the harpoon struck—fast, true, and deep.

The skin of the seal made footwear, boats, and sometimes summer tents. Its bones and teeth became tools, weapons, or ornaments. Its sinew had countless uses, and even the gut might be split and sewn into plastic-like rainwear, or stretched across an igloo opening to let in the light. But it was seal flesh and fat that was the main food of almost all Eskimo bands. The fats in particular were essential for survival. Stefansson reported that an exclusive diet of lean meat produced all the symptoms of starvation, for there are elements in fat that are vital to the human body. "We had an abundance of lean meat and would boil up huge quantities and stuff ourselves with it. We ate so much that our stomachs were actually distended with it. . . . But with all this gorging we were continually hungry."

In winter, when the band must move on or perish, it was the dogs that hauled the sturdy, flexible Eskimo sled, pieced together ingeniously out of driftwood, bone, and sinew, its runners smoothed with frozen mud. The dogs fanned out on separate lines, each picking its own way over the rough ice, while the driver cracked his long braided leather whip, to flick the flank of a lazy pup or break up a fight before the lines became snarled. The family rode or ran behind, depending on their age and whether the going was easy or rough.

As they stopped to camp in the early darkness, the igloo rose with magical speed, each block expertly cut from the wind-hardened snow with a bone snow knife and fitted in an ascending and closing spiral to form a durable dome. Within, a fire was kindled in the stone lamp.

No other people on the planet depended for light, warmth, and cooking on so frail a flame as this, gleaming through the gloom of the interior from its moss wick on the edge of a pool of seal oil. Above it hung a cooking pot of stone, kept packed with melting snow until the meltwater came to a gentle boil. But a hungry family on the move rarely waited for a hot seal-meat stew. Fish and meat were frequently eaten while still frozen, and were preferred that way when raw. The eating done — whether the meal were plentiful or meagre — the family stripped to the skin and crawled naked into their fur sleeping bags, preferably with a sibling or spouse if the cold was intense. In the morning they would beat the frozen body moisture from their fur-lined underclothes, for dampness was the subtle ally of frostbite and also loosened the hair of caribou-skin clothing.

A woman's skill at sewing and mending clothes — above all her ability to sew a watertight seam — was a matter of life and death. A man might borrow a friend's wife for a long hunting trip solely on the ground that she was the band's best seamstress, and this practice benefited everyone if the hunter were successful. Freuchen's portrait of such a seamstress is worth passing on. "Like a Turkish tailor, she sits with her legs stretched out at right angles to her body, her favourite position, with her work between her toes. Her most important tool is the *ullo*—a curved knife with a handle in the middle of the blade. From intuition, she cuts the skins in their proper places and sews them together, rarely measuring anything. The furs of the blue and white fox are woven together in intricate patterns, and her work puts the finest Paris furrier to shame. With small, hardly visible stitches she weaves her narwhal sinew thread in and out until the skin pieces look as if they had grown together."

Each region had its typical cut of clothing, commonly made from caribou skin with the hair left on. Local preferences, however, or a scarcity of the customary skins might determine that the clothing of a particular band was made out of none of the usual materials. Belcher Island natives, for example, have been known to piece together garments entirely of eider duck skins. Polar bear skin was often used for pants in the high arctic, and sealskin garments predominated among people lacking an adequate supply of caribou hides. Normally, however, a man's summer suit was made of caribou, with the hair turned in. Over this went the thicker winter hide, with the hair turned out. Both suits, with local variations, consisted of *kolitak* (tunic), knee-pants, and leggings, with waterproof sealskin boots. In winter, socks of caribou skin were worn under low sealskin boots, the hair of the latter turned out. A woman's tunic was made looser than the man's to allow a baby to be breast-fed or slid around on the mother's back without being exposed to the weather. Women of the Caribou Eskimo carried their babies in a hood that was capacious enough for their head and the baby too.

Arctic travellers have learned by bitter experience that woollen clothing, no matter in how many layers, is ineffective against winter temperatures in the high arctic, especially if worn tight to the skin. Intuitively the Eskimo discovered the principle of air convection. If the cold were intense, he tightened his tunic at the neck to hold the warm body air in. If he became too hot, he had only to loosen the neck, releasing the warmer air and automatically creating an upward flow of cooler air from the loose skirt of the tunic. Belts or girdles that would have inhibited this circulation were not worn. And, better than any other known material, the skin of the caribou combines lightness with weather and chill resistance. No Eskimo was handicapped by the weight of his winter wear.

Indoors, the Eskimo of the high arctic discarded all or most of his clothing, feeling quite comfortable in air that had to be kept close to freezing point lest the walls of his dwelling melt. While blizzards raged outside, the family ate, slept, worked, or played according to need or mood. Half of the floor space was raised to form a sleeping platform which was insulated from the cold beneath by furs over which the children played with the puppies or at hunting among imaginary ice floes. The women and the girls worked endlessly at the clothes while watching the melting snow or simmering food in the cooking-pot, and tending the lamp-wick, which needed constant trimming to get a maximum of heat and minimum of smoke. Clothes needed constant care: tough sealskin had to be chewed into softness, new garments made to replace the worn ones, and pulled seams repaired to waterproof tightness. The men were just as occupied: making or repairing harpoons, bows, arrows, snow goggles, knives, needles, thimbles, charms, ornaments, and toys for the children, who were spoiled shamelessly by all the adults. The hardest stone and toughest ivory yielded to the patient skill of the carvers. And young and old spent hours of leisure twisting a loop of string between the fingers of opposing hands, to make complicated "cat's-cradles" which were so ingeniously contrived that some could imitate the forms and even the actions of animals, birds, and men.

Coming of Age in the Arctic

A boy became a man once his hunting skills had developed to the point where he could provide a wife with the food and skins they would need for survival. In the eastern arctic it was customary to make a show of

force in taking a girl to wife. The girl allowed herself to be abducted — biting, scratching, and screaming, to show all and sundry that she had no need of this particular male, as well as to show him that life with her wasn't going to be all that easy. Then there was a brief honeymoon that scarcely interrupted the exacting routine of arctic life.

When starvation threatened, the first to be sacrificed were newborn baby girls. Consequently women tended to be in short supply and a man seldom had two wives, though it was not uncommon for two men to share a single wife. This sometimes produced a comic situation in which a woman's two husbands were running and fetching for her in eager rivalry. Such polyandrous marriages could be quite successful when they were the result of an agreement between friends. And even a less friendly arrangement could be tolerated in the knowledge that a bachelor with no woman to sew his clothes—unless his mother were old and widowed — had little chance of survival. Fatness in a woman made her peculiarly attractive, indicating for all to see that the husband was a bounteous provider. A woman's "chastity" was not important in Eskimo eyes, and sex play among children was regarded with tolerant amusement by the adults. Yet once children were born, husband and wife were usually faithful to each other.

Children were spoiled, which made it easier for them to learn by imitating their elders and so acquire, through play, the sense of responsibility that was imposed on them very early, by necessity rather than parental discipline. Children's mistakes were laughed at in a tolerant way, while among adults ridicule was a major means of discouraging anti-social behaviour. The rare meetings between wandering groups always led to an exchange of gossip, and there was a great hilarity whenever the topic of conversation was the breaking of unwritten rules. For example, men and women would roll on the snow with mirth on hearing that So-and-so's husband had nearly lost his foot from frostbite because one of his boots had leaked on a hunting trip. But his wife would be deeply humiliated, and she would sew her seams with double care thereafter. No other people were so consistently cheerful, or broke into hearty laughter on such small excuses. Practical jokes were particularly popular, but usually their victim enjoyed the merriment as keenly as the others.

For human groups that are small and intimately exposed to each other for months on end, it is obviously better to take reverses and irritations with a smile than with a murderous attack. Yet it would be false to think of the Eskimo as eternally cheerful people. In the dark of winter, when storms lasted for weeks and cooking-pots were empty, quarrels often arose, and dark deeds might be performed. Blood-feuds often began with a quarrel over a woman, and could last for years. Rasmussen encountered an Eskimo band west of Boothia Peninsula whose existence had been so harsh a dozen years previously that half the girl babies had been strangled at birth. A few years later, the resulting shortage of young females brought on so many wife-robberies and murders that, Freuchen relates, "no man knew himself safe. When families of a settlement undertook a trip, they fared with their sleds in single file. No man dared to step out of this formation, even to do necessary natural business, for a man in front of him would immediately suspect foul play, and being of quick tempers they preferred to shoot first and ask questions later."

The Narrow Margins of Life

The arctic could play cruel jokes. In the early spring of 1921, according to Freuchen, a small band of Eskimo was tempted against its better judgment to "go shopping" at the newly established Hudson's Bay Post at Pond's Inlet—a mere 400 miles away. But this was the eastern arctic, where, unlike the western arctic, wood was scarce. And so they improvised a sled in an extraordinary way: runners were made out of tightly rolled caribou skin, soaked with water, and then frozen solid, while the cross-pieces were fashioned out of frozen salmon chopped to size! At night, the sleigh and provisions were cached on top of the snow huts, out of reach of the voracious dogs. But one night, at the half-way point in their journey, a sudden spring thaw made the roofs sag, the sleigh tilted down within reach of the dogs, and when the travellers emerged in the morning the bulk of their sleigh rested comfortably in the bellies of the sated dogs! Only a single woman survived the gruelling, almost provisionless trek over the 200 miles that remained.

If sickness came, the people gathered in a large snow hut made of two or three igloos merged into a big one, and watched the healing performances of their *angakok*, or shaman, who drummed and danced himself into a frenzy and mouthed syllables that were unintelligible to the awed spectators but may have been relics of an archaic language. When the performance ended, the people learned what enemy had cast a spell on the sick person, or what broken taboo had angered the invisible powers. Most feared of all was a monstrous female Sea-Being, *Telliulik*, who could change the weather unpredictably and cause the seals to vanish. When such things happened, or the caribou failed to appear at their usual crossing places, individuals might be inspired — in the absence of their shaman — to literally dream up rites or charms to meet the emergency. Like other Amerindians, the Inuit were convinced of the reality of their dream experiences. Stefansson, discussing this with an Eskimo companion, was told that "If you remember on waking that you have dreamed about things at a great distance it is because your eyes have actually been there while you were asleep." He also relates an instance when an informant, after describing in detail the rites for dealing with a critical childbirth, warned him that he must not try to practise the rite until he "possessed" it. The Eskimo enabled him to do this by transferring possession to a stick, and then instructing Stefansson to pick it up.

The aged met death with a special dignity, of which Freuchen gives us a glimpse in a vivid piece of fact-based fiction. Weakening on the trail, the grandmother takes her son aside and tells him her time has come. But he protests vehemently and she agrees to go on. A day or two later, however, it is clear that her slowness on the trail, even her weight on the sleigh, are becoming a threat to the family's survival.

" 'My son,' she says, as they camp that night, 'now I have words that are firm, and which you must not contradict. My years are many, and my legs are tired. Build me an igloo.' "

So after the family igloo has been built and the wife and children are settled in it, the son builds his mother a second small snow house. That night she moves in with her personal possessions, taking only the oldest skins to make her bed.

"Night passed," relates Freuchen, "and when it was dawn . . . she heard them get up out there, heard them prepare the sled, and she followed everything in her thoughts. Now the dogs were rushing into the deserted igloo to eat the garbage. Now they strapped the load on the sled, and the children wanted to know if Grandmamma had walked on ahead. She heard that, too, and she heard the sled drive away. . . .

"And darkness came, and night closed about her. Old Naterk had been born, and had lived, and now her life had come to an end."

Two Technologies Meet

In spite of the fact that some Eskimo bands had been in contact with European explorers and American whalers for more than a century, the invading culture made little impact until the 1930s, when the arctic fox began to command high prices on the market and Hudson's Bay posts were established at strategic points in the high arctic. Then the usual effect of the fur trade on native society set in. With the Second World War the impact escalated. Along the DEW line, American bases hired Eskimo hunters as labourers and bulldozer operators. For a few years a gold mine at Rankin Inlet employed Eskimo as miners, housing them in modern buildings with full facilities. At Frobisher a large air base was built and maintained on the route to Europe — until the jet plane made it obsolete — and the local Eskimo camped near by to find casual employment and

178

a rich harvest of unused food in the garbage pails of the wasteful newcomers. Through the 1950s an alarming decline in the caribou population west of Hudson Bay threatened the inland Eskimo with starvation, and they were moved out to the coast where they could be housed and fed on welfare.

Two factors have modified the savage onslaught of the modern world on the morale and life style of the Eskimo. One is their apparent talent for three-dimensional thinking, which has emerged as an aptitude for mechanics and a special skill in sculpture. The second is the respect their art has won for them throughout the world.

Early in the 1950s, James Houston, a Canadian artist, was sent to Cape Dorset to encourage the Eskimo there to try their hand at soapstone sculpture. Although the Inuit had previously shown great skill at shaping bone, ivory, and stone into miniature forms for charms and ornaments, they had shown no interest in carving larger forms. Now, however, the whole band crowded into the little co-operative workshop at Cape Dorset and began to produce pieces of stone sculpture that in a few years were in demand around the globe. Co-operative workshops were set up in other Eskimo communities with such success that the more skilful sculptors were earning more by their art than by trapping. A Japanese technique of print-making was adapted to Inuit art with equal success. Recently, a whole range of Eskimo arts and crafts have been successfully marketed. But whether the superb sculpture of the Inuit can be maintained as the young people are detached from intimate knowledge of arctic life remains to be seen. It is encouraging, though, that their art has won them respect in far places, and in the government agencies that are attempting to ease their transition from the Stone Age to the Age of Technology. An additional reason for hope is that the Eskimo are native to an environment that southern Canadians find difficult to adjust to. Through on-the-job training, the Inuit could well provide a majority of the technicians required for the operation and maintenance of mining and oil-drilling equipment.

One of the grimmest effects of twentieth-century technology has been unintentional: the influence of radio-active fallout on arctic lichens. An important source of nutrients for these peculiar plants is the air itself, and their growth is so slow that they can accumulate radio-activity over years instead of a single growing season. Reindeer moss is such a lichen, and is the favourite forage of the caribou. Experiments on caribou show that, as a result of the testing of nuclear devices, the radio-active contamination of their meat had reached *ten times* what is thought to be the safe limit for man. The effect of this on the Eskimo has not been measured in Canada, but both Laplanders and Alaskans have been found to have absorbed dangerous levels of bone Strontium-90.

Equally serious is the increasing impact of resource development on the far north. Substantial oil and gas reserves have been discovered in the western arctic, and huge deposits of iron ore on Baffin Island. Inevitably the ancient hunting culture of the Inuit will pass into history. And already the prospect that pipelines could disturb the fragile balance of arctic ecology, coupled with the menace of oil spills in arctic waters, has raised grave doubts about the future. It will tax all the ingenuity and wisdom of the federal government, in consultation with the native people, to save those Eskimo bands that have not already been degraded from the fate of their Amerindian cousins to the south.

12 Aliens in Their Native Land

A Reservation at Mid-Century

It is a sunny day in midsummer of the year 1950. A Canadian family is driving along a section of the Trans-Canada Highway that passes through an Indian Reserve.

The grandfather, returning for the first time to the place where he had lived as a boy — the son of the mission school teacher — stares out in dismay and disbelief. His grandchildren see youngsters of their own age in shabby, ill-fitting hand-me-downs, playing listlessly by the roadside. They see the run-down shacks or sagging cabins and weed-grown yards, while visions of tipis and feathered savages fade. "Where," they ask their grandfather, "are the *real* Indians?"

But the grandfather is as confused and disappointed as they. In the place of the neat log cabins on the lake shore that he had known are these wretched dwellings on the highway. Women who would have been drying fish or smoking meat on wooden racks over an open fire are pumping an old, hand-powered washing machine in the yard, or carrying a parcel of groceries along the dusty shoulder of the highway. Youths who might have been stretching new canvas on a damaged canoe lean over the hood of a dilapidated car while one of them tinkers with the engine, regardless of the fact that three of the four tires are flat and there is only one headlight.

The family turns onto the ungraded Reserve road and drives down to the lake shore. The water level, dammed high to supply power for the nearby pulp and paper mill, had drowned out the sweeping curve of the beach that the grandfather knew, and partially flooded the old mission graveyard. The little white mission church is gone. So is the old Hudson's Bay trading post, 181 established more than a century ago, that used to stand a mile down the shore.

The family walks over to the graveyard, weed-grown and neglected, its picketed grave enclosures, with rotting, hand-carved corner posts all askew. The grandfather points to a few marble tombstones dated in the 1920s, when fur was plentiful and prices so high that the better trappers could pay to have expensive stones freighted in from the city 800 miles away. He points, too, to pathetic little graves almost lost in the bushes. Dimly discernible on the cracked, weather-beaten grave posts are the names and ages of four children of the same family — all under six — and the grim words carved below: "DIED OF T.B."

A girl in her mid-teens comes down to the rickety dock to dip a pail of drinking water from the lake. "Ahnde John Keezhik?" the grandfather asks her, using her own language to break the barrier of her shyness. "He's died," she says, so faintly he can barely hear her answer. What does her father do, he inquires. "He cut pulp sometime." Her brother, the family learns, worked in the pulp mill for a while, "but he get laid off." The grandfather questions her in her own language, but she invariably answers in English. She was sixteen when she reached Grade Six in school; then she dropped out to get married. Her husband operates a bulldozer for a construction company. Her eyes shine

and her voice is stronger as she tells them: "He does good. He's got a car now." They have a little daughter who is sick. When the grandfather asks her why she doesn't answer him in Indian, she explains, "I don't talk Indian too good."

Back in the car again the family drives out to the highway, then slows down to view a neat cluster of buildings: the government day-school, a small hospital, and the Council house — all freshly painted, although the grass needs cutting.

Soon they enter the bustling paper town with its trim houses, paved main street, and smart new shopping centre. As they sit around the table in a small restaurant they are all depressed about their visit to the Reserve. The children feel cheated. What had happened to the paint and feathers, the picturesque wigwams? Why, they want to know, are the Indians so poor? The mother blames the government for not spending more money. The father blames the Indians for not being more ambitious.

But the grandfather is buried in memories of the happy, hard-working, fun-loving people he had known fifty years ago. He remembers the last fur brigade before the railway came in, when twenty freight canoes loaded to the gunwales with tight bales of beaver, mink, bear, fox, and otter skins paddled away. And their return five weeks later laden with winter supplies: flour, salt pork, beans, sugar, wooden pails of candy, bolts of colourful cottons, axes, guns, ammunition, traps, fishnets, hammers, chisels, shovels, and a hundred other commodities. He recalls the festive Treaty gatherings in June, when the bands of three Reserves met on the point up the lake for a week of visiting, dancing, and celebration. Here the Indian Agent handed out to the head of each family five dollars a piece for each of its members, and the traders' booths near by did a flourishing business in candy and carnival gew-gaws.

There was no highway then, of course, and no bush planes, or even any "kickers", as the outboard motors came to be called by Northerners. And the Mounties had succeeded in keeping itinerant bootleggers from setting up business near by to get their share of the freely spent Treaty money.

The grandfather's memory went back far beyond the appearance of automobiles, aircraft, radios, and television. He had seen many changes in his lifetime, and had expected to find some here. But surely, after all these years of experience, when the decent men he had known as traders, teachers, missionaries, government agents, and Indian leaders had made honest efforts according to their lights to improve things — surely something better than this should have resulted.

How had it all happened?

Aca Nada

"Aca nada!" a Spanish skipper is dubiously reported to have said, after vainly seeking gold along the Gaspé coast — "Nothing here!" The story goes that Cartier, hearing the natives repeat this phrase, which they had overheard a dozen years earlier from the Spanish captain's lips, concluded that "Canada" was the name of the country.

A superficial look at the descendants of the first Canadians in the mid-twentieth century might have prompted the same comment. Stripped of the last vestiges of their material culture and reduced to the level of third-class citizens, they might seem neither to have retained any of their old, proud identity, nor to have acquired a new one to take its place. This is, in fact, far from the truth. But their situation does pose the question: how has it come about that a group of aboriginal Canadians, who comprise two per cent of the total population, shares less than one-thousandth of the wealth whose beginnings were based on their forefathers' skills and sweat?

The economic answer is simple enough. In the beginning, alien and native built a mutually profitable fur trade. For the alien this was only the preliminary to the farm-based economy and the supporting industries that his people had known in 183

Europe. But as the native was more and more committed to the fur economy, he became more and more dependent on the trade goods he could not produce himself. As long as the demand for his bush skills gave him a place in the economy, the trader depended on him, and when fur prices were high he lived better than his ancestors. But as farming, lumbering, and mining thrust rapacious fingers into the wilderness, and the fur trade declined, his whole economy collapsed. The only skill he knew became useless and he found himself at the bottom of a society that paid little attention to his predicament — an alien in his own land.

Sometimes, as with the otter hunters of the West Coast, the first years of contact were rosy. In the east, the skill of the Micmac and the Iroquois in bush fighting ensured their employment during the Franco-British struggle for power. While the bison lasted on the prairies, the Plains tribes got good prices for the pemmican that was used widely by the fur brigades. And briefly in the far north a few bands of Eskimo earned unheard-of wages during the building of the DEW line, for it was difficult to lure labour from the south to work in the bleak, remote radar stations of the arctic. Only in Newfoundland, where the fur trade never flourished, was the native's story tragic from the very beginning.

All through the Canadian Shield Woodlands, in the northern valleys of the Cordilleran interior, across the taiga of the Mackenzie plains, and in the high arctic, the native people of the hinterland survived the shock of the first devastating epidemics and built their lives around the isolated posts of the fur companies. Protected by rugged terrain and formidable distances from the predatory and degrading influences of the invading frontier, they enjoyed a stability that endured for decades, and sometimes a century or more. A closer look at the evolution and collapse of such communities may offer some insights into the dilemma that now faces two out of every hundred Canadians.

Few of those who have known such a wilderness society, based on an adequate supply of fish, game, and fur-bearing animals, can recall its heyday without nostalgia. Here, surely, was a successful partnership between the old culture and the new, each depending on and adapting to the needs of the other. In the beginning, only the leadership seemed to have changed. The place of the native hunter who had most to give away was taken by the European trader with his impressive store of goods, which he gladly "shared" with native trappers, knowing they would share their furs with him in return. In the early period the trader might even be native, though more usually he was of mixed

French and Amerindian blood. For reasons we have already seen, the French readily intermarried with the native people, and frequently adopted Amerindian ways so thoroughly that only their beards and pallor revealed an alien origin.

Once the Hudson's Bay Company became dominant, subtle changes began to take place. Although many a Scottish post manager took an Ojibway, Chipewyan, or Loucheux wife, English-bred managers began to import class distinctions. These linger to this day in a few isolated communities where a visiting outsider may still be greeted by a respectful touch of the forelock. Although a man of mixed blood might still be hired as a clerk or even book-keeper, most natives could now aspire to no more than the role of "Company servant". As such they were apprenticed to a trade: carpentry or blacksmithing in the main, while the women were employed as domestics. The growing of vegetables was also encouraged, but the skills which would have allowed a local industry to develop to replace imported goods were deliberately withheld. No one, for instance, learned to be a gunsmith. In the fur posts, time stood still, even as industries were developing in the rest of Canada.

Around the more strategic posts, a small settlement grew: whitewashed, red-roofed Company buildings, including servants' quarters, and a scattering of log cabins along the shore and on adjacent islands, used more and more as a place to stay during warm weather, between the journeys to fish-spawning grounds or wild-fruit concentrations. But from freeze-up to spring break-up, the traditional winter hunting and trapping left the cabins empty. When the lake ice melted and the streams ran free, the trappers and their families reappeared and there were busy days in the store, grading and baling the furs and balancing the value of the pelts against the outfitting debt of the previous fall. Credit that was allowed by the trader was based on his assessment of a man's trapping skill, and it is a curious fact that while this system lasted, the man with the largest "debt" had the highest status among his peers. In the affluent days of the fur trade, the post manager depended so much on the goodwill and fur-getting zeal of the native community that he was generous with credit, even in cases where he knew the return in pelts might not justify it. The desire of the trade for profit was still powerfully inhibited by the native community's tradition of sharing.

The missionary's arrival complicated this picture. He immediately outlawed his rival practitioners, the local shamans, but this was taken as an announcement of his own shamanistic role. If he brought some medical skills with him — as he frequently did — this role was all the more firmly planted in the local mind. Having nothing to lose, most of the 185 people were easily persuaded to adopt Christian practices. They did this cheerfully, for they knew that their own shamans (who were sometimes the most vocal Christians) would still be available on the sly if the missionary's magic failed. As a rule the trader co-operated with the missionary, regardless of his religious convictions, in the interest of the community stability. It was rare that a missionary like Duncan of Metlakatla attempted to take over complete leadership of a community.

The first task of the conscientious missionary was to become fluent in the native language. Frequently the result of his work was compiling of a dictionary, and the translation of the scriptures into the native tongue. In England the Society for the Propagation of the Gospel specialized in printing bibles and prayer books in the languages of preliterate peoples around the globe. In North America, a dozen attempts were made to devise systems that were more suitable than the Roman alphabet for rendering native languages. The most successful of these was a syllabary invented by James Evans, a Methodist missionary stationed at Norway House, the great Hudson's Bay depot at the north end of Lake Winnipeg. He invented thirty-six easily formed signs that reproduced all the basic syllables of Cree. Then he cast them in type by pouring melted

bullet lead into clay moulds, mixed soot with sturgeon oil to produce printing ink, and improvised a press from the screw-jack of a fur baler. In 1841 he produced the first literature to be printed in any language in the Canadian Northwest. Twenty years later a Roman Catholic missionary devised Déné syllabics, while the Anglicans early in this century adapted Evans's system for the Eskimo. Both Cree and Ojibway still make wide use of Evans's syllabics for trail messages and letters; and they are so admirably adapted to Algonkian dialects that children to this day quickly learn them in a few teaching sessions at home.

Not only did some missionaries succeed in making their converts literate in their native tongue, but they frequently offered training in religious leadership. An Anglican-trained Cree from York Factory, for example, converted most of the bands north of the Albany River to Fort Severn. He did this so effectively that they remained faithful until white missionaries were able to take up where he had left off. In Saskatchewan a school for native catechists at Prince Albert was so well organized that it developed into a theological college. Later it was moved to Saskatoon, where it became the nucleus of the University of Saskatchewan. When the university opened its doors in 1883, it offered courses in eight subjects: Theology, Moral Philosophy, Agriculture, Classics, Chemistry, Mathematics, Indian

Languages, and English Literature. At its peak the evangelical enthusiasm of the churches brought dedicated teachers and nurses into isolated native communities long before the government showed any interest in either health or education. Indeed, it was not until a band "took Treaty" that the government entered these fields.

Taking Treaty

The earliest such treaty goes back to 1680 when the Jesuit Order persuaded the French Crown to give a grant of land near Montreal where they could place a band of Christian Mohawk, both as a military buffer and "to augment their number and propagate more effectively the faith and gospel". Subsequent treaties varied greatly in their terms, and it was not until after Confederation that a consistent formula was arrived at. From the first the British Crown claimed absolute sovereignty over all the land, but recognized that the natives had a sort of "squatter's claim" because they in fact lived there. The object of a treaty was to "extinguish the native title" by a suitable exchange. The Crown agreed to give the band permanent title to a parcel of land, usually selected by the band's spokesmen in a favourite summer gathering place, and varying from 160 acres to 2 square miles per family. The band agreed to relinquish all claims to the surrounding territory — although it would still have the right to hunt and fish there. The Canadian government agreed to be responsible for the education and welfare of the band, to establish a band fund with an initial contribution, to supply specified fishing, trapping, or farming equipment, and to make annual payments of four or five dollars per head in perpetuity.

The payments continued a practice that went back to the beginning of Canadian history, when both British and French learned that annual gifts to native allies or trading partners were the best means of ensuring friendship and military aid. And while these grants might appear small to modern eyes, they seemed fair enough to both parties at the time. No one foresaw the day when the native population, which was then almost static, would explode beyond the capacity of local resources to support them, or that European settlement and industry — usually at the time of treaty-signing still far from the band's territory — would push to the very edges of the reserved land. It was in the interest, too, of the Canadian government, in view of the fierce warfare south of the border, and especially after the blunders made in the Riel uprising, to deal fairly with the native people. So, for the most part, the hinterland people went about their accustomed ways, which seemed — apart from the gifts and festivities at "Treaty time" — to have been unaffected.

For the more remote bands, the most noticeable change — the annual arrival of the Treaty party, consisting of agent, interpreter, bookkeeper, policeman, and doctor—was an exciting event. It was the agent's duty to distribute the annual head payments— which could amount to sixty dollars for a family of twelve, to register births and deaths, to hear local grievances, and sometimes to act as a magistrate. Several bands were often served at one centre, and the occasion became even more festive than the old pattern of summer gatherings around food concentrations. Gossiping, gambling, romances, secret visits to surviving shamans, and night-long dances characterized such events. The festivities included lining up in front of the doctor's tent for a quick medical check-up, which was usually verbal, with the help of an interpreter. After this, an assistant would hand each a bottle of harmless cough medicine dipped from a ten-gallon jar, and the recipient swallowed the contents appreciatively as soon as he stepped out of the line. Nevertheless, even the most careless medical reports accumulating in Ottawa made it more and more clear that infant mortality, malnutrition, and endemic tuberculosis were all but neutralizing an extraordinarily high birth rate.

Government involvement in native life brought new complications in the leadership roles. To implement treaty promises, both day-schools and residential boarding schools were built. The churches continued to provide education, but now that education costs were paid by the government, they became in effect its agents. Sometimes, too, the missionary's status was increased when the government made him the agent for distributing relief to needy families. Relieved of this role, the trader became more exacting in the credit he extended to trappers who were poor risks. Now, too, nursing stations began to appear, urging that the moss-bag and sphagnum be replaced with laundered diapers. This undoubtedly reduced infant mortality, but it created confusion in the women's minds by upsetting the ancient patterns of child-rearing. In some posts a radio transmitter and weather station increased the annual visits of government inspectors.

The established pattern of hiring native people only for menial tasks persisted. No attempt was made to train the local youth as radio operators, nurse's assistants, police constables, or teachers. The main excuse for this was the low grade of education they had received. But while this had some validity at first, when schooling would often be interrupted by trips to the winter traplines, it became less so as educational standards slowly climbed. An unhealthy barrier was growing between the white administrators and even the brightest young people. Students who stayed in school long enough to reach the secondary level lost their native skills, and yet had little opportunity of being employed in the community with their new ones.

At the same time, the administrators no longer felt any pressure to learn the people's language. Even the traders found they could get along with only an occasional interpreter. And as the native children learned more English, they began to lose their own language, creating a generation gap in the native community. Frequently the new generation found that it was fluent in neither language.

Theoretically, the treaties recognized the native capacity for democratic leadership, and provision was made for the annual election of a Chief and Councillors. In practice, however, it was the government agent who made such decisions as he had complete control — subject to Ottawa's approval — of the band funds. As it became clear to the band's leaders that they were not trusted to learn by making their own mistakes, that no real responsibility was being given them at any level, and that even their opinions were being ignored by an official "we-know-better" attitude, they ceased to stand for election. Voters stayed away in large numbers on election day, so that a small minority, dominated by the friends and relatives of a candidate, could elect a man who deliberately curried favour with the agent in return for special treatment for his supporters. Up to the middle of the present century the agent was at best a well-intentioned retired army officer with a paternalistic attitude towards his "wards". At worst, he was an ignoramus with political connections and a blind eye to the band's needs.

So, a fatal weakness developed. Potential native leaders with a knowledge of their people's needs acquired neither training nor experience in responsibility. And the rank and file became increasingly dependent on, and subservient to, an alien power group.

Nevertheless, while the fur economy functioned, these isolated communities endured and outside interference was minimal. Here, indeed, was the nearest approach made anywhere in Canada to a stable, working partnership between the native culture and the invading one. But the whole structure depended on the pelts harvested, the demands of the market, and the continuing isolation of the native community from the corrosive effects of settlement and industry. Regardless of the stability such communities achieved, all of them crumbled catastrophically under the first full impact of the dominant culture. Neither Church nor Company nor Treaty could save them. For the problems that con- 189 fronted them were massive, and the forces that thrust them — totally unprepared — into the mainstream of Canadian life were impersonal and implacable.

Even as the frontier approached, the symptoms of impending collapse appeared and multiplied. The building of a railway or a road, the location of a new lumber operation or mine, brought a motley collection of new faces: prospectors, surveyors, timber cruisers, fur and liquor bootleggers, loggers and sawmill hands, construction workers, business promoters, commercial fishermen, tourists, "Mounties", outfitters, and bush bums. Their multiple activities, regardless of how constructive some of them might have been, inevitably upset the wilderness ecology. The resources of game, fish, and fur were disrupted, bush fires increased, and social forces were introduced whose operations were beyond control.

The Collapse of the Fur-Trading Community

In the native fur community, production began to fall off. Trappers had to go farther inland to get their furs, and came out with smaller takes. The best trappers were offered higher wages for guiding surveyors, prospectors, and cruisers, and were lured away. The Company manager, in a desperate effort to keep his dwindling profits alive, began to cut off credit from the less successful trappers, who then brought their take to "free" traders who paid in cash instead of goods. Such trappers, with no experience in handling money, spent it freely — all too frequently on liquor that impaired their judgement and accelerated their degradation. Now they set up their tents or built their shacks near the settlement, and found that the demand of frontier males for the services of their wives and daughters could compensate for their own lack of employment. Meanwhile, the Company balance sheets were reaching the point of no return. In the old days the manager would simply have opened up a new post in the unexploited hinterland. But now trading prospects were brighter in the frontier settlement. There money flowed freely over the counters of the competing traders, and the Reserve was being deserted. The decision he had to make was obvious. So, though he still bought furs, he moved his business to the frontier settlement and became the manager of a general store catering to a growing non-native population. And, in this way, the Hudson's Bay Company began the great department stores that developed on sites like Fort Edmonton and Fort Garry, as the fur trade declined and the frontier settlements developed into major Canadian cities.

The native leaders that had been the mainstay of

the fur community were faced with a hard choice. Well aware of the degrading influences of the frontier, they hesitated to move to the settlements and expose their families to them. Yet, if they stayed on the Reserve, they would be unable to support their families. Meanwhile their sons and nephews, who would formerly have taken over their roles, were being irresistibly lured to the excitement and the prospects of employment offered in frontier settlements. At first work was plentiful, and they became packers and axemen on survey parties, or firefighters, tourist guides, fishermen's helpers, or construction labourers. Paid in cash, and laid off at unpredictable intervals, they fell into heavy drinking patterns and became less and less reliable as workers. At the same time, the demand for cheap, casual labour dwindled. Gradually these young men lost their self-reliance and ambition, and gravitated to the bottom of the labour force. Here they and their wives and sisters were fully exposed to the lowest elements of frontier society. And so some became transients with alcoholic addictions, or other social misfits, who worked only long enough to finance their next city spree, and often only enough to qualify them for the unemployment insurance that would see them through the winter in an urban slum.

As our fictitious Canadian family left the restaurant to return to their parked car, a man emerged from a nearby hotel and walked unsteadily toward them. The father pretended not to see him. The mother put her arm protectingly about the daughter's shoulder. "You mustn't stare, dear," she told her son, who was looking back to see what the man would do.

The man was talking to the grandfather, who reached into his pocket and pulled out some money.

"You're just encouraging them to be bums," was the father's critical comment as the grandfather got into the car.

"Maybe he has problems we don't know anything about," his wife suggested mildly.

"Too Bad!"

The wife's assumption that the man had been drinking to forget his problems was probably quite mistaken. Millennia ago his ancestors had learned to let tomorrow look after itself. The simplest explanation for his heavy drinking was that he had no other way of putting in his time. With the establishment of the local pulp and paper mill and the sudden appearance of an industrial community, he was simply a displaced person, his bush skills useless, his long apprenticeship as a trapper meaningless.

191

He had been on relief since the spring, after working all winter with a cutting crew on the right of way for a new highway. His clothes were shabby, but he had never been concerned about his appearance; he would have dressed at least as shabbily if he had been prosperous, to show that he didn't put himself above the others. Yesterday his outboard motor had seized; this morning he had sold it for a few dollars, collected a couple of friends, and converted the cash into beer. Like him, his friends were unemployed and bored. With the grandfather's handout they would enjoy another round. Perhaps another friend or a cousin would turn up with money in his pocket and they would all get really drunk.

Sentimentalists tend to close their eyes to the fact that there *is* excessive drinking among our Amerindian people, comparable in degree with the heavy drinking of the Canadian pioneers at a barn-raising, or the wild excesses of booming gold-rush camps. Before the Hudson's Bay Company acquired a monopoly of the fur trade, rival companies bribed the native fur-getters with French brandy, British rum, or American whiskey. But wherever the trade stabilized, drinking was controlled, simply because it was bad for business. In the remote native settlements from the 1850s on, drinking was almost unknown, even though it continued to be the rule in Canadian frontier communities, even during prohibition. But with the appearance of the bush plane, and winter tractor trains over the frozen lakes, the trickle of alcohol to the remote fur communities became a flow. Today a Cree trapper can "blow" his entire winter take on a few cases of rye whiskey that have been bought to treat his friends and relatives to a carousal, which sometimes ends with beatings, stabbings, gunshot wounds, and even suicide. Recently, too, a knowledge of home-brewing techniques has penetrated all through the hinterland, with tragic consequences.

It must be made crystal clear, however, that the reasons are cultural, and not genetic. In the cities a major reason is undoubtedly the boredom of unemployment and alienation. But there are deeper traditional factors, to which most Amerindian people still cling. A man's private life is his own business. Even the "ugly drunk" was shrugged off with a mere shake of the head and a "too bad". A man could get drunk openly, without social censure from his own people. But the very same people would not tolerate him in their midst if he failed to observe the sharing code.

Nor was a man judged harshly because he made no effort to control his drinking appetite. The

Amerindian was allowed from infancy to eat when he was hungry and drink when he thirsted, and so this kind of control was not expected. But he *was* expected to control his anger, and a striking feature of the Amerindian to this day is his reluctance to display it. This has resulted in an inbred tactfulness and courtesy that is seldom matched by those he meets outside his culture.

It is widely recognized that the more anger is repressed, the more explosive it is likely to be once a discharge of the pent-up feelings is triggered. So the smiling Eskimo, who needs to preserve peace within his small band through the winter darkness and the privations of the high arctic, has been known to break out into irrational violence when his abnormally high self-control is pushed beyond its limits. All across the continent, in fact, the Amerindian male learned as a child to endure excesses of privation, pain, and hostile taunting that are far beyond the endurance of other Canadians. But when alcohol reduces his inhibitions, the pent-up anger aroused by real or imaginary wrongs done him in the past, by rivalry over women, or by family frustrations, prompt him to a violence far beyond the normal expressions of anger. Then, his actions can range from smashing furniture to arson, manslaughter, and suicide.

Alcoholic addiction is probably far more severe among non-natives, perhaps because it is associated with the sexual impotence frequently induced by the stern suppression of sexual play in childhood. For the Amerindian, the pattern of alcoholism is cyclic rather than addictive. Each time his built-up anger finds an outlet, his heavy drinking subsides and returns to normal levels until a new accumulation is ready for discharge. Before the arrival of Europeans, there were traditional outlets for repressed anger in inter-tribal raids—as in the senseless slaughter of the Coppermine Eskimo band that Hearne witnessed, in blood feuds, and in sorcery. And perhaps because it is aware that anger needs an outlet, the native community does not condemn its heavy drinkers.

The most serious offence in a native community is not drunkenness but hoarding wealth.

The Sharing Code

"We have jealousy and so do you," an informant told the writer, "but it's not the same. When someone gets above you you try to get up there where he is. We don't do that. *We pull him down.*"

But few natives elect to defy the community code, or even get the chance. Word of a man's good fortune almost immediately brings a procession of 193 relatives and friends expecting to share the wealth, and shamelessly making it apparent. A loan is actually a gift, with the understanding that the giver can expect the borrower to be equally generous, if and when their fortunes are reversed. The only acceptable way of getting "above" — that is, of acquiring higher status — is to acquire a reputation for generosity.

The wife of a Manitoba resources official tells of an experience when she was a young unmarried school teacher in a hinterland community. It illustrates the sharp contrast between the native values and European ones.

On her first wash-day, she became aware of the silent presence of the only woman she had met who spoke any English, and who had been very friendly. The teacher sensed that the woman was waiting for something. Finally, with some reluctance, the woman said what was on her mind.

"You have two wash-tubs. I haven't any. You should give me one."

To the teacher this was a strange request, but she patiently explained that she needed two, one for washing, the other for rinsing.

The woman was equally patient, pointing out that one tub could serve both purposes if the dirty water was dumped out and the tub refilled with clean water.

When it became clear that the teacher was determined to keep both wash-tubs, her friend transferred her pressure to the sad-irons that were being heated on the wood stove for ironing the clothes. There were seven sad-irons, the teacher should give her two.

From wash-day to wash-day, the pressure continued until in desperation the teacher asked the missionary's wife, "What should I do?"

"Oh," was the reply, "just ignore her. These people are always scrounging. If you listened to one, you'd have the whole tribe on your back."

"Their willingness to share," comments a government conservation report, "can be a serious handicap in our way of life," and later referred to the northern Cree's "lack of interest in saving money".

A team of sociologists, in summarizing an intensive study of a large Albertan Reserve, states that: "To most Blackfoot Indians wealth is not so important in terms of accumulation of property as for prestige and security that can be acquired *by giving it away* [italics added]. Many Indians of prominence appear to lack the symbols of wealth we find necessary, e.g., good furniture, new clothes, many horses, etc. . . . but they are wealthy in terms of the prestige acquired from having given away their property. . . . The Blackfoot emphasized not a single demonstration of generosity but a continuous show of it."

The origin of this attitude towards sharing can be found in the conditions of Amerindian life before the European arrived. In aboriginal times it was a waste of energy — sometimes fatal — to accumulate stores of food beyond the needs of the coming winter. Survival depended on an immediate response to the rhythms of nature: the spawning seasons, the annual migrations of bird and beast, the alternations of heat and cold, rain and drought. Food surpluses, no matter how carefully cached, were subject to destruction by forest fires, spring floods, or the cunning strength of the wolverine. The food-seeking migrations of the people themselves would often take them far from the cache and make a return to it uncertain. So the surplus was limited to what could be carried as they went. Deliberate, long-term planning for the future was not merely impractical; it could be hazardous.

And so the Amerindian had to depend, in times of scarcity, on whatever food resources were available to the whole band. If any member had extra food, he was expected to share, and the man who was most honoured was he who had most to give away. The man who tried to hoard was a danger to the band and was regarded with contempt.

The strength of this taboo against hoarding was reinforced by religious belief. These men, at the mercy of the unpredictable whims of nature, looked to supernatural sources for guidance, and needed a faith to sustain them through their repeated confrontations with calamity. Through magic and ritual, they tried to win the favour of — or at least avoid offences against — the invisible powers around them, those powers who appeared in what was for them the most real of all experiences: the dream. One did not offend these dream powers, and so a man who broke the taboo against hoarding was clearly an evil person, with whom it was wise to have as little to do as possible. It might be dangerous to lose the favour of these powers by appearing to approve of the actions of a stingy man. Even the wealthy coast tribes, who need never have starved, and did accumulate enormous stores of food and goods, consumed them so lavishly in winter potlatches that they could actually starve in spring. In other words, the taboo against hoarding survived even in a situation where it was no longer needed.

The ancestors of our native peoples were taught 195

in the harsh school of nature to recognize and cherish the value of sharing, which enabled them to survive. And the standards of Christianity, which arose out of the equally harsh desert life of the Semitic nomads in the Near East, have much in common with this concept of helping others. Many basic Christian values have survived, even though the conditions in which they were born have disappeared. In much the same way, the Amerindian value system endures, even though the material cultures from which it arose have collapsed.

Conflict of Values

Today we are likely to dismiss the problem of exchanging the values of one culture for those of another as simply a matter of education. But education, we are learning, is not a simple matter. More and more it is being realized how difficult it is to change attitudes formed in infancy. And Amerindian values persist because the Amerindian system of raising children survives.

But what are the values that are taught to the majority of Canadians? We can best see what these are by taking an unsentimental look at how children are raised in the ethnic mainstream. Weaned and toilet-trained in their first year, infants are likely to be scolded and spanked before they can talk. Already, they are being prepared for the demands that will be made upon them by external pressures. Nursery school, kindergarten, primary school, and secondary school — all reinforce the attitudes taken in with the mother's milk. Schedules become progressively more demanding, even at play: hockey practice, music lessons, swimming instruction, or community recreation projects. And so the child learns the lesson: he or she must suppress feelings and obey instructions. Obedience, not independence, is what makes a complex industrial society function.

The purpose of the Amerindian system was quite different. A shrewd observation by the widely travelled English journalist Anna Jameson, made when she visited Michilimackinac in 1837, gets to the heart of the matter.

"The Indians, apparently, have no idea of correcting or restraining their children; personal chastisement is unheard of. They say that before a child has any understanding there is no use in correcting it; and when old enough to understand, no one has the right to correct it. Thus the fixed, inherent sentiment of personal independence grows up with the Indians from earliest infancy. The will of a child is not forced; he has nothing to learn but what he sees around him, and he learns by imitation. I hear no scolding, no tones of command or reproof; but I see no evil results from this mild system, for the general reverence and affection of children for parents is delightful."

No doubt she was over-impressed, but compare her comments with those of Lewis and Clark, describing the rearing of children 1,500 miles farther west and a generation earlier: "They seldom correct their children particularly the boys who soon become masters of their own acts, they give as a reason that it cows and breaks the spirit of the boy to whip him, and that he never recovers his independence of mind after he is grown."

In fact, light physical punishment *was* inflicted on children, and ridicule could be a sharp weapon on an adult's tongue. But Jameson put her finger on a point that has been almost totally overlooked: the purpose of the system was to create a sense of "personal independence . . . *from earliest infancy* [italics added]". This method of child-rearing persists among Amerindians to this day.

As in most cultures, it is the woman who is the most important teacher in infancy. But little has been written and less learned about the Amerindian woman. Traditionally she has stayed in the background; and even today in a northern town one may occasionally see her walking along the sidewalk a few paces behind her husband. The conventions of her people require that the husband be the spokesman with outsiders, and it is not until a stranger is accepted into the family circle that she feels free to speak for herself.

In many ways her traditional role of acceptance and passivity is an advantage that allows her to adapt to a Canadian society that finds little use for the independence of the Amerindian male. Always fertile, she welcomes each baby as it arrives, and treats all her children with gentle forbearance. And although she still loses infants more often than improved health services can prevent, her family is large enough that her Family Allowance cheque may be the main support of the family. The unemployed father, seeking work far and wide, or spending his time in hotel beer rooms, becomes more and more detached from the family. And this deprives the young males of the confidence engendered by a successful father. Frequently a deserted mother, attracted by a male from outside her native community, enters a common-law relationship which is likely to end by the time she has borne him three or four children. Back she goes to the Reserve, to bring up her family — some of them blue-eyed and fair-haired — at government expense. Sometimes she moves into the city for a year or more, taking 197 on some domestic work, but subsisting largely on welfare. The children, however, whether on the Reserve or in the city, regardless of how much or how little pigment they have in skin, hair follicle, or iris, become as Amerindian in identity as their mother. For, long before they reach school age, they have learned — gently, wordlessly, and by example — that it is shameful not to share, that it is bad manners to display your anger, that it is better to satisfy your needs today than to plan for tomorrow, and that independence is the mark of a man.

All too often the child who has taken in Amerindian values with its mother's milk will not fit into the rigid social scheme of modern industrialized society. Especially if he is a boy, he will gradually withdraw as the pressures of school increase, and become an early dropout. The chances of his marrying outside his ethnic stream are radically reduced, and he finds a Métis or predominant Amerindian mate, who passes on the ancient attitudes. Far more frequently than the man, the Amerindian woman marries outside of her ancestry. And yet she raises her children as she was raised. The total effect is to increase the proportion of persons raised with life styles and attitudes that bar them from absorption into the cultural mainstream.

In 1900 the Amerindian population was estimated to be less than half the aboriginal one. Journalists wrote about the Amerindian as the "vanishing American", and even the experts thought in terms of a dying race. Then a slow increase appeared. By the 1920s an upward trend was clear, and by mid-century the Amerindian population was pushing close to the estimated original figure of 200,000 — *plus* at least as many Métis. The fertility rate of the Amerindian mother, twice to three times that of other Canadian females, and relatively unaffected by the widening use of contraceptive devices elsewhere in Canadian society, may now be increasing the proportion of native people in the population. And the slow reduction of infant mortality, though still far above the Canadian average, will boost it further. Indeed the number of those of recognized Amerindian ancentry may reach a million persons by the end of the century. But there is no guarantee that this considerable population will be any less alienated from Canadian society.

Nor can we ignore the effect of sexual permissiveness, which is most strongly illustrated by the fact that sexual play among children is regarded with tolerant amusement. But such tolerance is only one facet of a broad permissiveness that pervades Amerindian communities. Racial discrimination is unknown, or of recent origin as a sort of backlash response to the discrimination of outsiders. In earlier times, most tribes adopted both children and adults from neighbouring ones, and the adoptees accepted new tribal ways with impressive permanence. Indeed this climate of acceptance has always attracted European males, some of whom — contemptuously labelled "renegades" or "squaw-men" by the society they rejected — rose to positions of high status and responsibility in their adopted community. This still happens.

Perhaps the Canadian Amerindian has accepted government paternalism with passivity because it seems as remote and powerful as those supernatural powers to whose will he has taught himself to submit. There is ample evidence, too, that underground shamanism and sorcery is practised by many Amerindians who profess Christianity. A Mistassini girl in northern Quebec, interpreting an old man's reminiscences of aboriginal beliefs for a museum interviewer, becomes uneasy, hesitates, begins to stutter. Fear shines in her eyes as she turns to the ethnologist and blurts out: "Those are all fairy tales that he's telling" — and adds, after a fearful sideglance at the old man—"*aren't they?*"

But for our Canadian family speeding along the highway, in the year 1950, the complex interplay of two cultures that has made the Amerindian an alien in his native land is beyond the range of their understanding. Uncomfortably aware that "something" is wrong and that "something" should be done about it by "someone", they soon find it easier to think of other things.

The grandfather, however, tossing restlessly in his luxurious motel bed that night, vainly seeks respite from the impact of his visit to the Reserve. Like a phonograph needle that keeps jumping back on its former track, a single question rasps endlessly and persistently in his brain. "But, whose fault is it? Whose fault — "

Men in the Midst of Change

Since beginning this book, I have written, revised, scrapped, and rewritten the "final" chapter half a dozen times, attempting to assess the present situation of our native peoples and to project what the future might hold for them. But changes are coming too thick and fast, and finalities escape me. All I can do is to end the book as I began it — in the first person, stating personal views that seem valid today but may have to be revised tomorrow.

I am both optimistic and pessimistic. Optimistic, because of the way attitudes are changing. There is new strength and articulation in the native voice, and a new willingness to listen among a growing number of Canadians. Pessimistic, however, in the shadow of the massive social problems around the globe which seem to point towards a future in which the rich continue to get richer and the poor poorer. In the meantime, an uncontrolled technology pushes us closer and closer towards total pollution and unthinkable wars. There seems to be no sign that those who have much are likely to settle for less, nor that those who have the least will continue to tolerate a gross imbalance of global wealth, of which they are becoming more and more aware.

In Canada native leaders are emerging who see this imbalance clearly. Even the *comfortable* Canadians are beginning to get the message, to ask, as they glance uneasily south of the border: "Could it happen here, too?"

As I have pointed out earlier, there is a different tradition in Canada than in the United States in dealing with native peoples. The discrimination that is undoubtedly present is neither so deep nor so widespread, if only because the native people were useful to us for a longer period than they were to the aggressive settlers of our southern neighbour. But technology has radically changed the scene. The search for fossil fuels and metallic ores, now technically possible in the remotest corners of the globe, has exposed even the Eskimo — to say nothing of his environment — to the familiar story of ruthless exploitation. The multinational corporation, however high it may temporarily boost our gross national product, has no interest in any nation or its people, except to the extent that either will be useful for its own self-aggrandisement.

Yet the pains we take to attract enterprise of this sort, in order to promote a steady rise in the gross national product, remind me of how eager the aborigines were to acquire European trade goods, without any awareness of how brief would be the upsurge of affluence, or how dependent they would become on the invading economy. To my mind there is a disturbing parallel between then and now. Already outposts of the great corporations are scattered — like the early fur-trading posts — through the Canadian hinterland, and have begun to dominate the centres of population.

To see this more clearly, we have only to glance at the formidable threat to the cultural identity of French Canada that has arisen because it allowed the growing domination of Anglo-American enterprise to continue for so long. Already, even though the natural and human resources of Quebec offer a logical economic base for the viability of a separate nation that would guarantee the survival of a French fact in North America, a separate Quebec state would be achieved at the expense of the substantial French-speaking populations of Ontario and New Brunswick, and would ensure the swift extinction of the islands of *Canadiens* elsewhere in the country.

But separate nationhood is not even remotely possible for the native people of Canada, scattered as they are in small communities across the length and breadth of half a continent. Their surest hope lies in the increasing strength and political sophistication of their native organizations and leaders, as they insist on a vital place in the Canadian sun. But to be successful, they need the support of a substantial body of public opinion. When heads are counted, as will inevitably come to pass if Canadians are able to keep any decision-making in their own hands, the public will have to decide whether the vision of a Canadian mosaic is mere wishful thinking, or something we are really serious about.

A White Paper on Indian Affairs issued recently

has dealt shrewdly with the problem of justice for the native people. It pointed out that if they want absolute equality, they must forget about the special status that gives them at least a minimal guarantee of survival as a distinct culture. This, in turn, brought out into the open the basic grievance of our Amerindian population: that their basic treaty rights, as they have understood them, have never been fully honoured, and that they fear that even those they have will be taken away from them. In fact, even while they accepted the material benefits of the invading culture, they have maintained a steady passive resistance to any change in their values. And there is no indication that anything they learn from us will weaken that resistance; rather, it will likely strengthen it. In addition, a single severe slump in the Canadian economy could create the kind of backlash against native rights that we have witnessed in the United States against the civil rights movement and the "war on poverty". Inevitably the first casualty of such a reaction would be the people with the weakest foothold in the economy: the Amerindians.

But in my view, we are rushing towards the bankruptcy of our society if we continue to be obsessed with increasing our material standard of living and, in order to do this, continue the rape of our non-renewable resources and refuse to meet the pollution problem head on. Our society is doomed unless new and more human values replace the old, and we begin to understand that affluence and poverty are two sides of the same dubious currency. The important issue is not that the Amerindian become a token white man. Rather, the question is, how much can we learn from the Amerindian about the values that can promote the quality of our life — before it is too late to learn anything.

I am not sentimentalizing here, being well aware that the native people are not noble red men but human beings with all the weaknesses, irrationality, and even absurdities that we are all prone to. Over the years I have passed through every kind of attitude towards Amerindians that I have observed in my fellow Canadians: the romanticism that wants to identify with "the Indian" (who never existed); the sentimentality that wants to "help" the Indian (which disguises the arrogance of an assumed superiority); and the hostility one feels on discovering that one's help is not wanted. Only as it became necessary for me, as a researcher of aboriginal art, to *learn* something about the Amerindian did I acquire some insights into the value systems that enabled him to survive, and discover how inadequate the value system of Western Man has proven to be in dealing with the changes that are sweeping around the globe.

We ignore at our peril the effects that the environment we are creating around us has on the way we respond to life. I am reminded of the contrast I observed in a single person, my friend A-Joe Ratt of La Ronge in northern Saskatchewan, a northern frontier town of some 1,500 persons equally divided between Cree and non-Indians. Hearing that A-Joe (there was also a "B-Joe" and a "C-Joe" Ratt) knew the Eulas River and upper Churchill River country, I looked him up and found he could pinpoint the location of six rock-painting sites in the area. Asking around, I learned that he was reputed locally to be a skilful "con" man and habitual drunk, spending a substantial proportion of his time in the local jail. I saw evidence to confirm this. Nevertheless he had the information I sought and I persuaded the local government agency to fly me, A-Joe, and my canoe up to Eulas Lake to record the sites.

Once there, I gave A-Joe the stern of my canoe — something I had never done with anyone before — and paddled bow for the rest of our five-day trip. Here, back in his home environment, the transformation in the man was little short of miraculous. No bush novice myself, I learned ten times as much from him in those few days — about the habits of birds and animals, about edible plants, and even about handling fast water in a canoe — than from any other person in my life. But the most impressive lesson he taught me was at Eulas Lake, as we stood in the tall weeds surrounding the trapper's cabin he had built for his family years before, and looked down at the silver paint that flaked off here and there from the cement surface of a cross he had fashioned to plant over his daughter's grave. I don't remember what he said, but I'll never forget the tears that streamed unashamedly down his face as he stood there.

In the harsh code of Western Man, riddled with his fear of sexual emasculation, this is sheer sentimentality. But place beside it the words of a Blackfoot of the Blood Tribe, speaking at Banff to an elite group of native leaders and educators from across Canada. Deeply disturbed by the kind of education his own children were getting in a government-supported school, he made an eloquent plea for the *humanizing* of Canadian education. He wanted *love* in the school his children went to, and he went on to spell out in the most personal terms exactly what he meant by the word. I took down the part of his speech that most impressed me, and so I can offer a fairly faithful transcript of his actual words.

"You know, when you get married, you feel   203

pretty good about it, and you think that's what love is. But you don't know anything about love. After a while your first kid comes along, and *then* you think, now I know what love is. But you still don't know. So your kids grow up and get married. Pretty soon there's a grandchild. And then you know. *That's* when you know what love is!"

He couldn't understand why white parents left their children at home when they went shopping or visiting. They didn't seem to want them around! And they didn't even want their own parents! He recalled how he and his wife used to vie with their brothers and sisters as to which of their families the old people would visit next.

Once I asked a wise and tranquil old Ojibway, whose guest I have been off and on over the years, what in his opinion his people wanted most. Typically, he thought this over carefully for a while. Typically, too, although he had been the elected chief of his band more than once, he prefaced his answer by saying he couldn't speak for his people but only for himself.

"I guess," he finally answered, "we just want to be free." As he enlarged on this, it was clear that he was talking about a freedom he already had but was afraid he might lose. A veteran of the First World War (with a deep leg scar from a shrapnel wound),

he had brought back a wife from England, where he convalesced, but she had died on the Reservation a few years later. He was both an elder of the Presbyterian Church and a practising *Midé* shaman, believing that the good points of both religions reinforced each other. He had travelled widely and lived in a Canadian city for a time, working for Indian Affairs. I asked him how he felt about living in the Canadian mainstream.

"Well," he said, "it's nice to have an indoor toilet, and my wife [an Ojibway woman who succeeded his first wife] sure appreciates a good washing-machine. And it's pretty nice to have a car to get around in — there's no doubt about that. But if you have to trade your *freedom* for all that — Well, the price is a bit too high."

Yet he was too gentle a man to express the real strength of his feelings about the price. I well knew, however, that in his heart he despised many of the things he had observed in his contacts with the prevailing culture, and presumptuous though it may be, I will put those unuttered words into print.

"I don't know why you white people talk so loud about freedom," he could have said. "As far as I can see you're a bunch of slaves. You're slaves to your clocks. You're tied down to your desks and factory benches. You worry all the time about something.

Maybe it's taxes or bills, or how to get ahead of the other guy. You worry if your neighbour has a better car, even when your own is working fine. You're a slave to sex. You must be, always talking about it and using it to sell everything. You're a slave to soap. If your kid comes in crying about something and his face is snotty your wife will tell him 'Go wash your face, *then* I'll love you.' You're a slave to comfort. You've got to take a pill as soon as you feel a little pain, and if you don't get your three meals a day you think you're going to die.

"Then you come to us and say, 'Why don't you live like me?'!!!"

But he was well aware that the freedom he had known was becoming a thing of the past.

The dilemma of the Southern Indian Lake community illustrates the basis of his fears. In the summer of 1967 I had the chance to investigate reports of rock-paintings in northern Manitoba by hitching an airlift with the Provincial Trapper Education Officer. We stopped off at Southern Indian Lake to visit a Cree band of commercial fishermen and trappers who were completely self-supporting, and I sat in on a meeting of some fifty heads of families gathered to discuss adjustments in registered traplines, fishing licences, and marketing problems. But the main discussion centred around a single community problem: should they, or should they not, admit two more families from a neighbouring area who wanted to move in? Each man in turn rose to give his opinion. A consensus was reached and the vote that followed was almost unanimous: their resources were too limited to make it practicable to admit any other families. One man stood up then, and called for a separate vote on each family that had applied. Far fewer spoke to this, and all who did offered arguments as to why an exception should be made for this or the other family. When it came to the vote, a majority voted in favour of breaking the rule in both instances. A number abstained from voting, but *nobody voted against.*

The vote was entirely predictable. For the incoming families had relatives who were already in the community. And while the relatives could agree to a *policy* that excluded the admission of more families, it was unthinkable that they should vote against the wishes of their own families. For the rest, it was equally unthinkable that they should reject either family specifically, knowing that the bad feeling so created would remain a sore point and create rifts in the community for years to come. And so all were willing, for the sake of the whole community, to tighten their belts a little, and cheerfully accepted the newcomers.

In the meantime, the entire community was being threatened by a society that operated on totally different values. Hydro engineers had been busy surveying the power potential of the Nelson River, and had devised a scheme whereby a dam at the outlet of Southern Indian Lake (an enlargement of the Churchill River) would be built to create an enormous reservoir that would swell the power potential of the site by hundreds of thousands of kilowatts. Incidentally, of course, it would wipe out the resources of the band at Southern Indian Lake, one of the last self-sustaining Cree communities in the north. Once the facts had been publicized, there was a popular outcry against so ruthless a displacement of a viable native community — possibly the first instance in Canadian history where values that would be gained by technology were measured against the human values they threatened. Alternatives were explored and a less radical flooding of the lake was undertaken, though it only partially reduced the basic problem.

The central issue has yet to be faced: energy needs versus the preservation of a healthy environment. Has a government or industry the right to deprive a northern minority of its means of livelihood in order to give more employment to a southern majority? It's an old dilemma in North American history, and Canadians have had to face it from the days when an expansionist American republic declared the doctrine of "manifest destiny".

More recently the same issues were raised when the Quebec government launched the Baie James Project, to construct a vast system of dams and river diversions that would make it possible to generate millions of kilowatts of hydro-electric power from the waters flowing into the east side of James Bay. No treaties to extinguish the aboriginal rights to the land had ever been made. Yet work began without any attempt to consult with native hunters, trappers, and fishermen who depended on the region for their livelihood or any consideration of the effect the project might have on the animal population. In this case, the native organizations, supported by federal funds, succeeded in forcing the Quebec government to negotiate a settlement. However inadequate this may prove to be from an environmental point of view, it did establish a precedent that is bound to affect the settlement of native land claims in other parts of the country. Above all, it proved that the native people's rights, wishes, and needs could no longer be ignored.

The insidious, indeed tragic, aspect of both of these cases is that there was no deliberate intention on anyone's part to exploit anyone — merely the massive inertia of an impersonal industrial machine. Under its domination, industrialists lack the imagination to see any alternative, governments lack the courage to implement one, and the voting public continues blindly to believe that the gross national product will go on expanding forever.

An even more insidious problem is the reaction of the non-expert to the scientist who informs him of the threats of environmental pollution. The non-expert may be told of the presence of a poisonous "trace element" in the food he eats, the water he drinks, or the air he breathes. But unless he is confronted in his own experience with the evidence of such dangers, being informed that minute particles of a toxic substance are a menace to his health not only fails to impress him, but tends to convince him that the experts are exaggerating the threat.

Here it may help to take a look at the history of the Wabigoon River in northwestern Ontario. I vividly recall, as my wife and I traversed the Wabigoon on a 500-mile canoe trip between Kenora and Red Lake in 1937, how crystal clear the water was, more than the water of any other stream I had known. Everywhere in those days one could drink the water. But twenty years later, crossing the same river on the trans-Canada Highway, we were puzzled by the sight of dirty brown foam, flotillas of which were drifting downstream, until my wife pointed to the sign "POLLUTED WATER". We had just come from Dryden, the site of a large kraft paper mill and the source of both the polluting effluent and of an odour that dismays newcomers to the town. I had asked a Dryden man whom I knew about the heavy stench, only to get a grin and the explanation "Oh, didn't you know? That's the smell of money!"

But a decade later there was a sequel to that encounter involving two Ojibway communities, known in my youth as stable, even prosperous, trapping and fishing centres. These were Grassy Narrows, a community on the English River a mere dozen miles downstream from where the Wabigoon enters it, and White Dog, on the junction of the English River and the Winnipeg River. As this is being written, the people of Grassy Narrows and White Dog have been warned that mercury pollution in the fish they eat daily has reached levels hazardous to human health. Commercial fishing has been banned on the whole river system over the past five years, and the tourist industry on which many of the men depended for summer employment as guides has collapsed.

There is no more eloquent illustration of how profoundly and unpredictably the exploitation of our natural resources can affect the northern environment and the people who depend on its wildlife for their living.

Yet most Canadians, seemingly secure in their urban environment, are slow to realize how vulnerable the whole economy is to the winds of technological change. If the multinational corporation that owns the Dryden mill decides to automate the plant, half the town's population would be thrown out of work. But technological change is not the only threat. Inadequate reforestation programs, escalating energy costs, political decisions made in foreign countries — any one or any combination of these and other factors could cause the mill to shut down permanently. The fate of former mining communities, once the last vein has been gouged out, has already shown what happens to the miner and his family when his skills are no longer needed in the town where he was born. So it is not only the native people who suffer when we "mine" our non-renewable resources. In some parts of Canada, notably sections of the Maritimes, the fate of marginal farmers and pulpwood cutters already resembles the plight of our native people. And in spite of the warnings of foresters and ecologists, the rape of our resources, the displacement of people and soil, the pollution of water and air, and the flooding of huge areas of the northern hinterland go on apace, with no more than token efforts to check them. Canadians cannot afford to separate their interests from those of the native people: over the long term, our needs and dangers are identical.

Indeed, so complex and cumbersome has the administration of federal and provincial agencies become, in an effort to provide for the sick, the aged, the disabled, the displaced, and the unemployed, that the idea is being seriously mooted of setting up a *guaranteed annual income* for which every citizen would qualify, regardless of income. So it may be that the native people are merely a few steps ahead of us to the extent that a substantial proportion of them are already on total welfare. As Duke Redbird astutely remarked in a television interview, our increasing dependence on the fruits of technology is bringing us closer to the aborigine's dependence on the affluence of nature. And it is perhaps symptomatic that an increasing number of young Canadians are becoming disinterested in the Protestant ethic of work for its own sake, taking to heart the barrage of messages from the mass media: that technology can eliminate, or at least relieve, the monotony of clock slavery, that only what is new is good, and that sexuality is the prime reason for existence.

The White Paper issued by the Canadian government a decade ago, though it recommended an approach to the "Indian problem" that had been tried and abandoned in the United States, did succeed in clarifying the wishes and interests of the native people. When it proposed that the federal government pass responsibility for the native people to the provinces, and that the reservation system be phased out as they assumed full citizenship, a storm of protest was aroused. And it was realized that for all the faults of the Indian Act and the Indian Affairs Branch of the federal government, the proposed changes would leave the native people in a more confused and vulnerable situation than already existed. The proposal further stimulated the development of native organizations to fight for what they felt to be their rights, and their protests against inadequate prior consultation prompted attempts by the federal government to communicate more directly with native leaders. Non-status Indians, or Métis, who as yet have had no federal assistance, even though in many instances their need for adequate housing and education is as great, have also formed pressure groups to which the governments have begun to respond. Articulate and highly educated young men and women, too, are making the Canadian public more and more aware of how its own attitudes, more of apathy than of conscious discrimination, have handicapped the first Canadians.

These young people have acquired a renewed belief in their own identity and ancestral values. Increasingly insistent that changes be made *now* for their people, they are equally aware that their own values may be more durable than ours. Better than we, they know that the earth cannot be "owned" by anyone, and that for everything we take out, something must be put back. Society must be based on sharing. And the only valid status is that earned by those whose strength and skills enable them to give the most away. To save time is to waste living, and to save money is miserly. To compete is to poison society, for even the successful competitor must strain his resources to stay "on top". In fact, there is an old Indian jibe about the white man who slaves and saves for fifty weeks of the year so he can live like an Indian for two!

The following excerpt from an essay by Wilfred Pelletier, an Ottawa from Manitoulin Island, is relevant here:

"If you can't somehow or another have a community movement which is a spontaneous sort of urge which results in something coming about, then the only alternative you have is to build some kind of pyramid and put the toughest guy on top, or maybe you don't put him there, he just automatically gets there. From there on down, you have an organization within which there is no communication, there is simply a passing down of orders from the various levels and this is no longer society — this is a machine."

No one could put it more succinctly than that.

The ancient Amerindians shared to survive. An urgent question now faces Canadians, and it is posed by their descendants: can *we* survive if we *fail* to share?

Index